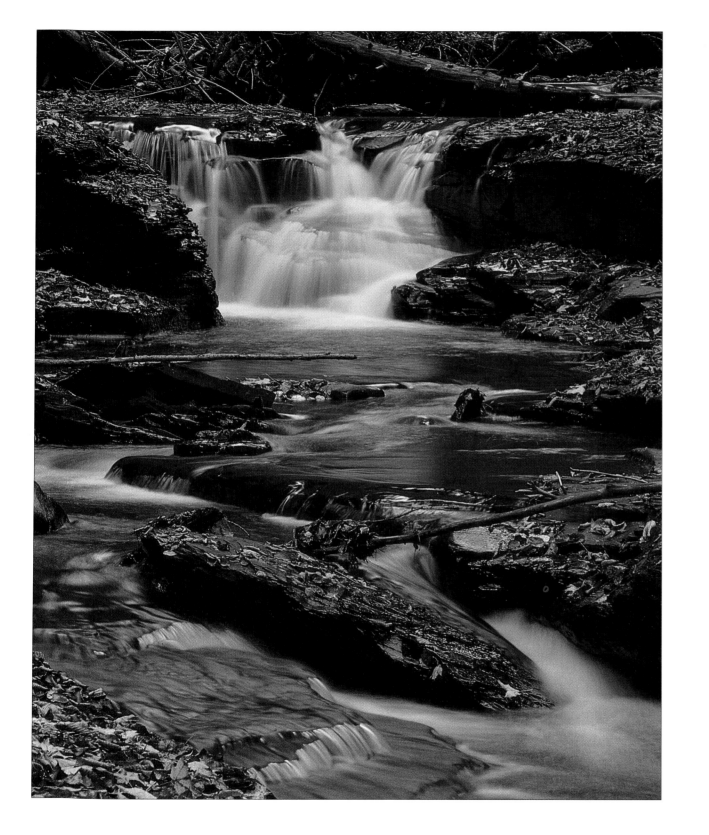

Contemporary Atlas of the United States

Catherine M. Mattson
Mark T. Mattson

Organization and Editing
Yvonne Keck Holman

Photography
Stephen B. Shore

Text Contributor
Chester Zimolzak

Macmillan Publishing Company
NEW YORK

Collier Macmillan Canada
TORONTO

Maxwell Macmillan International
NEW YORK   OXFORD   SINGAPORE   SYDNEY

Macmillan Publishing Company
A Division of Macmillan, Inc.
866 Third Avenue, New York, N.Y. 10022

Collier Macmillan Canada, Inc.
1200 Eglinton Avenue East, Suite 200
Don Mills, Ontario M3C 3N1

Library of Congress Catalog Card Number: 90-675182

Printed in the United States of America

printing number
1 2 3 4 5 6 7 8 9 10

Library of Congress Cataloging-in-Publication Data

Mattson, Catherine.
    Contemporary atlas of the United States.

Includes index.
    1. United States—Maps.   2. United States—Economic conditions—1981–   —Maps.
3. United States—Social conditions—1980–   —Maps.   I. Mattson, Mark T.
II. Macmillan Publishing Company.   III. Title.
G1200.M355 1990   912.73   90-675182
ISBN 0-02-897281-3

This book is dedicated to our daughters Maryanne Frances and Erin Anne. May they give us lots of grandchildren, buy houses in our neighborhood, and be rich enough to support us when they grow up.
It is also dedicated to Chester Zimolzak whose geographic inspiration was the source of much that is contained herein. As always, thanks Chet.

CONTENTS

Sources:

Pages 7, 11, 14, 16, 21, 84, 88, 110, 111

Mason, Robert J., Mattson, Mark T. Atlas of United States Environmental Issues. New York: Macmillan, 1990.

Page 17

United States Water Resources Council. The Nation's Water Resources, 1975–2000: Summary. Washington, DC: Government Printing Office, 1979.

Page 19, 26, 27, 29, 34, 35

The National Atlas of the United States of America. The United States Department of the Interior, Geologic Survey. Washington, DC: Government Printing Office, 1970.

Page 110

United States Fish and Wildlife Service. National Wetlands Survey. Washington, DC: Government Printing Office, 1988.

Page 111

Omernik, James M. Alkalinity of Surface Waters. Corvallis Environmental Research Laboratory. Corvallis: United States Environmental Protection Agency, 1982.

Page 112

Brown, R. S., et al. Solid Waste Programs in the States. Journal of Resource Management and Technology. vol. 15 (3): 137-144 (September 1987).

Waste Age. Refuse Incineration and Refuse to Energy. vol. 19 (3): 195-212 (November, 1988).

Franklin Associates, Ltd. (for the United States Environmental Protection Agency, Office of Solid Waste and Emergency Response). Characterization of the Municipal Solid Waste in the United States, 1960 to 2000, Update 1988: Final Report. Prairie Village: Franklin Associates, 1988.

United States Environmental Protection Agency, Office of Solid Waste and Emergency Response. Non-Hazardous Waste Programs. Washington, DC: Government Printing Office, 1986.

Page 113

United States Environmental Protection Agency, Office of Policy and Planning. Environmental Progress and Challenges. Washington, DC: Government Printing Office, 1988.

United States Environmental Protection Agency, Office of Air and Radiation Programs. Areas with Potentially High Radon Levels. Washington, DC: Government Printing Office, 1987.

Page 113 (diagram)

The Atlas of Pennsylvania. Philadelphia: Temple University Press, 1987.

Page 114

Scott Ridley. State of the States: 1988. Washington, DC: Fund for Renewable Energy and the Environment: 1988.

League of Conservation Voters. The Environmental Scorecard. Washington, DC: League of Conservation Voters, 1987.

Page 115

United States Environmental Protection Agency, Office of Toxic Substances. The Toxic Release Inventory; A National Perspective, 1987. Washington, DC: Government Printing Office, 1989.

Unspecified pages

U.S. Bureau of the Census. County and City Data Book, 1983. 10th ed. Washington, DC: Government Printing Office, 1983.

U.S. Bureau of the Census. State and Metropolitan Area Data Book, 1982: A Statistical Abstract Supplement. Washington, DC: Government Printing Office, 1982.

U.S. Bureau of the Census. Statistical Abstract of the United States. Washington DC: Government Printing Office, 1879–1990 (annual).

Bureau of Labor Statistics, U.S. Department of Justice. Report to the Nation on Crime. 2nd ed. Washington: Government Printing Office, 1988.

PREFACE

Opening this book will give you a lively, factual, and engaging look at the United States as it is today. While the *Contemporary Atlas of the United States* serves as a simple reference filled with basic facts about such things as physiography, climate, population, and agriculture, it also makes connections between the geography of the United States and the issues and events which shape the daily lives of every American.

The book is easily accessible with maps and graphics that are eye catching and interesting. The graphics are supported by text which is lively and informative, explaining not only where things are, but how phenomena interact and relate.

Using the latest technology, this book was produced entirely on computer. The computer used was Macintosh and to the Apple Corporation we owe a debt of gratitude to their ingenuity. From assembling data-based statistics to producing graphics and text, sophisticated methods have been harnessed to produce a colorful book that will reach America's students at a time when geographic literacy concerns teachers at all levels of education.

Intended for anyone who desires a straightforward yet stimulating look at America, the *Contemporary Atlas of the United States* is most appropriate for students, and for teachers leading their students in classroom discussions of current events and events from America's past. Much can be gained from mere surface perusal, but this book invites a peeling away of the layers for a deeper look at the statistics and the integrated, interpretive ideas presented in its text.

Among the salient and timely topics presented here is a look at drugs and their use in the United States. While a map traces supply routes of various narcotics, graphs show the change in drug use over time and suggests the social impact which increased usage brings. The text points out the necessity for programs focusing on social change to combat drug use in addition to the efforts now being made to decrease drug supplies at U.S. borders.

A section on environmental issues presents an overview of the problems facing planet earth. As one of this volume's most important contributions, this section focuses on such subjects as the nature of wetlands and their importance; the impact of acid rain; solid waste, its increased volume, and the need for solutions to its management; and hazardous wastes and their disposal. Attention is also focused on those *who are* and *who are not* contributing to solving environmental problems in a section that looks at laws, environmental programs, and voting records of elected officials in U.S government.

No less attention is paid to the social issues facing America. The dilemma of health care is discussed with maps and graphs showing the availability of and the increasing expenditures for health care. Topics also covered are the pervasiveness of teenage pregnancy, births to unwed mothers, and the current high rate of U.S. infant mortality. Included also are sections on the American family, its composition, housing, and budgets.

A good amount of space is devoted to the Native American, both past and present. A part of society that is often overlooked as America focuses on more visible segments of its society, Native Americans are not neglected here. Careful reading will introduce concepts calling for further investigation into the events that led to the loss of Indian land and to the alienation of Native Americans from the rest of society as manifested in their lack of employment, poverty, and problems with suicide and alcohol consumption.

Despite the wealth of topics covered in this volume, geography does not stop with knowing the location of major rivers or the capitals of all states. This book embraces a higher ideal. It is our hope, as educators, that we have contributed to the analytical resources of our student readership by demonstrating fundamental relationships that will endure in their minds long after isolated facts have been forgotten. It is with this hope that we say to the bright, young minds that will understand our intent—have fun, learn, and be clever. This book is for you.

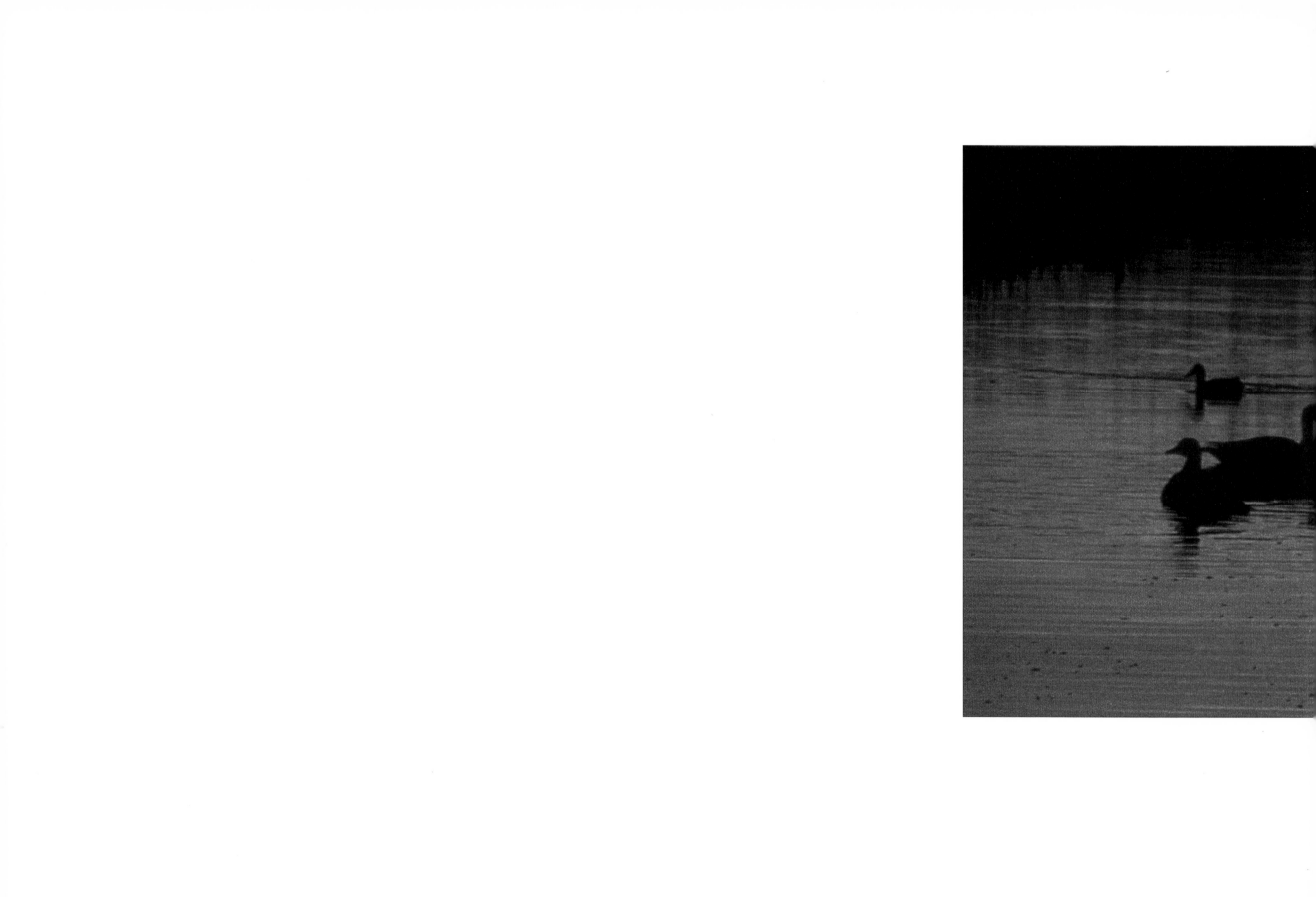

The traditional division of the United States into 50 states and the District of Columbia does not always suit the needs of students and researchers. At times, states are collected into larger groupings called "regions" for easier analysis. Each region contains states that share a common general location, exhibit similar population characteristics, occupy similar physical environments, and sometimes display strong similarities in culture.

The concept of "regionalization" will be used throughout this atlas as a way of organizing information. The regions shown on the next page were developed by the Bureau of the Census, and are used by many federal agencies. Each region is colored and labeled for easy identification. Borders and names are shown for each state, and every state's capital is indicated with the appropriate symbol.

In the simple scheme used here, four regions predominate. They are the Northeast, the South, the Midwest, and the West. Hawaii and Alaska are grouped with the western states. A further subdivision is also used. In it, nine regions are created by subdividing the four primary regions. These nine regions, which are shown on the following page, are the Northeast, the Mid-Atlantic, the East North Central, the West North Central, the South Atlantic, the East South Central, the West South Central, the Mountain, and the Pacific.

Also included on this page is a simple yet useful table that can be referred to for the area and population of each state, its rank by area and population, water and land measures, and interesting facts such as the official flower and state bird.

United States Facts, 1988

	Abbre-viation	Population	Area (sq. mi.)	Land Area	Water Area	State Flower	State Bird	Rank by Population		Rank by Size	
United States	**US**	**245,807,000**	**3,618,770**	**3,539,289**	**79,481**			**4**		**4**	
Alabama	AL	4,127,000	51,705	50,767	51,705	Camellia	Yellowhammer	1	California	1	Alaska
Alaska	AK	513,000	591,004	570,833	591,004	Forget-Me-Not	Willow Ptarmigan	2	New York	2	Texas
Arizona	AZ	3,466,000	114,000	113,508	114,000	Saguaro Cactus Blossom	Cactus Wren	3	Texas	3	California
Arkansas	AR	2,422,000	53,187	52,078	53,187	Apple Blossom	Mockingbird	4	Florida	4	Montana
California	CA	28,168,000	158,706	156,299	158,706	Golden Poppy	Calif. Valley Quail	5	Pennsylvania	5	New Mexico
Colorado	CO	3,290,000	104,091	103,595	104,091	Rocky Mt. Columbine	Lark Bunting	6	Illinois	6	Arizona
Connecticut	CT	3,241,000	5,018	4,872	5,018	Mountain Laurel	American Robin	7	Ohio	7	Nevada
Delaware	DE	660,000	2,045	1,932	2,045	Peach Blossom	Blue Hen Chicken	8	Michigan	8	Colorado
Dist. of Col.	DC	620,000	69	63	69	American Beauty Rose	Wood Thrush	9	New Jersey	9	Wyoming
Florida	FL	12,377,000	59,664	54,153	59,664	Orange Blossom	Mockingbird	10	North Carolina	10	Oregon
Georgia	GA	6,401,000	58,910	58,056	58,910	Cherokee Rose	Brown Thrasher	11	Georgia	11	Utah
Hawaii	HI	1,093,000	6,471	6,425	6,471	Hibiscus	Hawaiian Goose	12	Virginia	12	Minnesota
Idaho	ID	999,000	83,564	82,412	83,564	Syringa	Mountain Bluebird	13	Massachusetts	13	Idaho
Illinois	IL	11,544,000	56,345	55,645	56,345	Native Violet	Cardinal	14	Indiana	14	Kansas
Indiana	IN	5,575,000	36,185	35,932	36,185	Peony	Cardinal	15	Missouri	15	Nebraska
Iowa	IA	2,834,000	56,275	55,965	56,275	Wild Rose	Eastern Goldfinch	16	Tennessee	16	South Dakota
Kansas	KS	248,7000	82,277	81,778	82,277	Native Sunflower	Western Meadowlark	17	Wisconsin	17	North Dakota
Kentucky	KY	372,1000	40,410	39,668	40,410	Goldenrod	Cardinal	18	Maryland	18	Oklahoma
Louisiana	LA	4,420,000	47,752	44,521	47,752	Magnolia	Eastern Brown Pelican	19	Washington	19	Missouri
Maine	ME	1,206,000	33,265	30,995	33,265	White Pine Cone/Tassel	Chickadee	20	Louisiana	20	Washington
Maryland	MD	4,644,000	10,460	9,837	10,460	Black-Eyed Susan	Baltimore Oriole	21	Minnesota	21	Florida
Massachusetts	MA	5,871,000	8,284	7,824	8,284	Mayflower	Chickadee	22	Alabama	22	Georgia
Michigan	MI	930,0000	58,527	56,954	58,527	Apple Blossom	Robin	23	Kentucky	23	Michigan
Minnesota	MN	4,306,000	84,402	79,548	84,402	Pink Lady's Slippers	Common Loon	24	South Carolina	24	Illinois
Mississippi	MS	2,62,7000	47,689	47,233	47,689	Magnolia	Mockingbird	25	Arizona	25	Iowa
Missouri	MO	5,139,000	69,697	68,945	69,697	Hawthorn	Bluebird	26	Colorado	26	Wisconsin
Montana	MT	804,000	147,046	145,388	147,046	Bitterroot	Western Meadowlark	27	Oklahoma	27	Arkansas
Nebraska	NE	1,601,000	77,355	76,644	77,355	Goldenrod	Western Meadowlark	28	Connecticut	28	North Carolina
Nevada	NV	1,060,000	110,561	109,894	110,561	Sagebrush	Mountain Bluebird	29	Iowa	29	Alabama
New Hampshire	NH	1,097,000	9,279	8,993	9,279	Purple Lilac	Purple Finch	30	Oregon	30	New York
New Jersey	NJ	7,720,000	7,787	7,468	7,787	Purple Violet	Eastern Goldfinch	31	Mississippi	31	Louisiana
New Mexico	NM	1,51,0000	121,593	121,335	121,593	Yucca	Roadrunner	32	Kansas	32	Mississippi
New York	NY	17,898,000	49,108	47,377	49,108	Rose	Bluebird	33	Arkansas	33	Pennsylvania
North Carolina	NC	6,526,000	52,669	48,843	52,669	Dogwood	Cardinal	34	West Virginia	34	Tennessee
North Dakota	ND	663,000	70,702	69,300	70,702	Wild Prairie Rose	Western Meadowlark	35	Utah	35	Ohio
Ohio	OH	10,872,000	41,330	41,004	41,330	Scarlet Carnation	Cardinal	36	Nebraska	36	Virginia
Oklahoma	OK	3,263,000	69,956	68,655	69,956	Mistletoe	Scissortailed Flycatcher	37	New Mexico	37	Kentucky
Oregon	OR	2,741,000	97,073	96,184	97,073	Oregon Grape	Western Meadowlark	38	Maine	38	Indiana
Pennsylvania	PA	12,027,000	45,308	44,888	45,308	Mountain Laurel	Ruffed Grouse	39	New Hampshire	39	Maine
Rhode Island	RI	995,000	1,212	1,055	1,212	Violet	Rhode Island Red	40	Hawaii	40	South Carolina
South Carolina	SC	3,493,000	31,113	30,203	31,113	Yellow Jessamine	Carolina Wren	41	Nevada	41	West Virginia
South Dakota	SD	715,000	77,116	75,952	77,116	Pasque Flower	Ringnecked Pheasant	42	Idaho	42	Maryland
Tennessee	TN	4,919,000	42,144	41,155	42,144	Iris	Mockingbird	43	Rhode Island	43	Vermont
Texas	TX	16,780,000	266,807	262,017	266,807	Bluebonnet	Mockingbird	44	Montana	44	New Hampshire
Utah	UT	1,691,000	84,899	82,073	84,8991	Sego Lily	Seagull	45	South Dakota	45	Massachusetts
Vermont	VT	556,000	9,614	9,273	9,614	Red Clover	Hermit Thrush	46	North Dakota	46	New Jersey
Virginia	VA	5,996,000	40,767	39,704	40,767	Dogwood	Cardinal	47	Delaware	47	Hawaii
Washington	WA	4,619,000	68,139	66,511	68,139	Western Rhododendron	Willow Goldfinch	48	Dist. of Col.	48	Connecticut
West Virginia	WV	1,884,000	24,232	24,119	24,232	Big Rhododendron	Cardinal	49	Vermont	49	Delaware
Wisconsin	WI	4,858,000	56,153	54,426	56,153	Wood Violet	Robin	50	Alaska	50	Rhode Island
Wyoming	WY	471,000	97,809	96,989	97,809	Indian Paintbrush	Meadowlark	51	Wyoming	51	Dist. of Col.

Washington
• Seattle
Olympia • • Spokane
• Portland
• Salem
• Eugene
Oregon

Idaho
• Missoula Montana
• Helena
• Billings
• Boise

North Dakota
• Bismarck Fargo •
Minnesota
St. Paul • • Minneapolis Duluth •
Green Bay •
Wisconsin

Maine
• Bangor
Montpelier • • Augusta
Burlington • Portland •
Vermont New Hampshire
• Concord
Syracuse • Albany • Boston •
Buffalo • New York Massachusetts
Hartford • Providence •
New Haven • Rhode Island
Connecticut

Sacramento
San Francisco •
San Jose •
Nevada
California

Carson City •
Salt Lake City •
Utah
Cheyenne •
Wyoming
Denver •
Colorado

South Dakota
• Pierre
Rapid City •
Sioux Falls •

Nebraska
Omaha •
Lincoln •

Iowa
Davenport •
Des Moines •

Madison •
Lansing •
Milwaukee •
Detroit •
Chicago •

Michigan

Pennsylvania
Cleveland • New York
Harrisburg • • Trenton New Jersey
Pittsburgh • • Philadelphia
Baltimore • Dover • • Atlantic City
D.C. Annapolis • Delaware
Richmond • Maryland

Ohio
Columbus •
Indiana
Indianapolis •
Illinois
Springfield •
Topeka •
Kansas City •
Missouri
Jefferson City •
St. Louis •
Kansas
Wichita •
• Springfield

Cincinnati •
Frankfort • West
• Lexington Virginia
Louisville • Charleston •
Kentucky

Virginia
Norfolk •
Raleigh •
North Carolina

Las Vegas •

Los Angeles •
San Diego •
Arizona
Phoenix •

Santa Fe •
• Albuquerque
New Mexico

Tulsa •
Oklahoma
Oklahoma City •

Arkansas
Little Rock •

Nashville • Knoxville •
Tennessee
Memphis •

Columbia •
South Carolina
• Charleston

El Paso •

Dallas •

Mississippi Alabama
Birmingham • Atlanta •
Georgia
Savannah •

Texas

Louisiana
Mobile •
Jackson •
Baton Rouge •
New Orleans •
Montgomery •
Tallahassee •
Jacksonville •

Austin •
Houston •
San Antonio • Galveston •

Orlando •
St. Petersburg • Tampa •
Florida
Miami •

• Nome
• Fairbanks

Honolulu •

Key West •

• Anchorage
• Juneau

• Hilo

Alaska Hawaii

0   200   400
Miles

• Major cities
• Capital cities

U.S. Regions

New England
Middle Atlantic
East North Central
West North Central
South Atlantic
East South Central
West South Central
Mountain
Pacific

907 Alaska

808 Hawaii

TIME ZONES 5

Mountain Standard Time

Central Standard Time

Pacific Standard Time

Eastern Standard Time

- Major cities
- Capital cities

Bering Standard Time (9:00)

Yukon Standard Time (11:00)

Pacific Standard Time

Alaska/Hawaii Standard Time (10:00)

Alaska

Hawaii

0   200   400
Miles

The United States encompasses vast areas of land, most of it level, and much of it with the potential for farming. This tremendous land resource forms the basis for much of American wealth.

Although the United States is mostly level, three mountain chains extend north-south from the Canadian border. In the east, the remnants of an ancient mountain chain make up the Adirondack and Appalachian Highlands. The Rockies, which spill southward through the western third of the states, constitute a much younger and higher mountain group. The Pacific Mountain complex, where coastal highlands are backed with broad valleys, ends in the massive Sierra-Cascades. In this westernmost chain, active volcanoes and earthquakes indicate that the process of earth upheaval and change continues through a process known as "plate tectonics."

Between the Pacific Mountains and the Rockies is an area of higher land that is characterized as plateaus and basins with occasional higher mountains and a dry climate. The Rockies themselves are divided between a massive, blocky set of ranges in the north and more regular lines of parallel ridges in the south. Between, yet really a part of the Rockies, is the Wyoming Basin.

Beyond, to the east, is a vast interior plain that encompasses almost half the country. Its higher, drier western portion is called the Great Plains. These high plains gradually merge eastward into the Central Lowland, where the Mississippi and its tributaries have relentlessly leveled the land through the natural processes of erosion and deposition. The Central Lowland contains a few higher areas, where nature has uplifted sections of the continent. These areas are the Superior Upland, the Ozark Plateau, and the Eastern Uplands containing the Nashville Basin and the Kentucky bluegrass country. Southward, the Central Lowland merges with the vast Coastal Plain; eastward it abuts the Appalachian Highlands.

The Appalachian Highlands, the complex remains of a prehistoric continent that has been folded and crushed through the collision of land masses, represents a portion of the earth that has been worn down to nubs by eons of erosion. The Appalachian Highlands, like the Adirondacks to the north and the Superior Uplands to the west, are an ancient outlier of the vast Canadian Shield. New England, which is only marginally useful for agriculture, is typified by rolling, rocky hills that are the folded and contorted remains of the Piedmont.

The Atlantic Coast, with its good harbors and welcoming level land, is a vast plain that becomes ever wider as it stretches southward, from Long Island through Florida to the Mexican border in southern Texas.

Alaska's landscape sandwiches a highland basin between the tectonically active Pacific Mountain Complex and a frozen, inhospitable Arctic Lowland.

The map on the following page organizes the landscape of the United States into 18 physical regions that share similar characteristics based on the discussions outlined above.

The Landscape

| | Percent | | Elevation (feet) | | |
	Land	Water	High	Low	Mean
Alabama	98.0	2.0	2,407	•	500
Alaska	97.0	3.0	20,320	•	1,900
Arizona	99.6	.4	12,633	70	4,100
Arkansas	98.0	2.0	2,753	55	650
California	98.5	1.5	14,494	-282	2,900
Colorado	99.5	.5	14,433	3,350	6,800
Connecticut	97.0	3.0	2,380	•	500
Delaware	94.5	5.5	442	•	60
D.C.	91.0	9.0	410	1	150
Florida	91.0	9.0	345	•	100
Georgia	99.0	19.0	4,784	•	600
Hawaii	99.0	1.0	13,796	•	3,030
Idaho	99.0	1.0	12,662	710	5,000
Illinois	99.0	1.0	1,235	279	600
Indiana	99.0	1.0	1,257	320	700
Iowa	99.0	1.0	1,670	480	1,100
Kansas	99.0	1.0	4,039	680	2,000
Kentucky	98.0	2.0	4,145	257	750
Louisiana	93.0	7.0	535	-5	100
Maine	93.0	7.0	5,268	•	600
Maryland	94.0	6.0	3,360	•	350
Massachusetts	94.0	6.0	3,491	•	500
Michigan	97.0	3.0	1,979	572	900
Minnesota	94.0	6.0	2,301	602	1,200
Mississippi	99.0	1.0	806	•	300
Missouri	99.0	1.0	1,772	230	800
Montana	99.0	19.0	12,799	1,800	3,400
Nebraska	99.0	1.0	5,426	840	2,600
Nevada	99.0	1.0	13,143	470	5,500
New Hampshire	97.0	3.0	6,288	•	1,000
New Jersey	96.0	4.0	1,803	•	250
New Mexico	99.8	.2	13,161	2,817	5,700
New York	96.5	3.5	5,344	•	1,000
North Carolina	92.7	7.3	6,684	•	700
North Dakota	98.0	2.0	3,506	750	1,900
Ohio	99.0	1.0	1,550	433	850
Oklahoma	98.0	2.0	4,973	287	1,300
Oregon	99.0	1.0	11,239	•	3,300
Pennsylvania	99.0	1.0	3,213	•	1,100
Rhode Island	87.0	13.0	812	•	200
South Carolina	97.0	3.0	3,560	•	350
South Dakota	98.0	2.0	7,242	962	2,200
Tennessee	98.0	2.0	6,643	182	900
Texas	98.0	2.0	8,749	•	1,700
Utah	97.0	3.0	13,528	2,000	6,100
Vermont	96.5	3.5	4,393	95	1,000
Virginia	97.0	3.0	5,729	•	950
Washington	97.0	3.0	14,410	•	1,700
West Virginia	99.5	5.0	4,863	240	1,500
Wisconsin	97.0	3.0	1,951	581	1,050
Wyoming	99.0	1.0	13,804	3,100	6,700

• sea level

Elevation Extremes

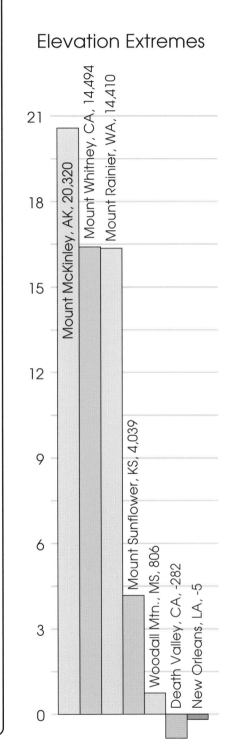

Mount McKinley, AK, 20,320
Mount Whitney, CA, 14,494
Mount Rainier, WA, 14,410
Mount Sunflower, KS, 4,039
Woodall Mtn., MS, 806
Death Valley, CA, -282
New Orleans, LA, -5

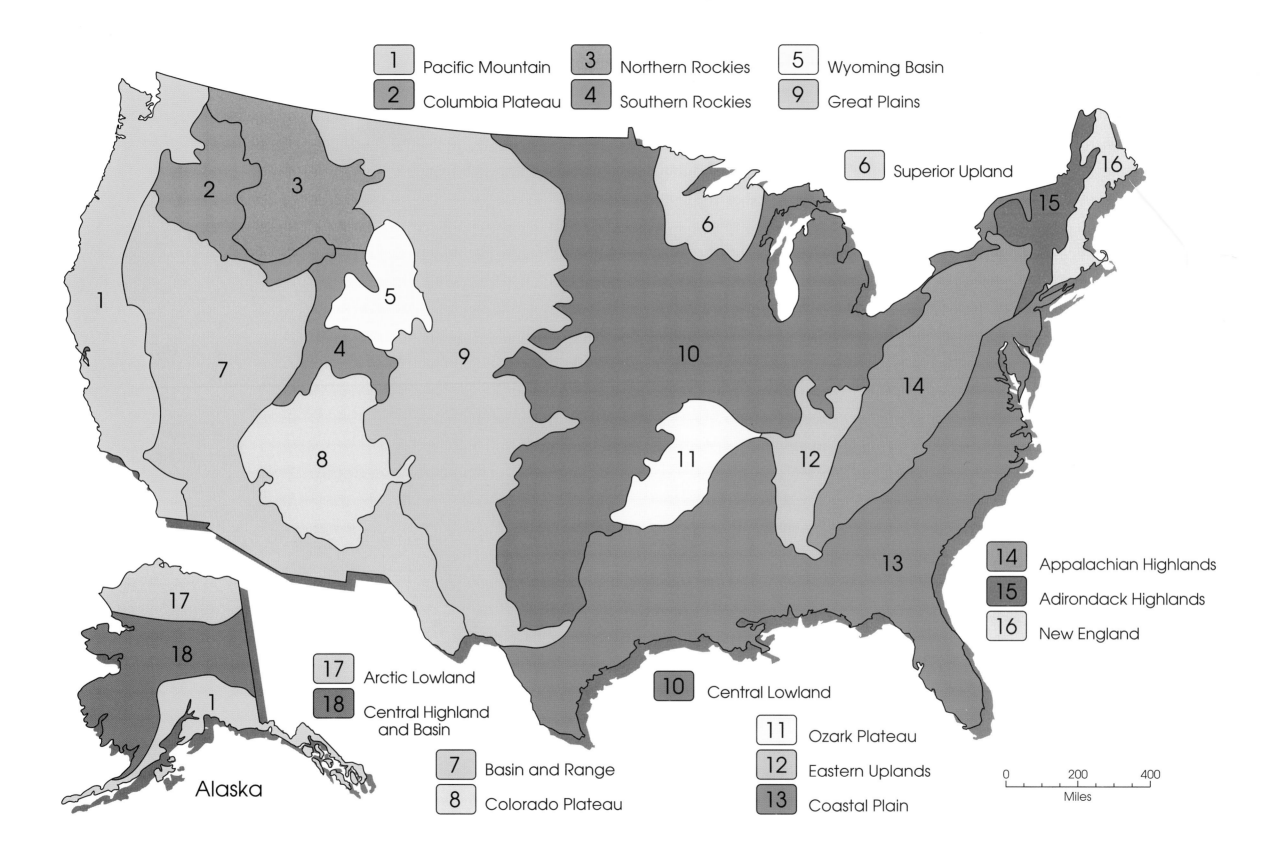

| 1 | Pacific Mountain | 3 | Northern Rockies | 5 | Wyoming Basin |
| 2 | Columbia Plateau | 4 | Southern Rockies | 9 | Great Plains |

6 Superior Upland

14 Appalachian Highlands

15 Adirondack Highlands

16 New England

17 Arctic Lowland

18 Central Highland and Basin

Alaska

10 Central Lowland

7 Basin and Range

8 Colorado Plateau

11 Ozark Plateau

12 Eastern Uplands

13 Coastal Plain

0   200   400
Miles

SOILS 8

Superimposed on a landscape that alternates between vast highland and lowland complexes is a thin covering of pulverized earth material called soil. There are literally tens of thousands of individual soils, each with a name and a set of characteristics. Even within some soils there are further minor differences called phases. Compared to the massive rock that underlies it, soil would appear to be unimportant. What gives this thin layer of soil its importance is that it is the medium for the production of food.

Soils are the result of many individual factors in the natural environment: the rock from which they were made, the climatic conditions of the past and present, the rainfall, the vegetation that grows in them, and the action of water and ice upon them.

Most soil classification systems identify ten to twenty great soil groups, and all the individual soils within each group have some similarities. The oldest classification, done by a Russian, uses unfamiliar Russian names. The latest effort at classification, which resulted from an international conference in the United States in 1950, is called the Seventh Approximation. A dozen groups are used here to show general patterns within the United States.

In general, dry areas have soils full of mineral nutrients—the foods that growing plants need. Wetter areas tend to be less fertile—the nutrients are washed out of the topsoil to great depths in the lower soil where crops cannot reach them. Soil forms faster in hotter, wetter areas, but also erodes faster and water rinses it of minerals. Soils

called "Subtropical" and "Tropical" often have fertility problems for this reason.

True Tropical soils are found only in Hawaii in the United States. Normally low in plant food in other parts of the world, the soils are exceptionally rich in Hawaii because they are renewed by volcanic activity. Subtropical soils are usually of low to moderate fertility. Exceptions occur where they were made from mineral rich rock or where they have been enriched by a cover of grass.

Cooler, seasonal areas are divided between fair and poor soils depending on location conditions. Soils are generally weak in the Northeast and the northern Midwest. Many soils in both those areas were deposited by ice during continental glaciation. They will yield good crops only with careful use and intense fertilization. Where these soils were covered with grass for thousands of years, nature has enriched them. These "Wet Prairie" soils are the nation's most productive. The "Dry Prairie" soils are also rich, but suffer from a lack of water.

Arctic areas consist far more of bare rock than soil. Soils there are thin and unproductive. Mountain areas contain extremely varied soils. Often thin and stony, they may run from extremely rich to absolutely worthless over short distances.

Alluvium is soil deposited by running water. Where thick, stone-free, and deposited by annual floods, it is often superior.

Standing water, like rainfall, can also rinse out plant nutrients. Years of dead vegetation piling up in swamps and lakes, however, can make such waterlogged soils reasonably

fertile. When drained, some of these bog soils yield good crops.

Comparing the map on the following page with the one on page 80, students can see that the western states, being covered with dry desert/semi-desert, dry prairie, and mountain soils, are primarily used for grazing. Intensive agricultural use, as shown on page 81, is associated with wet prairie, temperate, subtropical, and alluvial soil groups. Agricultural heartland states, with these soil types, account for 44 percent of the value of the nation's agricultural output while having only 35 percent of the nation's cropland.

The map below demonstrates the interrelationship between soil and America's agricultural activity.

Productive Soils and Prime Cropland

Brown area shows extent of fertile soil

★ States of the "Agricultural Heartland" (see page 81)

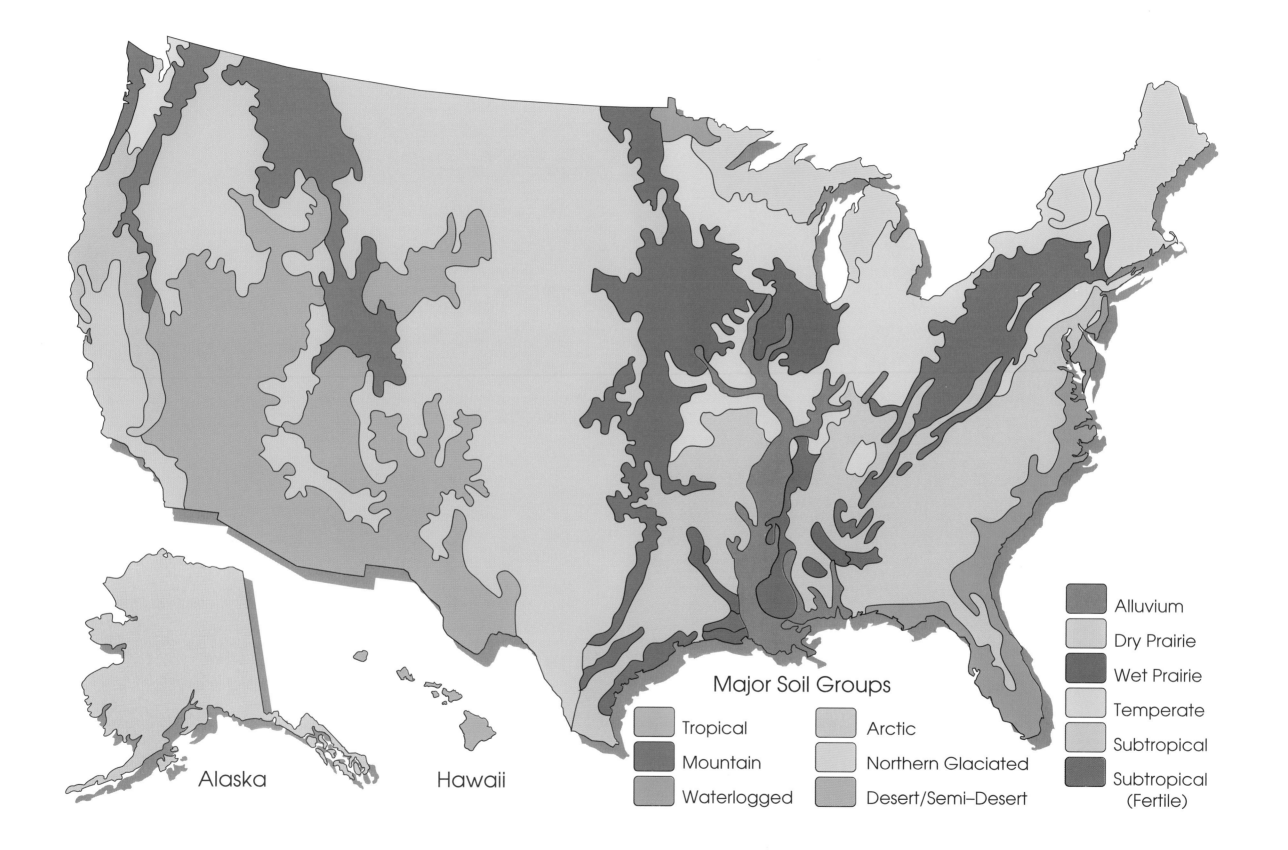

Alaska

Hawaii

Major Soil Groups

Tropical

Mountain

Waterlogged

Arctic

Northern Glaciated

Desert/Semi–Desert

Alluvium

Dry Prairie

Wet Prairie

Temperate

Subtropical

Subtropical (Fertile)

Vegetation is the mosaic of plant communities that cover the landscape. It consists of a combination of life forms that are distributed according to common requirements such as sun, soil, temperature, and moisture. A significant portion of the vegetation existing in America today was not original to this continent. It was brought here from other lands accidently or for the purpose of cultivation. A larger proportion of America's fauna is not indigenous to its present location due to influences caused by man's development and life style. Vegetation that exists in its original ecology can be termed *natural vegetation*. Natural vegetation is defined as that vegetation that would have existed if humans had not altered natural ecological progression. In contrast to natural vegetation is *actual* or real vegetation, i.e. vegetation as it exists at a precise moment in time at a specific place.

One of the most critical factors in vegetational cover is whether an area is wet or dry. Wet areas support tree growth, while dry climatic areas cannot support forest but favor grasses. (A review of the precipitation section on pages 20 and 21 will help the reader understand the relationship between vegetation and rainfall.)

The grass and shrubland of the U. S. interior is largely natural vegetation west of the Missouri River. East of that river, the grasslands were human induced. That is, Native Americans repeatedly burned the area to encourage the growth of grass to increase the range of the buffalo, their chief food source.

Northern areas with their sharply cold winters favor the growth of needle-leaf trees like oak, beech, and maple. Mixed forest areas are just that—evergreens on drier, sandier soils and broad-leaf trees on soils that retain water better.

The mixture of tree species gives character to each of the forest zones. In New England, maple and birch mix with spruce and other evergreens. This variety is responsible for that region's famed autumn colors. In the Eastern Deciduous forest, evergreens are infrequent, and oak, beech, tulip, and other valuable hardwoods dominate. Pines intersperse with oaks in the Southern forests, and such species as magnolia and gum trees replace hardier hardwood species.

Western forests are different from one another and contain different species. In the Pacific Northwest, evergreens dominate overwhelmingly. Douglas fir is the most important species. Southward, the forests progress through the stately and enormous redwoods in the Sierras of northern California to the scrubby and gnarled pines of southern California. As the climate becomes drier, shrub replaces tree. Herbs, laurel, and flowering bushes mix with grass and stunted pine in the Mediterranean and Chaparral climates of middle and southern California.

The deserts are rich and varied in their plant cover. The majestic saguaro cactus of the Sonoran desert contrasts sharply with the dull, almost gray weed and shrub of the salt flats. Wetter spots grow mesquite bushes and joshua trees. In the mountains there may be sufficient moisture to support ponderosa pines.

Grasses of the plains and prairies vary tremendously in height. Little variety in species is noted from a distance, but in spring and summer flowers highlight the variety and beauty of the natural grasslands.

In Alaska, remoteness and sparse population have combined to preserve natural vegetation. Introduced species are few and the landscape is covered with a uniform native tundra interspersed with birch, spruce, hemlock, and alder thickets.

In contrast to Alaska's uniform tundra is Hawaii's highly complex and diverse vegetation. More than two-thirds of all Hawaiian plants have been introduced. Some species such as mesquite and guava have literally crowded out native vegetation. Vegetation has also been affected by goats and pigs which have run wild throughout forests and hillsides in a most destructive manner.

Much of the natural vegetation of the United States was cleared for farming and/or was intensely lumbered. Very little of the original cover remains. The map on page 11 shows what would be on the land naturally were it not put to other uses. States and the federal government have reserved a few areas of virgin forest and grassland, preserving a portion of nature as a part of our national heritage. Large areas are preserved as national forests and government ranges, but they are no longer in their natural state. As of 1987, 430,600,000 acres of federal land had been set aside for forests and wildlife. Added to this figure is another 154,400,000 acres of rangeland that is devoted to grazing. Held in the public trust, these federal lands are valued at $1.497 billion.

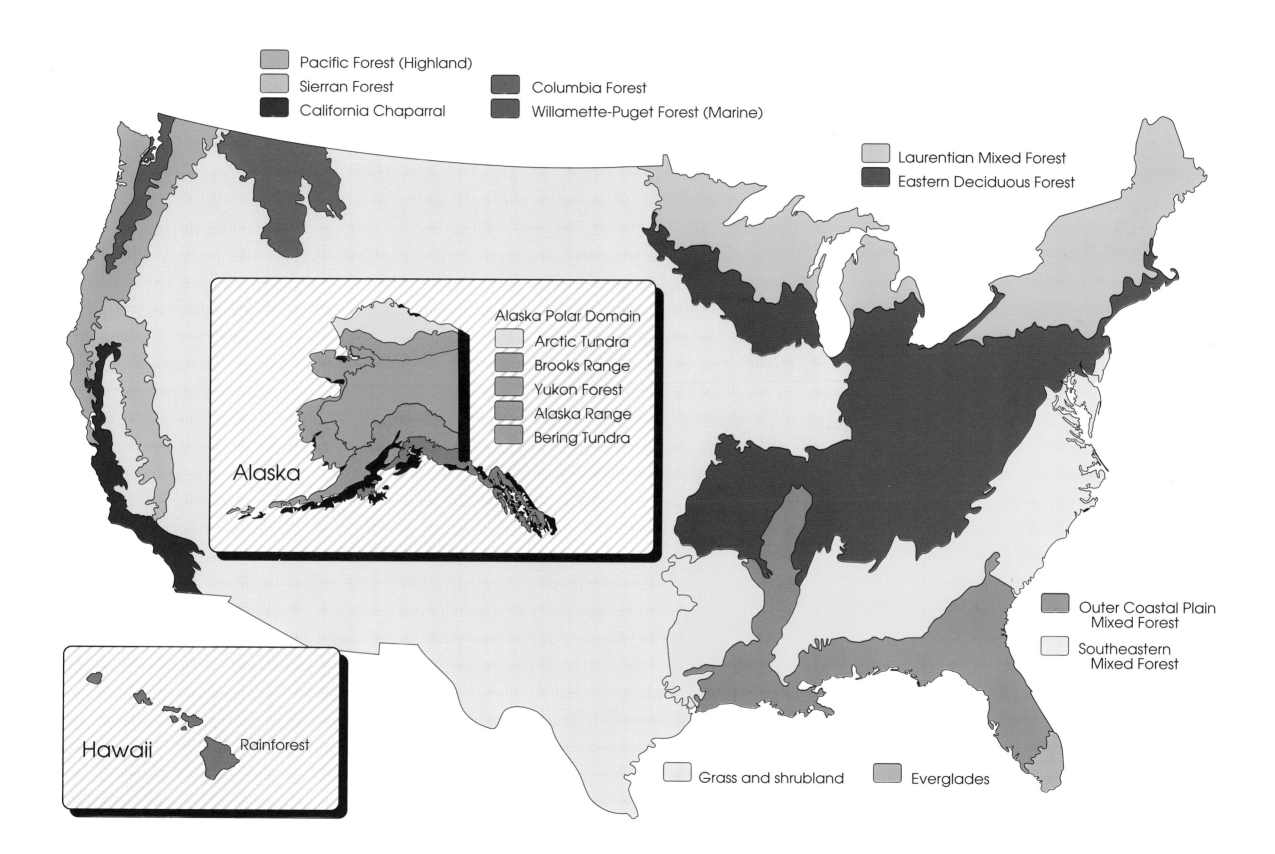

Pacific Forest (Highland)
Sierran Forest
California Chaparral
Columbia Forest
Willamette-Puget Forest (Marine)

Laurentian Mixed Forest
Eastern Deciduous Forest

Alaska Polar Domain
Arctic Tundra
Brooks Range
Yukon Forest
Alaska Range
Bering Tundra

Alaska

Outer Coastal Plain
Mixed Forest
Southeastern
Mixed Forest

Hawaii   Rainforest

Grass and shrubland   Everglades

Two immense river systems, the St. Lawrence-Great Lakes and the Mississippi-Missouri-Ohio, drain most of America. Both systems have been improved for navigation and carry immense amounts of freight by boat or barge.

The St. Lawrence Seaway, as the system is called, allows ocean-going vessels of medium size to reach deep into the northern interior of the country. The Mississippi System, while suitable only for barges over most of its length, allows navigation into the Appalachian coalfields, America's rich prairielands, the oil fields of Oklahoma, and parts of the Great Plains. The St. Lawrence flows eastward into the Atlantic; the Mississippi System southward to the Gulf of Mexico. The two systems are joined by a canal at Chicago. The St. Lawrence itself carries an enormous amount of water; the Great Lakes may contain as much as 20 percent of the world's total fresh water. Immense boats carrying ore, fuel, and grain shuttle between and among the lake ports of eight major industrial states and Canada's largest province, Quebec. Three major bottlenecks in the natural system—the Thousand Islands, Niagara Falls, and the rapids at Sault Sainte Marie—have been bypassed by canals. The St. Lawrence Seaway, opened in the 1950s, cannot accommodate the huge vessels that carry much of today's commerce, so domestic shipments far outweigh foreign trade.

The St. Lawrence has few tributaries of any size on the American side of the border. The Mississippi System, on the other hand, sends out branches in all directions. The main stream is navigable to Minneapolis-St. Paul. Its Ohio River tributary carries the largest amount of freight. Deepened, straightened, dredged, and canalized, the Ohio provides an east-west complement to the north-south traffic of the mainstream. The Ohio and its tributaries are lined with coal mines, steel mills, chemical plants, power generating stations, oil refineries, and industrial complexes. Eighty percent of its traffic involves facilities and locations along its banks, with 20 percent entering the Mississippi proper.

The Tennessee-Cumberland tributary generates hydroelectric, thermal (coal-fired), and nuclear power and is lined with lakes that have become extremely popular with American tourists. The entire system was improved during the 1930s under the Tennessee Valley Authority. This government agency engineered and developed a series of projects that changed the area it drains from one of poverty to one of plenty. A similar multi-purpose project along the Arkansas-Canadian tributary to the west has been less successful in accomplishing that change. There, the lakes that resulted have come to be a magnet area for retirees. Navigation and power generation are far less important.

The rivers of the West have smaller drainage basins. They are used primarily for irrigation and hydroelectric power generation. Three major systems drain the area west of the Rockies: the Colorado, Columbia-Snake, and the Sacramento-San Joaquin. Adjoining these three is a desert area with interior drainage and salt lakes that do not drain to the sea.

The Columbia has some of the world's largest dams. Its waters irrigate the farms and orchards of the Columbia Plateau. Its Snake River tributary irrigates the rich soils of southern Idaho. The dams on this system create huge amounts of cheap electricity that is used in producing much of the country's aluminum.

California's rivers irrigate the lush Central Valley of that state producing valuable farm products such as grapes, citrus, rice, and cotton. The Colorado's tortuous course is scenic rather than navigable with the Grand Canyon as its most famous feature. In its lower reaches, together with its Gila tributary, it irrigates the farms of desert Arizona.

The main function of the Rio Grande is to serve as a border with Mexico. Most of the irrigation provided by its waters is on the Mexican side.

The Atlantic and Gulf Coasts are characterized by many short individual rivers. Some of these rivers perform tasks out of proportion to their size. The Connecticut and Merrimack were lined with waterwheels that powered New England's early industries. The Hudson connects New York to the St. Lawrence System with the aid of three canals. These provide America's largest port with access to both the Midwest and Canada. The Susquehanna is lined with enormous power plants that generate a huge share of the Northeast's power. Rivers of the South Atlantic states have been dammed to create immense reservoirs that do double duty as flood control and recreational facilities. The Tombigbee River accesses the Mississippi System by canal, providing a second entrance from the Gulf to the nation's interior.

Ten Longest Rivers

	Miles
Mississippi/Missouri/Red Rock	3,710
Missouri/Red Rock	2,540
Mississippi	2,348
Missouri	2,348
Rio Grande	1,760
Arkansas	1,459
Colorado	1,450
Ohio	1,310
Columbia	1,243
Red	1,179

Ten Largest Lakes

	Square Miles
Lake of the Woods	1,697
Great Salt Lake	1,361
Iliamna	1,000
Okeechobee	700
Pontchartrain	625
Becharof	458
Red Lake	451
Champlain	435
St. Clair	432
Salton Sea	374

Area of the Great Lakes

	Square Miles
Lake Michigan	22,178
Lake Superior	21,118
Lake Huron	8,975
Lake Erie	5,002
Lake Ontario	3,033

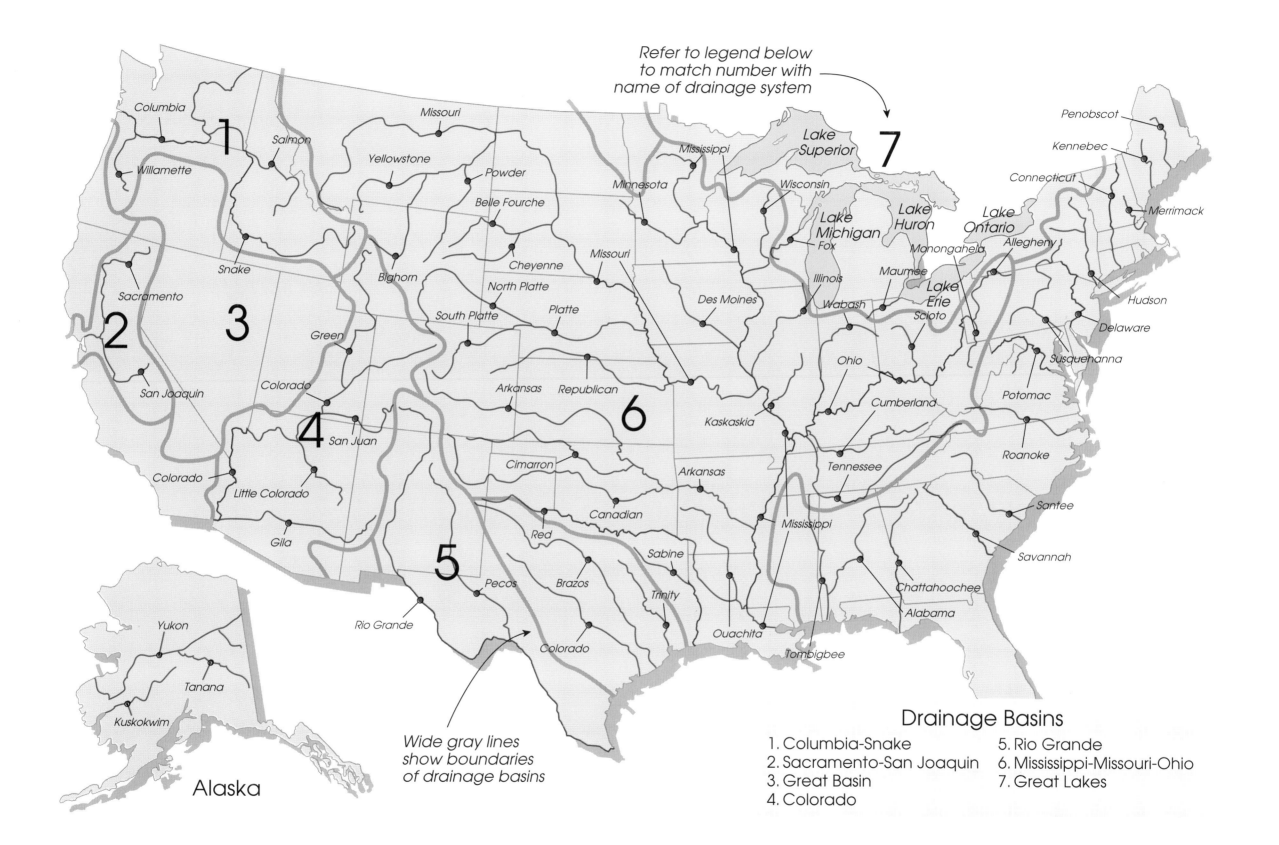

Refer to legend below to match number with name of drainage system

Columbia *Salmon* 1

Willamette *Missouri* *Yellowstone* *Powder*

Snake *Belle Fourche*

Sacramento 3 *Bighorn* *Cheyenne*

2 *Green* *North Platte* *South Platte* *Platte*

San Joaquin *Colorado* 4 *San Juan*

Little Colorado 6 *Arkansas* *Republican*

Gila *Cimarron* *Arkansas*

5 *Pecos* *Brazos*

Rio Grande *Red* *Sabine* *Trinity*

Canadian *Ouachita*

Colorado *Tombigbee*

Mississippi *Minnesota* *Wisconsin*

Des Moines *Illinois* *Fox* *Wabash*

Kaskaskia *Ohio* *Cumberland* *Tennessee*

Mississippi

Chattahoochee *Alabama*

Lake *Superior* 7

Lake *Michigan* Lake *Huron* Lake *Ontario*

Monongahela *Allegheny*

Maumee Lake *Erie* *Scioto*

Penobscot *Kennebec* *Connecticut* *Merrimack*

Hudson *Delaware* *Susquehanna* *Potomac* *Roanoke*

Santee *Savannah*

Yukon *Tanana* *Kuskokwim*

Alaska

Wide gray lines show boundaries of drainage basins

Drainage Basins

1. Columbia-Snake
2. Sacramento-San Joaquin
3. Great Basin
4. Colorado
5. Rio Grande
6. Mississippi-Missouri-Ohio
7. Great Lakes

The United States is divided into three regions based on the availability of water. In the *humid* eastern region drought is a rarity, with dry periods that are neither prolonged nor severe. Most of this region produces crops without irrigation despite high water consumption for industrial and human needs.

The *marginal* region is water-short by definition with yearly rainfall that is less than the potential for evaporation. One year in five is a drought year, and multi-year droughts such as the one that caused the "Dust Bowl" of the 1930s are common.

Except for coastal mountain ranges and areas of the Pacific Northwest, the entire western third of the country belongs to what can be called an *arid* region. In this region, with its desert and semi-desert soils, drought is the normal condition and rainy years are the exception.

While the Pacific Northwest experiences heavy rainfall in its mountains and coastal hills, most of California is rainless during the summer months in what could be called a cycle of seasonal drought. When winter rains are light or absent, the area suffers.

Regardless of average water conditions, floods are a danger in each of the three regions. The Northeastern states, for example, experience flooding almost every year due to the increase in "runoff" that accompanies the removal of trees and the paving of land during development. Instead of soaking into the soil, rain runs off into streams or drains causing local flooding. Some roads and parking lots in coastal areas flood after every rain and water seeps into basements often enough for many households to use sump pumps and dehumidifiers on a regular basis.

In the Appalachian region, torrential rains are frequent, causing localized but potentially severe flooding. After storms, small streams may rise 20 to 40 feet above normal. When rapid melting of heavy winter snow combines with spring rains, narrow valleys of major rivers are prone to spectacular flooding that can result in the destruction of entire communities.

The entire Mississippi Basin experiences heavy flooding on a frequent basis. In its higher reaches, the flooding affects fairly limited areas. In its lower course, the floodwaters may spread for tens or hundreds of miles across land that is mostly level. Higher natural levees along the river banks prevent water from returning to the river bed. Under flood conditions, standing water may cover thousands of square miles for weeks on end.

The sluggish lower Mississippi changes course frequently. Shifts in sandbars and silt deposits that result from flooding block navigation channels. Periodic floods literally rearrange the landscape as well as the river bottom. Dense population and intense farming here make the costs associated with flooding extremely high.

Western floods can occur instantly. A severe thunderstorm anywhere in a stream basin can turn a dry streambed into a raging torrent in minutes. The natural absence of water-retaining vegetation creates a severe flood hazard. An additional problem in hillier areas is the mudslide. Rain-saturated soil on sloping land may literally run like water downhill, burying or demolishing structures and forests.

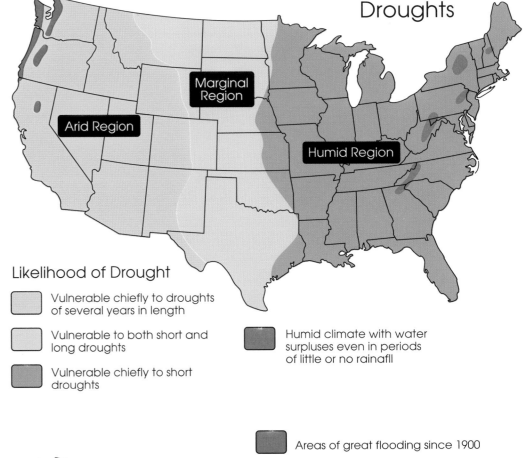

Droughts

Arid Region

Marginal Region

Humid Region

Likelihood of Drought

Vulnerable chiefly to droughts of several years in length

Vulnerable to both short and long droughts

Vulnerable chiefly to short droughts

Humid climate with water surpluses even in periods of little or no rainafll

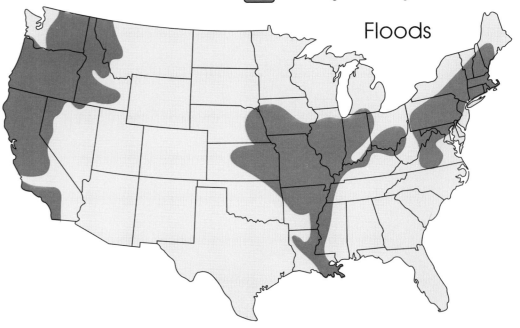

Areas of great flooding since 1900

Floods

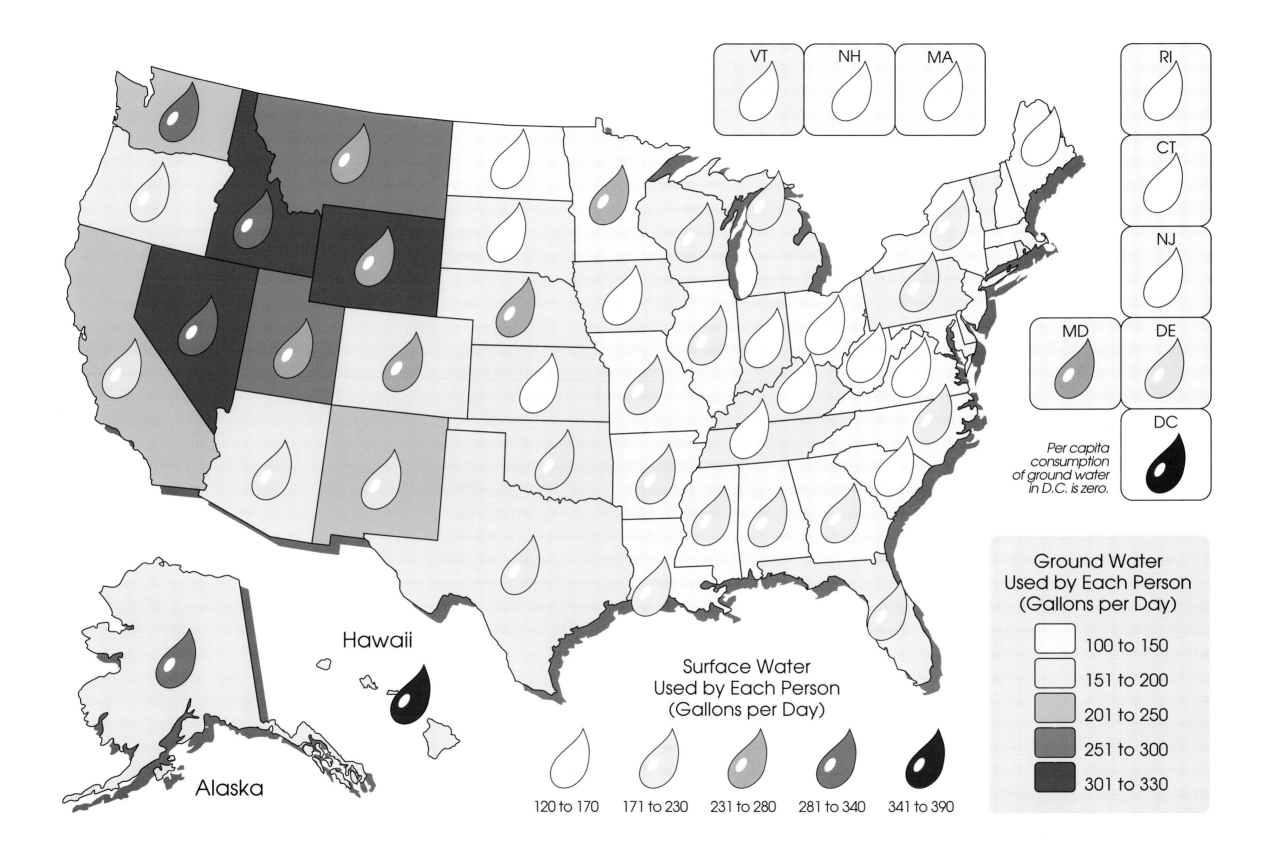

VT

NH

MA

RI

CT

NJ

MD

DE

DC

Per capita
consumption
of ground water
in D.C. is zero.

Hawaii

Alaska

Surface Water
Used by Each Person
(Gallons per Day)

120 to 170   171 to 230   231 to 280   281 to 340   341 to 390

Ground Water
Used by Each Person
(Gallons per Day)

100 to 150

151 to 200

201 to 250

251 to 300

301 to 330

There are two basic sources for water supply systems. One is surface water flowing in rivers or stored in lakes and reservoirs. The other is groundwater, the rainfall naturally stored in soil and underground rock. Groundwater use is heaviest in the West where surface supplies are scarce. The creation of huge, man-made lakes and reservoirs behind dams built by the federal government has increased surface water supplies there. Because of high temperatures, however, there is more evaporation from these water surfaces than normal. Western states consume far more water than Eastern states because of irrigation needs.

Although historically industry consumed more water than other users, this has now reversed. American industry is now conserving and recycling more water than the general public. A growing population and lifestyles that use more water have increased public consumption. In the past, apartment dwellers did not have lawns to water and fewer Americans had cars to wash. Increases in the number of swimming pools adds to the consumption of water.

Aquifers are rock and soil layers that collect and carry water. There are 27 major aquifer systems in the lower 48 states. In wetter areas, they are recharged yearly as water enters the aquifer on a consistent basis. In drier areas, the water is often in finite supply. Withdrawal reduces the amount of water in the aquifer, and natural conditions do not return enough water to maintain the supply.

Declining groundwater levels are a serious problem in many parts of the country. Even in wetter climatic areas, water users may withdraw water at faster rates than nature can return it. Lowering the amount of groundwater also reduces the flow of streams. In severe cases, soil compacts and the surface collapses as groundwater is taken out.

In the desert Southwest, particularly in Arizona and parts of Nevada, a severe water shortage exists. A potential water shortage encompasses most of the Great Basin and Rio Grande Valley. While water supplies are classed as adequate in California, the Rockies, and the Great Plains, these areas experience water shortages at fairly frequent intervals. A vast area of the southern Great Plains is over-using its groundwater supply. In southern California and the densely settled Phoenix area, there will certainly be problems as a result of overuse. Water supplies will not disappear, but water quality will certainly decrease there, and the salt content will undoubtedly increase through a process that scientists call "salinization."

In the northern glaciated area around Lake Michigan, as well as in the lower Mississippi Valley, the withdrawal of groundwater has caused settling of the soil. In some cases this causes walls to crack and structures to tilt, lean, and in extreme cases, collapse.

Water Consumption

Public Water Use   Industrial Water Use

Billion Gallons Per Day

'55 '70 '85

Aquifer Systems

1. Northern Great Plains
2. High Plains
3. Central Valley, California
4. Northern Midwest
5. Southwest Alluvial Basins
6. Floridan
7. Northern Atlantic Coastal Plain
8. Southeastern Coastal Plain
9. Snake River Plain
10. Central Midwest
11. Gulf Coastal Plain
12. Great Basin
13. Northeast Glacial
14. Upper Colorado River Basin
15. Oahu Island, Hawaii
16. Columbia Plateau Basalt
17. Edwards-Trinity
18. Southern California Alluvial Basins
19. Michigan Basin
20. San Jaun Basin
21. Ohio-Indiana Glacial Deposits and Carbonates
22. Pecos River Basin
23. Illinois Basin
24. Appalachian Valleys and Piedmont
25. No. Rockies Intermontane Basins
26. Puget-Willamette Trough
27. Alluvial Basins, OR, CA, and NV

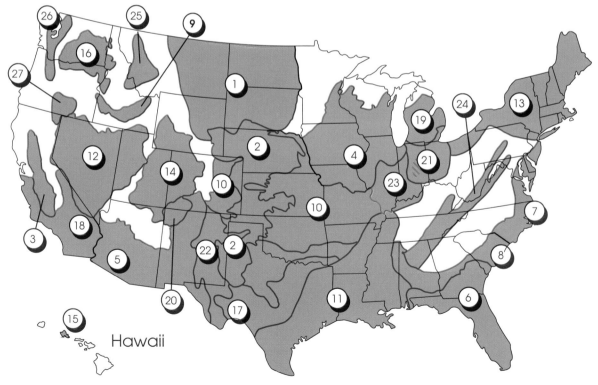

Hawaii

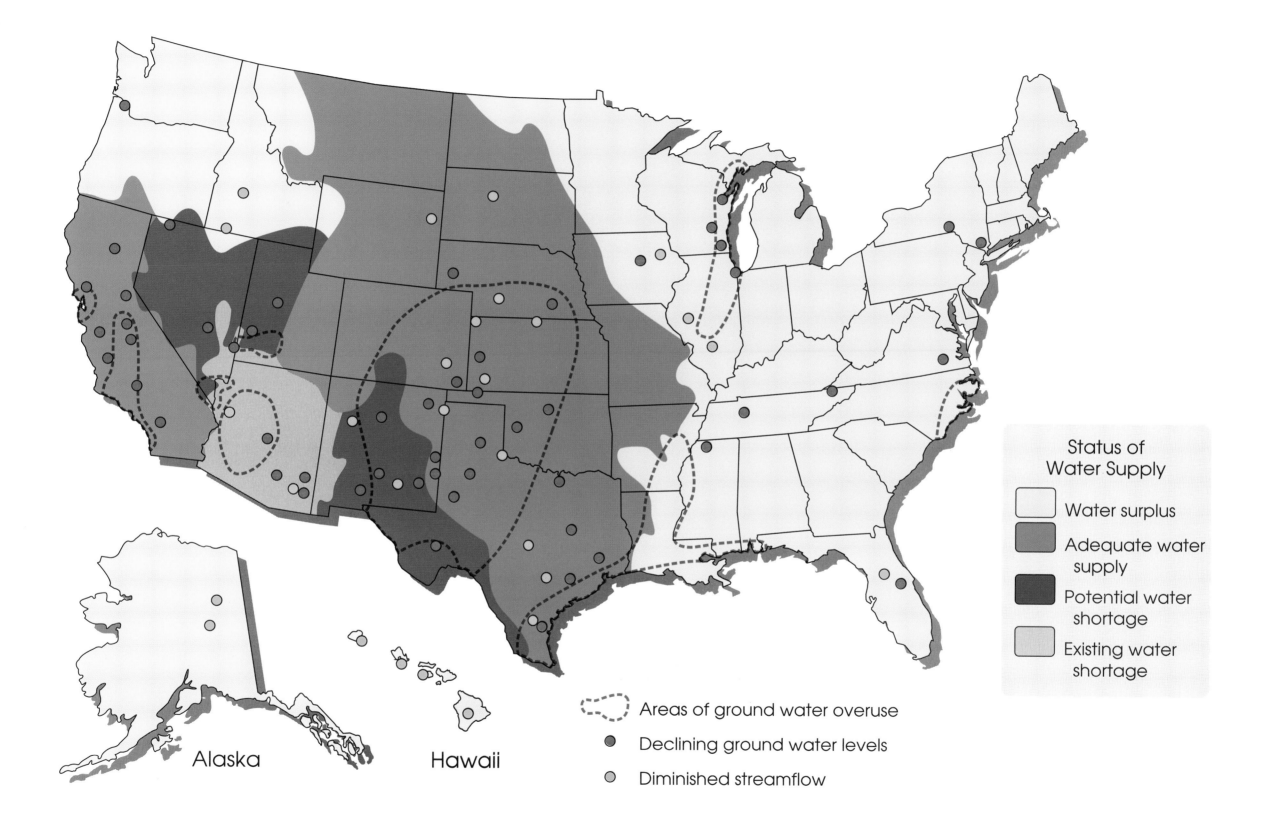

Status of
Water Supply

Water surplus

Adequate water
supply

Potential water
shortage

Existing water
shortage

Alaska   Hawaii

⌇ Areas of ground water overuse

● Declining ground water levels

● Diminished streamflow

Weather can be defined as the daily variations in temperature and precipitation that occur at any location. Climate is the long-term average of seasonal weather conditions. While daily changes in sunlight, cloud cover, temperature, and precipitation vary constantly, long term trends can be observed and generalizations about those trends can be made in defining average climatic conditions throughout the country.

In general, latitude, elevation, and proximity to the sea affect temperature. Climate is affected by human activities such as the discharge of aerosols and the generation of carbon dioxide from fossil fuels in what is referred to as the "greenhouse effect."

The accompanying maps show temperature averages for the months of January (winter) and July (summer). On the winter season map the spread of temperature (from warmest to coldest) is much greater than on the summer map. Isotherms (lines connecting points of equal temperature) indicate the effect of latitude over two-thirds of the country. In the heat of summer, this latitudinal zonation is less pronounced. In both seasons, the mountainous West exhibits strong temperature variations as altitude reduces temperatures. That is why mountains contain popular summer and ski resorts.

In general, temperatures are milder along the ocean shores. Oceans heat and cool less rapidly than land, tending to warm nearby land areas in winter and to cool them in summer. In the United States, this marine effect is more pronounced on the Pacific Coast, where winds are onshore.

U.S. Temperature Facts

		Mean Temperature (°F)		Annual Record (°F)		Annual Mean (°F)	Seasonal Degree Days
		January	July	High	Low		
Alabama	Mobile	50.8	82.2	104	3	67.5	1,695
Alaska	Juneau	21.8	55.7	90	-22	40.0	9,105
Arizona	Phoenix	52.3	92.3	118	17	41.2	1,442
Arkansas	Little Rock	21.8	52.7	112	-5	61.9	3,152
California	Los Angeles	56.0	69.0	110	23	62.6	1,595
	Sacramento	45.3	75.6	115	20	60.6	2,772
	San Diego	56.8	70.3	111	29	63.8	1,284
	San Francisco	48.5	62.2	106	20	56.6	3,161
Colorado	Denver	29.5	73.3	104	-30	50.3	6,014
Connecticut	Hartford	25.2	73.4	102	-26	49.8	6,174
Delaware	Wilmington	31.2	76.0	102	-14	54.0	4,986
Dist. of Col.	Washington	35.2	78.9	103	-5	57.5	4,122
Florida	Jacksonville	53.2	81.3	105	7	68.0	1,402
	Miami	67.1	82.4	98	30	75.6	199
Georgia	Atlanta	41.9	78.6	105	-8	61.2	3,021
Hawaii	Honolulu	72.6	80.1	94	53	77.0	0
Idaho	Boise	29.9	74.6	111	-23	51.1	5,802
Illinois	Chicago	21.4	73.0	102	-27	49.2	6,455
	Peoria	21.5	75.0	103	-25	50.4	6,226
Indiana	Indianapolis	26.0	75.1	104	-22	52.1	5,650
Iowa	Des Moines	18.6	76.3	108	-24	49.7	6,554
Kansas	Wichita	29.6	81.4	113	-21	56.4	4,787
Kentucky	Louisville	32.5	77.6	105	-20	56.2	4,525
Louisiana	New Orleans	52.4	82.1	102	14	68.2	1,490
Maine	Portland	21.5	68.1	103	-39	45.0	7,501
Maryland	Baltimore	32.7	75.6	105	-7	55.1	4,706
Massachusetts	Boston	29.6	73.5	102	-12	51.5	5,593
Michigan	Detroit	23.4	71.9	102	-21	48.6	6,563
	Sault Ste. Marie	13.3	62.9	98	-36	39.7	9,305
Minnesota	Duluth	6.3	65.3	97	-39	38.2	9,901
	Minneapolis-St. Paul	11.2	73.1	104	-34	44.7	8,007
Mississippi	Jackson	45.7	81.9	106	2	64.6	2,389
Missouri	Kansas City	25.9	78.5	109	-21	54.1	5,283
	St. Louis	28.8	78.9	107	-18	55.4	4,938
Montana	Great Falls	18.7	69.3	106	-43	44.7	7,766

		Mean Temperature (°F)		Annual Record (°F)		Annual Mean (°F)	Seasonal Degree Days
		January	July	High	Low		
Nebraska	Omaha	20.2	77.7	114	-23	51.1	6,194
Nevada	Reno	32.2	69.5	105	-16	49.4	6,030
New Hampshire	Concord	19.9	69.5	102	-37	45.3	7,482
New Jersey	Atlantic City	31.8	74.4	106	-11	53.1	5,086
New Mexico	Albuquerque	34.8	78.8	105	-17	56.2	4,414
New York	Albany	21.1	71.4	100	-28	47.3	6,927
	Buffalo	23.5	70.7	99	-20	47.6	6,798
	New York	31.8	76.7	106	-15	54.5	4,868
North Carolina	Charlotte	40.5	78.5	104	-5	60.0	3,342
	Raleigh	39.6	77.7	105	-9	59.0	3,531
North Dakota	Bismark	6.7	70.4	109	-44	41.3	9,075
Ohio	Cincinnati	28.9	75.4	102	-25	53.4	4,950
	Cleveland	25.5	71.6	103	-19	49.6	6,178
	Columbus	27.1	73.8	102	-19	51.7	5,686
Oklahoma	Oklahoma City	35.9	82.1	110	-4	59.9	4,691
Oregon	Portland	38.9	67.7	107	-3	53.0	4,947
Pennsylvania	Philadelphia	31.2	76.5	104	-7	54.3	5,950
	Pittsburgh	26.7	72.0	99	-18	50.3	5,908
Rhode Island	Providence	28.2	72.5	104	-13	50.3	2,629
South Carolina	Columbia	44.7	81.9	107	-1	63.3	7,885
South Dakota	Sioux Falls	12.4	74.0	108	-36	45.3	3,207
Tennessee	Memphis	39.6	82.1	108	-13	61.8	3,756
	Nashville	37.1	79.4	107	-17	59.2	2,407
Texas	Dallas-Fort Worth	44.0	86.3	113	4	66.0	2,664
	El Paso	44.2	82.5	112	-8	63.4	1,549
	Houston	51.4	83.1	107	11	68.3	5,802
Utah	Salt Lake City	28.6	77.5	107	-30	51.7	7,953
Vermont	Burlington	16.6	69.6	101	-30	44.1	3,446
Virginia	Norfolk	39.9	78.4	104	-3	59.5	3,960
	Richmond	36.6	77.8	105	-12	57.7	5,121
Washington	Seattle-Tacoma	36.1	64.8	99	0	51.4	6,882
	Spokane	25.7	69.7	108	-25	47.2	4,697
West Virginia	Charleston	32.9	74.5	102	-15	54.8	7,326
Wisconsin	Milwaukee	18.7	70.5	101	-26	46.1	7,310
Wyoming	Cheyenne	26.1	68.9	100	-34	45.7	7,310

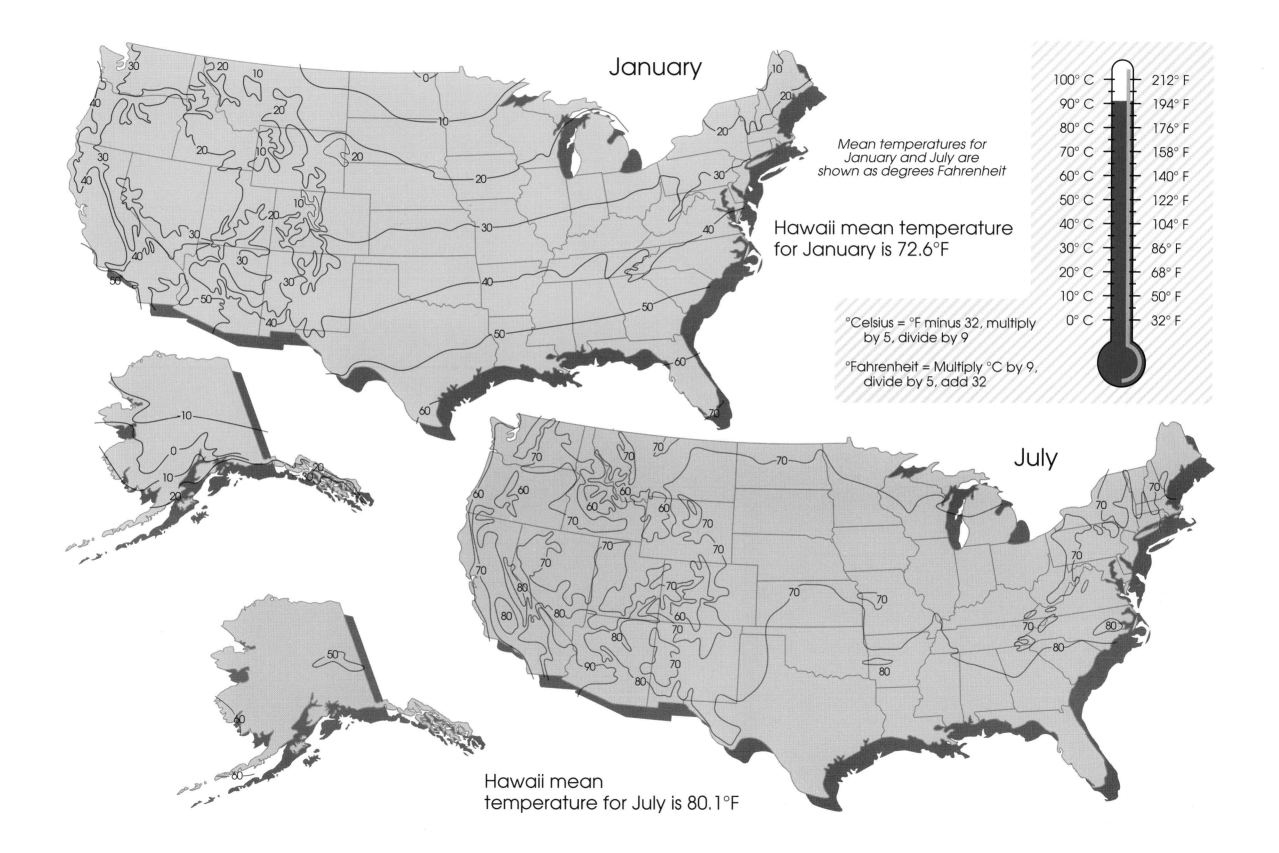

January

Mean temperatures for January and July are shown as degrees Fahrenheit

Hawaii mean temperature for January is 72.6°F

100° C	212° F
90° C	194° F
80° C	176° F
70° C	158° F
60° C	140° F
50° C	122° F
40° C	104° F
30° C	86° F
20° C	68° F
10° C	50° F
0° C	32° F

°Celsius = °F minus 32, multiply by 5, divide by 9

°Fahrenheit = Multiply °C by 9, divide by 5, add 32

July

Hawaii mean temperature for July is 80.1°F

The United States can be divided into an eastern, wetter region and a western region in which drier conditions prevail. The amount of rainfall any area receives depends on a great many individual factors. In the United States, both the direction of rainbearing weather systems and the arrangement of mountains in relation to the winds are important in explaining the pattern of rainfall.

Moisture-bearing weather systems are most frequently generated over the northern Pacific Ocean or the warm tropical water to the south and southeast of the mainland. These systems are caught up and pushed along by the prevailing winds that cross America from west to east. The average paths these storms take are called storm tracks. Major storm tracks are indicated by arrows on the map to the immediate right.

The dry western areas of the United States result from the position of mountains in relation to the winds and weather systems. As eastward moving storms pass over these mountains—the coastal ranges, Sierras, and Cascades—the air masses rise, cool, and drop their moisture. After crossing the mountains, most of the moisture is lost. Rains occur on the western side of the mountains leaving the eastern side arid. This blocking of rainfall by mountains is called the "rainshadow effect."

Storms originating over the Gulf of Mexico move north toward the land, but are soon picked up by winds moving from west to east. The dry west is isolated from Pacific weather systems by mountains, and from tropical weather systems by wind patterns that favor movement from west to east.

U.S. Precipitation Facts

		Normal Annual Precipitation (inches)	Average Days with Precipitation of .01 or More	Annual Snow & Ice (inches)			Normal Annual Precipitation (inches)	Average Days with Precipitation of .01 or More	Annual Snow & Ice (inches)
Alabama	Mobile	64.64	123	0.3	Nebraska	Omaha	30.34	98	30.5
Alaska	Juneau	53.15	220	99.9	Nevada	Reno	7.49	51	24.8
Arizona	Phoenix	7.11	36	Trace	New Hampshire	Concord	36.53	125	64.3
Arkansas	Little Rock	49.20	103	5.3	New Jersey	Atlantic City	41.93	112	16.6
California	Los Angeles	12.08	36	Trace	New Mexico	Albuquerque	8.12	61	10.9
	Sacramento	17.10	58	0.1	New York	Albany	35.74	134	65.5
	San Diego	9.32	43	Trace		Buffalo	37.52	169	92.3
	San Francisco	19.71	62			New York	44.12	121	28.6
Colorado	Denver	15.31	89	60.3	North Carolina	Charlotte	43.16	111	5.8
Connecticut	Hartford	44.39	127	48.8		Raleigh	41.76	111	7.5
Delaware	Wilmington	41.38	117	21.3	North Dakota	Bismarck	15.36	97	41.0
Dist. of Col.	Washington	39.00	111	17.4	Ohio	Cincinnati	40.14	129	23.6
Florida	Jacksonville	52.76	116	Trace		Cleveland	35.40	156	54.1
	Miami	57.55	129	0		Columbus	36.97	137	28.5
Georgia	Atlanta	48.61	115	1.9	Oklahoma	Oklahoma City	30.89	82	9.3
Hawaii	Honolulu	23.47	100	0	Oregon	Portland	37.39	152	6.8
Idaho	Boise	11.71	91	21.4	Pennsylvania	Philadelphia	41.42	117	21.8
Illinois	Chicago	33.34	127	39.8		Pittsburgh	36.30	154	44.2
	Peoria	34.89	114	25.2	Rhode Island	Providence	45.32	124	36.3
Indiana	Indianapolis	39.12	125	22.9	South Carolina	Columbia	49.12	109	1.8
Iowa	Des Moines	30.83	107	34.4	South Dakota	Sioux Falls	24.12	97	39.7
Kansas	Wichita	28.61	86	17.0	Tennessee	Memphis	51.57	106	5.7
Kentucky	Louisville	43.56	125	17.3		Nashville	48.49	119	10.9
Louisiana	New Orleans	59.74	114	0	Texas	Dallas-Fort Worth	29.46	78	3.0
Maine	Portland	43.52	128	71.5		El Paso	7.82	48	5.8
Maryland	Baltimore	41.84	113	21.9		Houston	44.76	106	0.4
Massachusetts	Boston	43.81	126	41.5	Utah	Salt Lake City	15.31	91	58.0
Michigan	Detroit	30.97	135	42.0	Vermont	Burlington	33.69	154	77.9
	Sault Ste. Marie	33.48	165	114.9	Virginia	Norfolk	45.22	114	7.5
Minnesota	Duluth	29.68	134	76.8		Richmond	44.07	113	14.6
	Minneapolis-St. Paul	26.36	115	49.1	Washington	Seattle-Tacoma	38.60	156	12.6
Mississippi	Jackson	52.82	109			Spokane	16.71	113	51.2
Missouri	Kansas City	35.16	107	20.3	West Virginia	Charleston	42.43	151	32.7
	St. Louis	33.91	111	19.7	Wisconsin	Milwaukee	30.94	125	46.7
Montana	Great Falls	15.24	101	58.3	Wyoming	Cheyenne	13.31	99	54.1

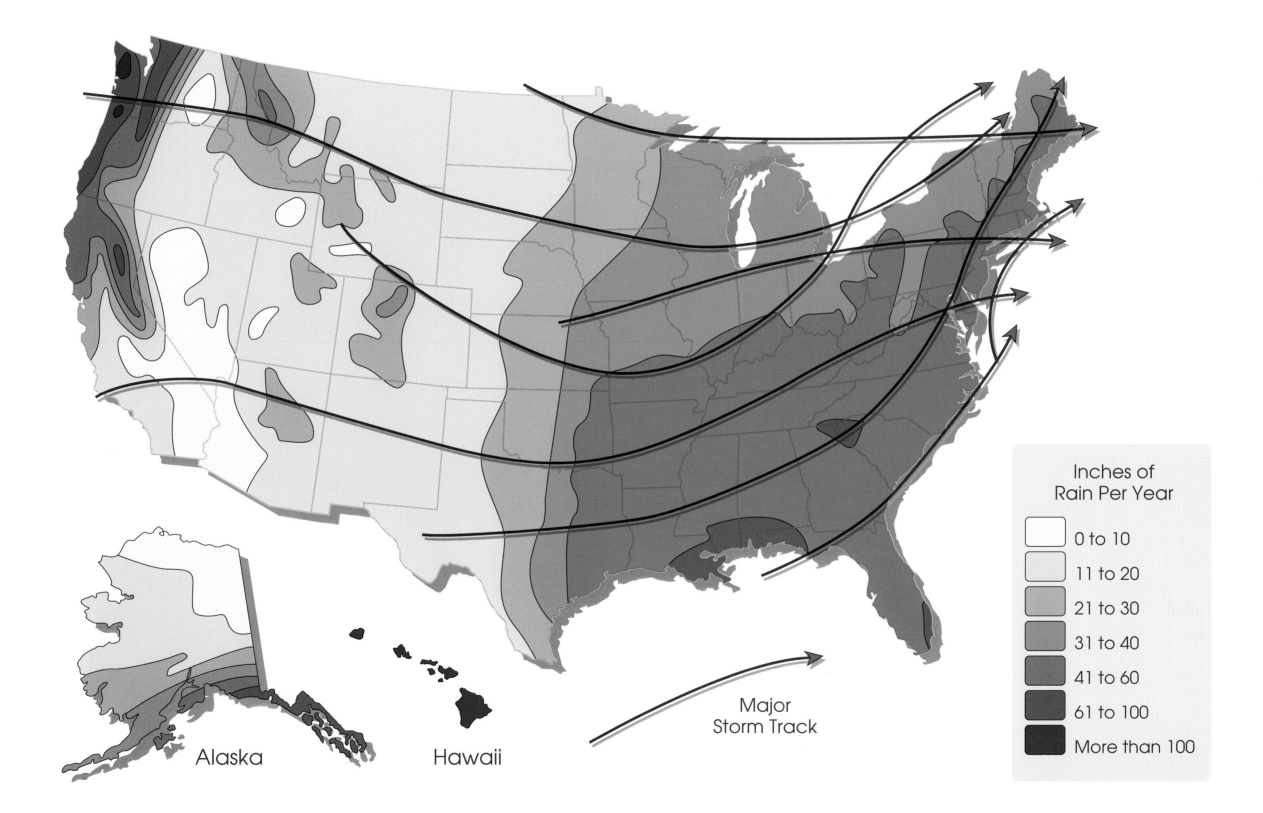

Inches of
Rain Per Year

0 to 10

11 to 20

21 to 30

31 to 40

41 to 60

61 to 100

More than 100

Major
Storm Track

Alaska

Hawaii

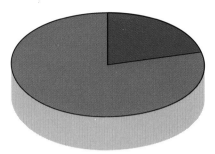

Federal/NonFederal

It seems at times that America's forests and farms are rapidly being converted to housing developments, shopping centers, and office parks. This is not really the case. In fact, urban development occupies only 3 percent of the total land area, and it has taken almost 50 years to increase that figure from 2 percent. Forest occupies 22 percent of the country, and the forested area has been growing consistently for reasons that are explained later in this discussion.

Area devoted to farming reached its peak in 1944. Since then the percent of farmland has been decreasing rapidly. Valuable farmland has been lost, particularly in California and Florida. Some fertile cropland has been lost to urban expansion in states like Ohio, Indiana, Illinois, and Iowa. In desert areas, as urban centers are built up, the cropland is simply "moved" to areas that were once used for grazing or were simply wasteland. Water, rather than land, is the valuable commodity being lost in much of the West.

Most of the land that is no longer used for farming has returned to forest. Since small family farms find it difficult to compete with agribusiness (large corporate farms), many small holdings have been abandoned and simply revert to forest. This is particularly common in the Northeast, the northern Midwest, and the Appalachian region. Federal programs such as the Soil Bank were designed to aid the transition of the South from a rural to an urban economy and to promote conservation. This program and later ones have created vast new forests in the South.

The federal government is the largest landowner in the United States. Federal ownership includes Indian reservations, national parks, national forests, military bases, and vast areas of rangeland. Most of these holdings are in the West or in Alaska. Some citizens in western states feel that federal ownership limits development. Still others feel that states with few federal holdings have an unfair advantage since privately held land yields taxes while federal land does not.

The government allows local farmers to graze cattle and sheep on federal rangelands. Lumbering and some mining are also allowed on federal holdings. All these functions are strictly controlled in order to prevent destruction of the environment. Very few of these federal lands are total wilderness areas, and fewer still are completely closed to the public.

Most lands east of the Rockies were already in private hands when the federal government became concerned with conservation. This concern was influenced by the destruction of forests by irresponsible lumber interests in the past. Acquisition of remaining unsettled areas concentrated federal lands in the West. Many of the areas held in national parks and forests have unique features and majestic scenery.

Urban/Rural

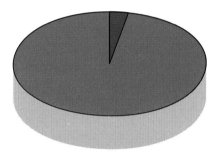

Rural Land

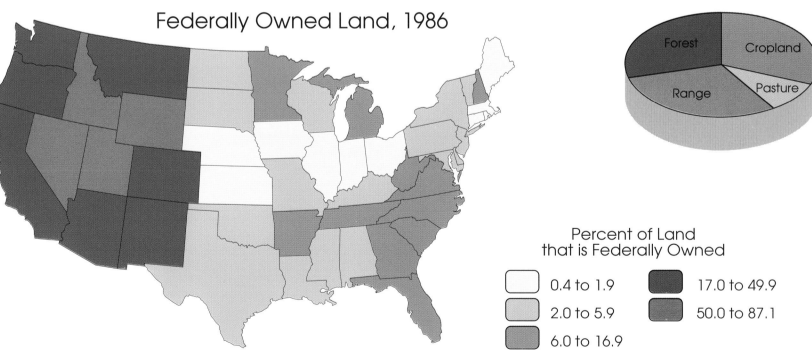

Federally Owned Land, 1986

Percent of Land that is Federally Owned

0.4 to 1.9   17.0 to 49.9

2.0 to 5.9   50.0 to 87.1

6.0 to 16.9

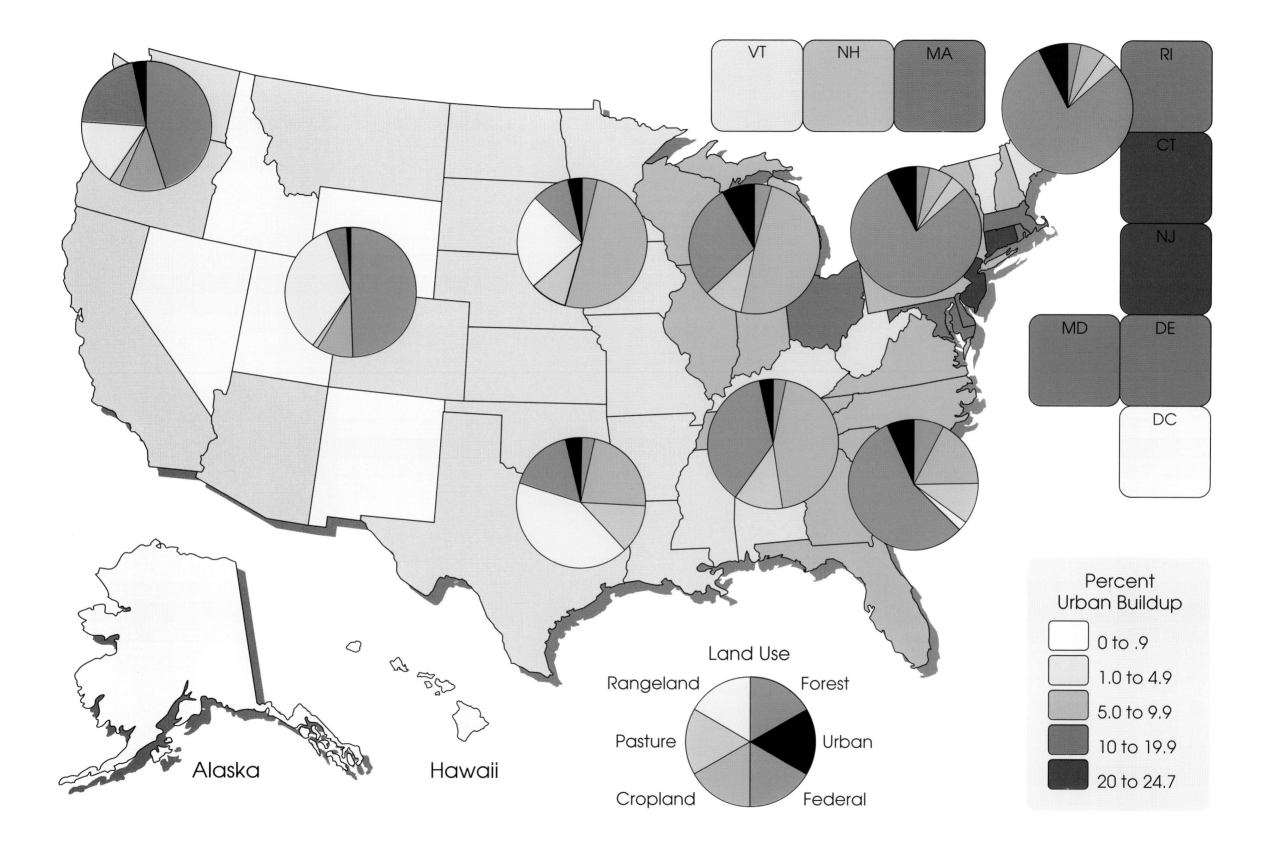

VT | NH | MA | RI | CT | NJ | MD | DE | DC

Land Use

Rangeland | Forest
Pasture | Urban
Cropland | Federal

Percent
Urban Buildup

0 to .9
1.0 to 4.9
5.0 to 9.9
10 to 19.9
20 to 24.7

Alaska | Hawaii

THE PAST   25

The date of the original settlement of North America has been pushed back time and time again as archeologists have uncovered progressively older sites. It is believed the ancestors of today's Native Americans reached the New World from Asia 20,000 to 40,000 years ago by crossing a land bridge then located near the Bering Strait. Dated remains uncovered thusfar go back to 10,000 B.C.

Native Americans entered the country through Alaska, and extended their settlements slowly and progressively down the rocky and inhospitable coast to what is now the state of Washington. From there they migrated inland in all directions. They had reached the Atlantic Coast before 5000 B.C.

Each settlement existed separately. Lifestyle was closely adapted to a particular natural environment, with the occupants of each territory using different building materials, building different types of structures, and consuming different diets. By the time Europeans arrived to explore, Native Americans had extended settlement to virtually all parts of the land.

The exploration party of Leif Eriksson, a Norse sailor, was apparently the first of the Europeans to arrive here. Columbus, who discovered the New World for Spain in 1492, never did set foot on what was to become the United States. Verrazano, in the employ of France, was the first of the European explorers to journey through the coastal waters of what became the United States. He was followed by a host of explorers from Spain, Portugal, France, and England, allowing each country to lay claim to certain areas of the new world.

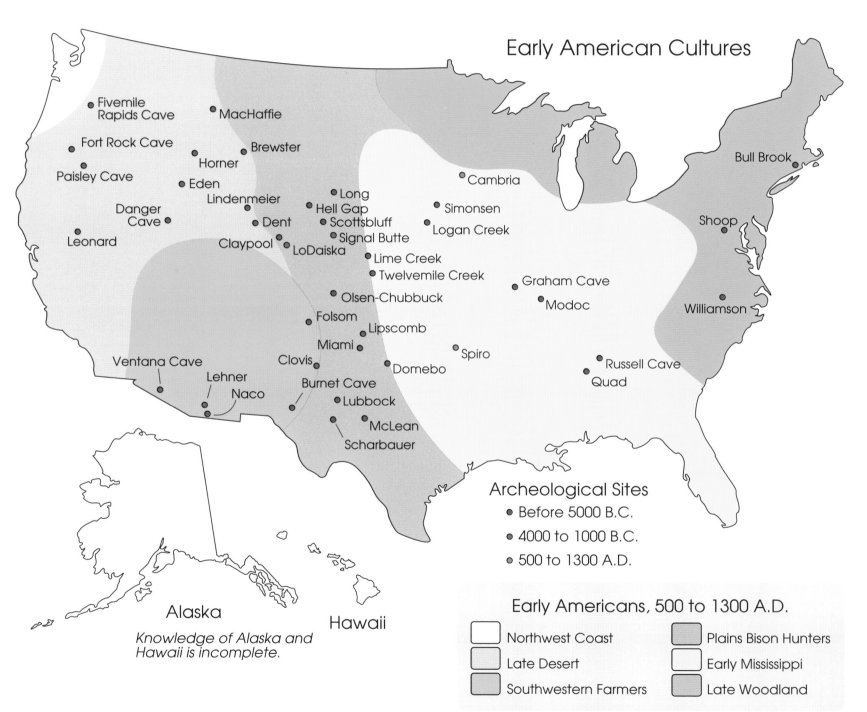

Early American Cultures

Fivemile Rapids Cave
MacHaffie
Fort Rock Cave
Brewster
Horner
Paisley Cave
Eden
Lindenmeier
Danger Cave
Dent
Leonard
Claypool
LoDaiska
Long
Hell Gap
Scottsbluff
Signal Butte
Cambria
Simonsen
Logan Creek
Lime Creek
Twelvemile Creek
Graham Cave
Olsen-Chubbuck
Modoc
Folsom
Lipscomb
Miami
Spiro
Ventana Cave
Clovis
Domebo
Russell Cave
Lehner
Quad
Naco
Burnet Cave
Lubbock
McLean
Scharbauer
Bull Brook
Shoop
Williamson

Alaska   Hawaii
Knowledge of Alaska and Hawaii is incomplete.

Archeological Sites
● Before 5000 B.C.
● 4000 to 1000 B.C.
● 500 to 1300 A.D.

Early Americans, 500 to 1300 A.D.
☐ Northwest Coast
☐ Late Desert
☐ Southwestern Farmers
☐ Plains Bison Hunters
☐ Early Mississippi
☐ Late Woodland

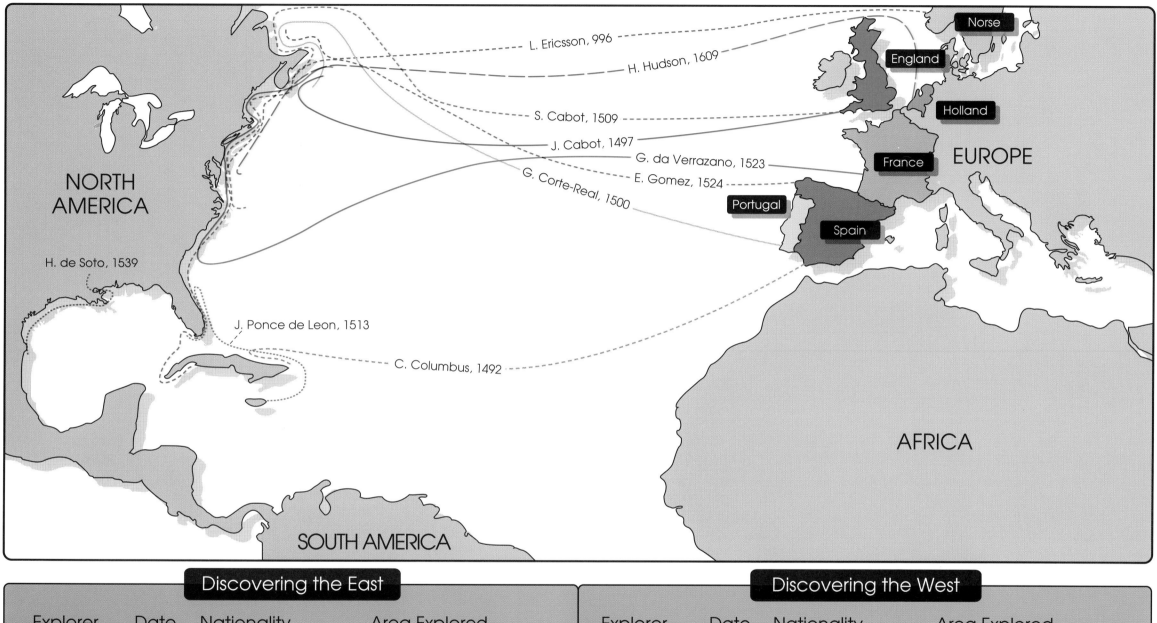

L. Ericsson, 996

H. Hudson, 1609

S. Cabot, 1509

J. Cabot, 1497

G. da Verrazano, 1523

G. Corte-Real, 1500

E. Gomez, 1524

H. de Soto, 1539

J. Ponce de Leon, 1513

C. Columbus, 1492

NORTH AMERICA

SOUTH AMERICA

EUROPE

AFRICA

Norse

England

Holland

France

Portugal

Spain

Discovering the East

Explorer	Date	Nationality	Area Explored
L. Ericsson	996	Norse	Newfoundland, Greenland, Davis Strait
C. Columbus	1492	Spanish	Cuba and Haiti
J. Cabot	1497	English	Nova Scotia and Newfoundland
G. Corte-Real	1500	Portuguese	Greenland and Newfoundland
S. Cabot	1509	English	Labrador, East Coast of US to Carolinas
J. Ponce de Leon	1513	Spanish	Puerto Rico and Florida
E. Gomez	1524	Spanish	Newfoundland Along Coast to Cuba
H. de Soto	1539	Spanish	Gulf Coast of Florida
S. de Champlain	1603	French	Gulf of St. Lawrence
H. Hudson	1609	Dutch	Hudson Bay

Discovering the West

Explorer	Date	Nationality	Area Explored
H. de Alarcon	1540	Spanish	Mexico, Gulf of California
J. Cabrillo	1542	Spanish	Mexico, Baja California, Coast of California
A. de Arellano	1565	Spanish	Northern California Coast to Southern Mexico
F. Drake	1577	English	Cape Horn, So. America, Washington, Oregon, California Coast
S. Cermenho	1595	Spanish	Northern California Coast to Southern Mexico
V. Bering	1741	Russian	Bering Sea and Bering Strait
J. Cook	1776	English	Pacific Northwest, Canadian Coast, Alaska, Bering Sea, Arctic Ocean
G. Vancouver	1791	English	West Coasts of North and South America

Prior to actual settlement, many European states sent explorers to the interior of the North American continent. Spaniards Ponce de Leon, De Soto, and Diaz were among the first as they scoured Florida and areas as far inland as Arizona in search of gold. Military leaders, such as de Portola, were followed by missionaries up California's coast and later through Texas and New Mexico. The Indians who were converted to Christianity became farmers and lived on the grounds of the mission. In the process, many intermarried with Spaniards. Others were simply assimilated into the Spanish culture. Regardless of origin, they were effectively "settlers" and helped to confirm Spain's claims to the areas they occupied.

Sailing due west from France, in a futile search for a *Northwest Passage,* Champlain found a land much colder and far less usable than his homeland. What he and other French explorers found were furs. France laid claim inland to the Great Lakes (Brule) and ultimately to the Mississippi Valley (Marquette and Joliet) using the St. Lawrence and Mississippi rivers as main trade arteries.

Henry Hudson explored for both the Dutch and the British. The establishment of Dutch settlements along the Hudson River followed his travels. Although he explored the Delaware also, it was the Swedes who settled there first.

The English, with an economic interest in tobacco, settled in Virginia (1607). Their control extended to Canada after they defeated the French in the French and Indian War which ended in 1763. It later

diminished as American colonialists won independence in 1781. With the Treaty of Paris (1783), England ceded all land east of the Mississippi River, resulting in a surge of westward settlement.

Earlier Americans and their descendants gradually extended control over the entire continent, purchasing the Louisiana territory from France, Florida and the Gulf Coast from Spain, annexing Texas from Mexico, and, ultimately, fighting that country for control of the Southwest. Britain agreed (under pressure) to cede the Oregon Country in the 1850s.

With the addition of each new piece of territory, and the pacification or defeat of the native Americans, settlement pushed relentlessly westward. By 1835 it had crossed the Mississippi. By 1845, settlement extended to Texas. The California gold rush (1849) drew settlers to the Pacific, and the Oregon territory was colonized immediately thereafter. Pious Mormons colonized the Utah oasis during the same era (1847). The land in between awaited the technology that allowed farming of the dry prairies—farm machinery.

By 1890, the last frontier had been reached on the Great Plains, while mining camps had brought settlers to the Rockies. Only Oklahoma and the Southwest, the last Indian territories, remained. These areas were sufficiently settled to become states only in the 20th century.

Alaska, explored and settled by Russians, was purchased by the U.S. during the Lincoln administration. Hawaii, explored and settled by Polynesians, was the last area annexed (1898). Alaska is something of a modern frontier area since settlement continues there at present.

Major Explorers of the United States

Explorer	Date	Area Explored
M Díaz	1540	Sonora, Mexico to lower Colorado R. to Baja California.
H. Hudson	1609	Hudson R.
S. de Champlain	1609	St. Lawrence to L. Champlain.
S. de Champlain	1613	Montréal to Ottawa R.
É. Brulé	1615–1618	L. Simcoe to Niagara R. to L. Oneida to Susquehanna R. to Chesapeake Bay. Return to Geogian Bay to L. Huron.
É. Brulé & Grenolle	1623	Manitoulin I. to Sault Ste. Marie.
J. Nicolet	1638	Sault Ste. Marie to Green Bay to Fox R.
L. Joliet	1668–1669	Ottawa R. to Sault Ste. Marie to L. Huron to L. Erie to L. Ontario.
L. Joliet & J. Marquette	1672	St. Ignace to Fox R. to Wisconsin R. to Mississippi River. Return via Illinois R.
L. Hennepin	1679	Ft. Crevecoeur to Illinois R. to Mississippi R. to Falls of St. Anthony.
R. de La Salle	1679–1680	Ft. St. Joseph to Kankakee R. to Ft. Crevecoeur. Return to Ft. St. Joseph to L. Ontario to Ft. Frontenac.
R. de La Salle	1682	L. Michigan to Illinois R. to Mississippi R. to Gulf of Mexico.
M. Chartier	1684–1692	Sonioto to Ohio R. to Susquehanna R. to Chesapeake Bay.
R. de La Salle	1686	Ft. St. Louis at Matagorda Bay to Neches R. area.
R. de La Salle & H. Joutel	1687	Ft. St. Louis to Trinity R. La Salle killed and Joutel reaches Arkansas Post.
P. & P. Mallet	1738–1741	Missouri R. to Platte R. to Santa Fe to Canadian R. to Mississippi R. to New Orleans.
C. Gist	1750–1752	Potomac R. to Allegheny Mts. to Ohio R. to Shawnee country to New R.
D. Boone	1767–1771	Big Sandy R.; Licking R. to Ohio R. to Kentucky R.; Cumberland R.
G. de Portolá	1769–1770	San Diego to San Francisco Bay to Monterey Bay.
M. Lewis & W. Clark	1804–1806	St. Louis to Missouri R. to Three Forks to Lolo Pass to Columbia R. to Ft. Clatsop. Back to Traveler's Rest. W. Clark to Three Forks. Both meet at Missouri and Yellowstone Rivers and return.
M. Lewis	1806	Traveler's Rest to Mirias R. to Missouri R. at Yellowstone R. Meets W. Clark.
W. Clark	1806	Traveler's Rest to Bozeman Pass to Yellowstone R. at Missouri. Meets M. Lewis.
Z. Pike	1804	St. Louis to upper Mississippi R. to Leech L. and return.
Z. Pike	1805–1807	St. Louis to Pawnee villages to Colorado Rockies to Rio Grande. Captured and taken to Mexico. Return via El Camino Real.
S. Long	1817	Ft. Smith to Hot Springs to Cape Girardeau.
S. Long	1819–1820	Ft. Atkinson to Platte R. to Pikes Peak to Canadian R. to Ft. Smith.
P. Ogden	1824–1825	Ft. Nez Perce to Flathead House to Pierre's Hole to Great Salt L.
P. Ogden	1826–1827	Ft. Vancouver to southern Oregon to Malheur L.
P. Ogden	1828–1829	Malheatu L. to Great Salt L. to Ft. Nez Perce to Malheur L.
J. Frémont	1842	Independence to Oregon Trail to Ft. St. Vrain to Fremont Peak.
J. Frémont	1843	Independence to Republican R. to Ft. Hall to Great Salt L. to Ft. Vancouver to San Joaquin Valley to Old Spanish Trail to Bent's Fort to Independence.
J. Frémont	1845	Independence to Bent's Fort to Salt Lake City to Humboldt R. to California via Sutter's Fort and Walker Pass to Klamath R.
J. Frémont	1848	Independence to Pueblo to Sangre de Cristo Mts. to Pool Table Mt. to Taos.

With an area of over three million square miles, America is the fourth largest country (in area) in the world. The original colonies occupied a much smaller and less well-defined area. The treaty of 1783 that ended the War of Independence granted the new country title to a large unsettled area between the Appalachian frontier and the Mississippi River. This territory of almost 900,000 square miles made the fledgling country one of the world's largest even at that time.

The area of the United States nearly doubled with the purchase of Louisiana. Through a combination of purchase and cession, Florida became a part of the country (1815–1819), and the United States held clear title to everything east of the Rockies and south of Canada to the borders of the area known as Texas. In 1818, a treaty with Britain straightened the northern border at the 49th parallel. In 1845, a then much larger Texas was annexed after it had declared independence from Mexico. United States control along the Pacific was established after Mexico's defeat in the Mexican War. In 1846, in the midst of that war, Britain agreed to a division of the disputed Oregon territory between the U.S. and Canada. The 49th parallel border was extended to the Pacific. The Gadsden Purchase of 1853 established the current border between Mexico and the United States.

Settlement sometimes preceded acquisition, and statehood generally followed settlement. All 48 contiguous states were in existence by 1912. The last two additions (Alaska and Hawaii) were made in 1959.

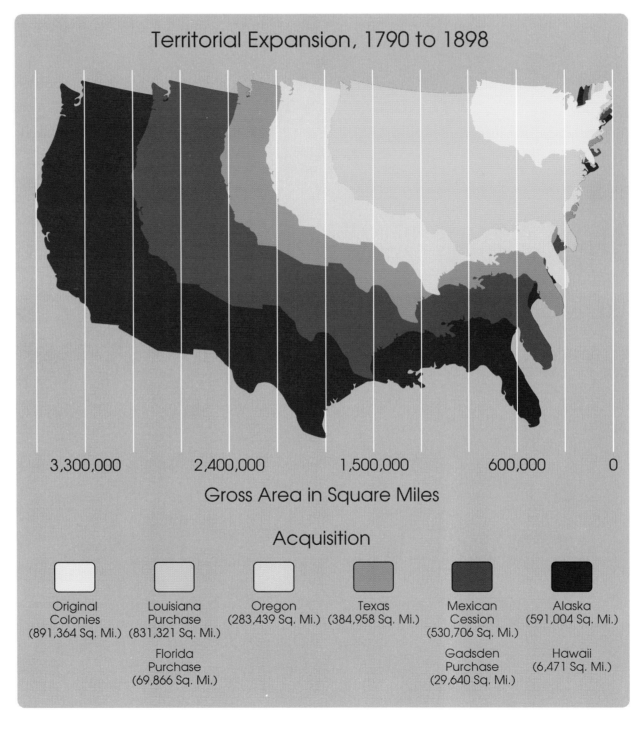

Territorial Expansion, 1790 to 1898

3,300,000   2,400,000   1,500,000   600,000   0

Gross Area in Square Miles

Acquisition

Original Colonies (891,364 Sq. Mi.)
Louisiana Purchase (831,321 Sq. Mi.)
Oregon (283,439 Sq. Mi.)
Texas (384,958 Sq. Mi.)
Mexican Cession (530,706 Sq. Mi.)
Alaska (591,004 Sq. Mi.)
Florida Purchase (69,866 Sq. Mi.)
Gadsden Purchase (29,640 Sq. Mi.)
Hawaii (6,471 Sq. Mi.)

Year of Statehood	
Alabama	1819
Alaska	1959
Arizona	1912
Arkansas	1836
California	1850
Colorado	1876
Connecticut	1776
Delaware	1776
Florida	1845
Georgia	1776
Hawaii	1959
Idaho	1890
Illinois	1818
Indiana	1816
Iowa	1846
Kansas	1861
Kentucky	1792
Louisiana	1812
Maine	1820
Maryland	1776
Massachusetts	1776
Michigan	1837
Minnesota	1858
Mississippi	1817
Missouri	1821
Montana	1889
Nebraska	1867
Nevada	1864
New Hampshire	1776
New Jersey	1776
New Mexico	1912
New York	1776
North Carolina	1776
North Dakota	1889
Ohio	1803
Oklahoma	1907
Oregon	1859
Pennsylvania	1776
Rhode Island	1776
South Carolina	1776
South Dakota	1889
Tennessee	1796
Texas	1845
Utah	1896
Vermont	1791
Virginia	1776
Washington	1889
West Virginia	1863
Wisconsin	1848
Wyoming	1890

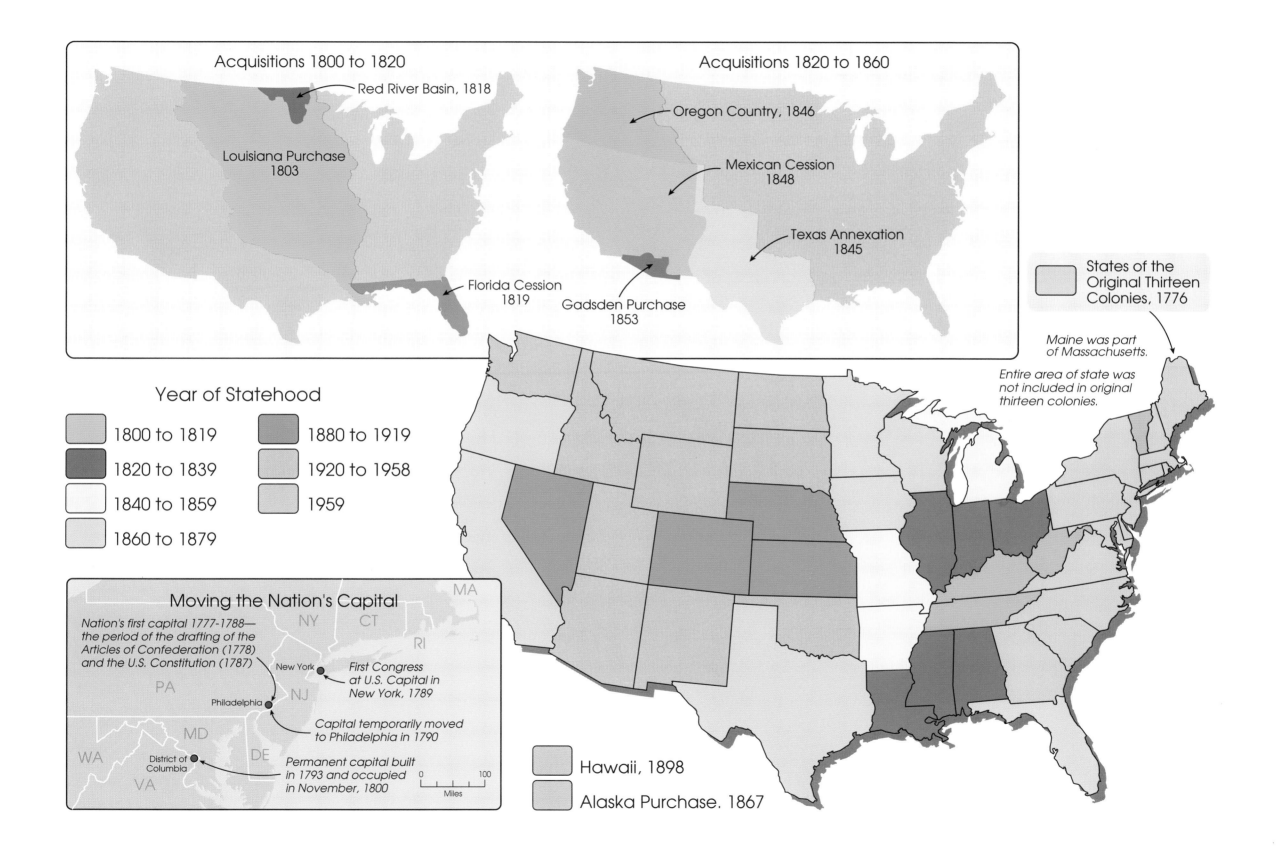

Acquisitions 1800 to 1820

Red River Basin, 1818

Louisiana Purchase
1803

Florida Cession
1819

Acquisitions 1820 to 1860

Oregon Country, 1846

Mexican Cession
1848

Texas Annexation
1845

Gadsden Purchase
1853

States of the
Original Thirteen
Colonies, 1776

Maine was part
of Massachusetts.

Entire area of state was
not included in original
thirteen colonies.

Year of Statehood

- 1800 to 1819
- 1820 to 1839
- 1840 to 1859
- 1860 to 1879
- 1880 to 1919
- 1920 to 1958
- 1959

Moving the Nation's Capital

MA

NY   CT

RI

PA

NJ

New York

Philadelphia

MD

DE

WA

District of
Columbia

VA

*Nation's first capital 1777-1788—
the period of the drafting of the
Articles of Confederation (1778)
and the U.S. Constitution (1787)*

*First Congress
at U.S. Capital in
New York, 1789*

*Capital temporarily moved
to Philadelphia in 1790*

*Permanent capital built
in 1793 and occupied
in November, 1800*

0   100

Miles

Hawaii, 1898

Alaska Purchase. 1867

Native Americans, misnamed *Indians* by European explorers, reached this continent between 20,000 and 40,000 years ago having migrated from Asia over a land bridge in the area that is now the Bering Strait. Most continued to move through North America, settling areas from Mexico through Argentina and Chile. Only two million or so Native Americans remained to inhabit areas that are today the United States and Canada.

A few great language groups called "nations" dominated among Native Americans. Each nation was divided into tribes that either farmed or lived by hunting, fishing, and gathering in their native environment.

European settlers quickly came into conflict with Native Americans as they dispossessed them from their tribal lands. While some early settlers treated Indians fairly, many exploited and cheated their less technologically sophisticated neighbors. In retaliation, Native Americans sided first with the French, and later with the British, in a series of wars involving colonial settlers.

In a series of conflicts with U.S. military forces during the mid-19th century, Indians were dislodged from their last strongholds: the forests of the Deep South, the Great Plains, and the deserts of the Southwest. Those who survived were placed on Indian reservations, primarily in the Plains, the Southwest, Oklahoma, and the areas surrounding the Great Lakes. This relocation is

reflected in the distribution of today's Native American citizens.

At the end of the hostilities, Native Americans of the 1880s held lands amounting to 138 million acres. In 1887, however, the "Dawes Act" stipulated that all Indian land was to be broken into 160-acre plots to be given to each Indian head of household and that the government could hold those plots until their

rightful owners were deemed competent to take possession of them. Under this discriminatory and arbitrary system, lands were often leased to non-Indian developers on the basis of 99-year leases. Other Indian land was broken up and sold to settlers. By its repeal in 1934, the Dawes Act left an indigenous Indian population with only one-third of the land that it had held prior to 1887.

Please note that the use of teepees to symbolize tribe locations is a matter of graphic convenience and is not meant to represent a stereotypical idea of the vast and various aspects of traditional Indian life.

Major Indian Tribes and Eskimo Groups

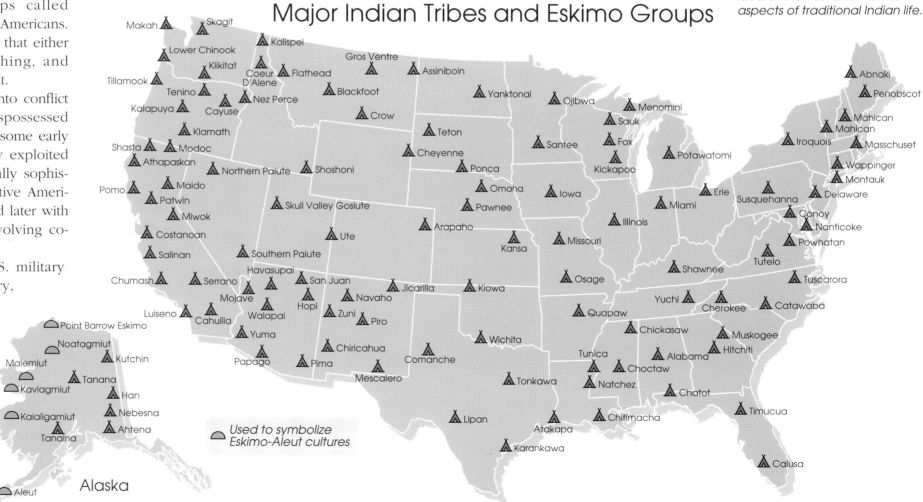

Used to symbolize Eskimo-Aleut cultures

Alaska

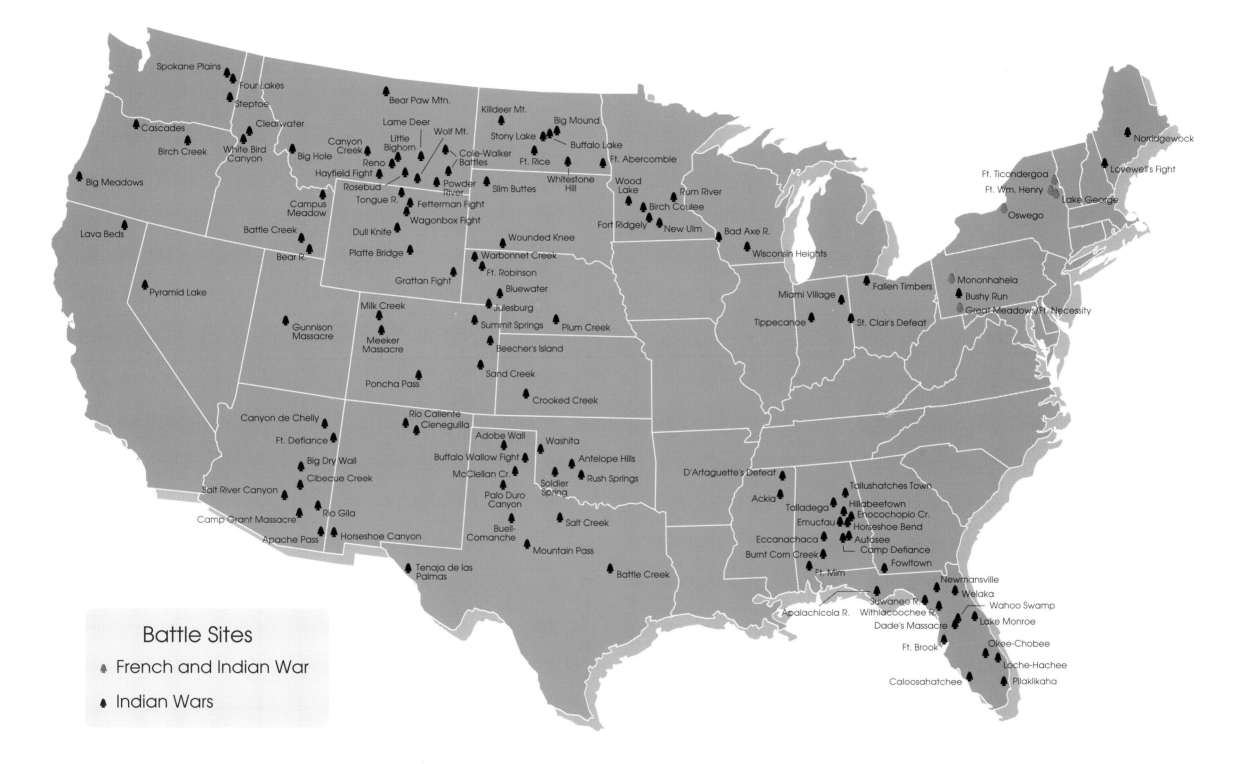

Spokane Plains
Four Lakes
Steptoe
Cascades
Clearwater
Birch Creek
White Bird Canyon
Big Hole
Bear Paw Mtn.
Lame Deer
Wolf Mt.
Canyon Creek
Little Bighorn
Reno
Hayfield Fight
Rosebud
Powder River
Tongue R.
Fetterman Fight
Campus Meadow
Wagonbox Fight
Big Meadows
Battle Creek
Dull Knife
Platte Bridge
Lava Beds
Bear R.
Pyramid Lake
Gunnison Massacre
Milk Creek
Meeker Massacre
Grattan Fight
Killdeer Mt.
Big Mound
Stony Lake
Buffalo Lake
Ft. Rice
Slim Buttes
Whitestone Hill
Ft. Abercombie
Wood Lake
Birch Coulee
Rum River
Fort Ridgely
New Ulm
Bad Axe R.
Wisconsin Heights
Wounded Knee
Warbonnet Creek
Ft. Robinson
Bluewater
Julesburg
Summit Springs
Plum Creek
Beecher's Island
Sand Creek
Poncha Pass
Crooked Creek
Canyon de Chelly
Ft. Defiance
Rio Caliente
Cieneguilla
Adobe Wall
Washita
Big Dry Wall
Cibecue Creek
Buffalo Wallow Fight
Antelope Hills
Salt River Canyon
McClellan Cr.
Rush Springs
Soldier Spring
Camp Grant Massacre
Rio Gila
Palo Duro Canyon
Apache Pass
Horseshoe Canyon
Buell-Comanche
Salt Creek
Tenaja de las Palmas
Mountain Pass
Battle Creek
Cole-Walker Battles

Miami Village
Tippecanoe
Fallen Timbers
St. Clair's Defeat
Mononhahela
Bushy Run
Great Meadows/Ft. Necessity

Ft. Ticondergoa
Ft. Wm. Henry
Oswego
Norridgewock
Lovewell's Fight
Lake George

D'Artaguette's Defeat
Ackia
Talladega
Emucfau
Eccanachaca
Burnt Corn Creek
Ft. Mim
Apalachicola R.
Tallushatches Town
Hillabeetown
Enocochopio Cr.
Horseshoe Bend
Autosee
Camp Defiance
Fowltown
Newmansville
Suwanee R.
Withlacoochee R.
Dade's Massacre
Ft. Brook
Welaka
Wahoo Swamp
Lake Monroe
Okee-Chobee
Loche-Hachee
Pilaklikaha
Caloosahatchee

Battle Sites
🌲 French and Indian War
🌲 Indian Wars

Of America's 240 million people, 0.6 percent are indigenous to North America. Two hundred sixty-six tribes in the continental states, added to 216 Eskimo and Indian communities in Alaska, make up a "Native American" community that is approximately 1.5 million strong.

Of the Native American population, over half lives in the Pacific and Mountain regions. Another 16 percent lives in the West South Central region. The map on the following page shows that most reservations are west of the Mississippi River.

The majority of indigenous Americans have not fared well since being alienated from their lands in the mid-1800s. Unemployment, poverty, inadequate heath care, and poor education have become the standard on reservations and in U.S. cities alike. Unemployment on Indian reservations exceeds 40 percent in many cases. Alcoholism and diseases such as tuberculosis, which are controlled in other portions of the country, are widespread on Indian reservations. Likewise, rates of infant mortality and suicide are high, being four and two times the national average of 10.4 per 1,000 live births and 11.9 per one hundred thousand population respectively.

Of the 50 million acres owned by Indians, many are not suitable for farming, being located in excessively dry areas. Where land is not used for grazing it is often leased to large, outside energy companies who have returned to Indian communities less than one percent of the market value of mined uranium and 25¢ for each ton of strip mined coal which sells for $70.00 a ton on the open market.

Unemployment on the Reservation, 1989

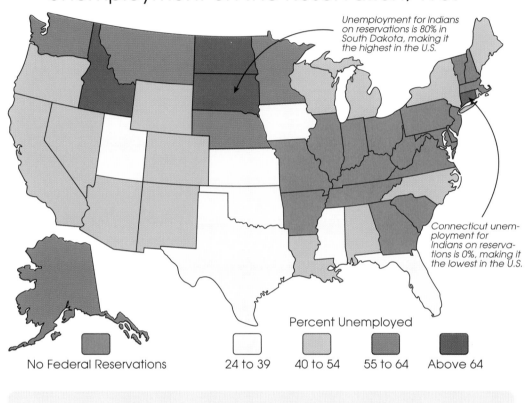

Unemployment for Indians on reservations is 80% in South Dakota, making it the highest in the U.S.

Connecticut unemployment for Indians on reservations is 0%, making it the lowest in the U.S.

Percent Unemployed

| No Federal Reservations | 24 to 39 | 40 to 54 | 55 to 64 | Above 64 |

Where Indians Live in America

New England 1.5%
Pacific 25%
Middle Atlantic 3.9%
South Atlantic 7.7%
East North Central 7.4%
East South Central 1.6%
West North Central 10%
Mountain 26.9%
West South Central 16%

American Indian Tribes of Over Thirty Members Living on Reservations

Tribe	Population	Tribe	Population
Navajo	101,369	Sac and Fox	453
Sioux	34,101	Umatilla	443
Pueblo	30,114	Stockbridge	412
Chippewa	17,849	Mandan	411
Apache	14,333	Penobscot	380
Pima	8,125	Coeur d'Alene	340
Papago	6,993	Luiseno	317
Cherokee	6,497	Cahuilla	313
Iroquois	6,422	Washo	302
Blackfoot	5,423	Chinook	285
Paiute	4,188	Kootenai	270
Yakima	4,093	Clallam	267
Shoshone	3,820	Chemakuan	252
Crow	3,718	Creek	240
Yuman	3,421	California Tribes	232
Colville	3,415	Kickapoo	229
Ute	3,248	Miccosukee	225
Cheyenne	2,843	Cupeno	212
Choctaw	2,834	Shinnecock	181
Flathead	2,562	Chitmacha	170
Arapaho	2,241	Bannock	139
Menominee	2,146	Ponca	138
Puget Sound Salish	2,039	Nomalaki	135
Assiniboine	2,028	Wailaki	122
Osage	1,679	Chehalis	116
Cree	1,559	Chumash	111
Nez Perce	1,326	Pomo	111
Lummi	1,299	Serrano	86
Colorado River	1,241	Long Island	83
Warm Springs	1,234	Cowlitz	82
Gros Ventres	1,060	Ottawa	76
Catawba	982	Miwok	74
Hoopa	843	Walla-Walla	70
Spokane	843	Karok	67
Quinault	803	Chemehuevi	66
Passamaquoddy	802	Konkow	62
Potawatomi	796	Delaware	59
Winnebago	776	Mono	58
Fort Hall	761	Kalispel	52
Seminole	751	Pawnee	52
Tsimshian	747	Mattaponi	48
Makah	706	Tlingit	47
Omaha	688	Cayuse	46
Diegueno	634	Pamunkey	45
Yurok	618	Kaw	41
Arikara	527	Shawnee	41
Yaqui	526	Kiowa	37
Yokuts	501	Mission	32
Alabama-Coushatta	481	Chickasaw	30

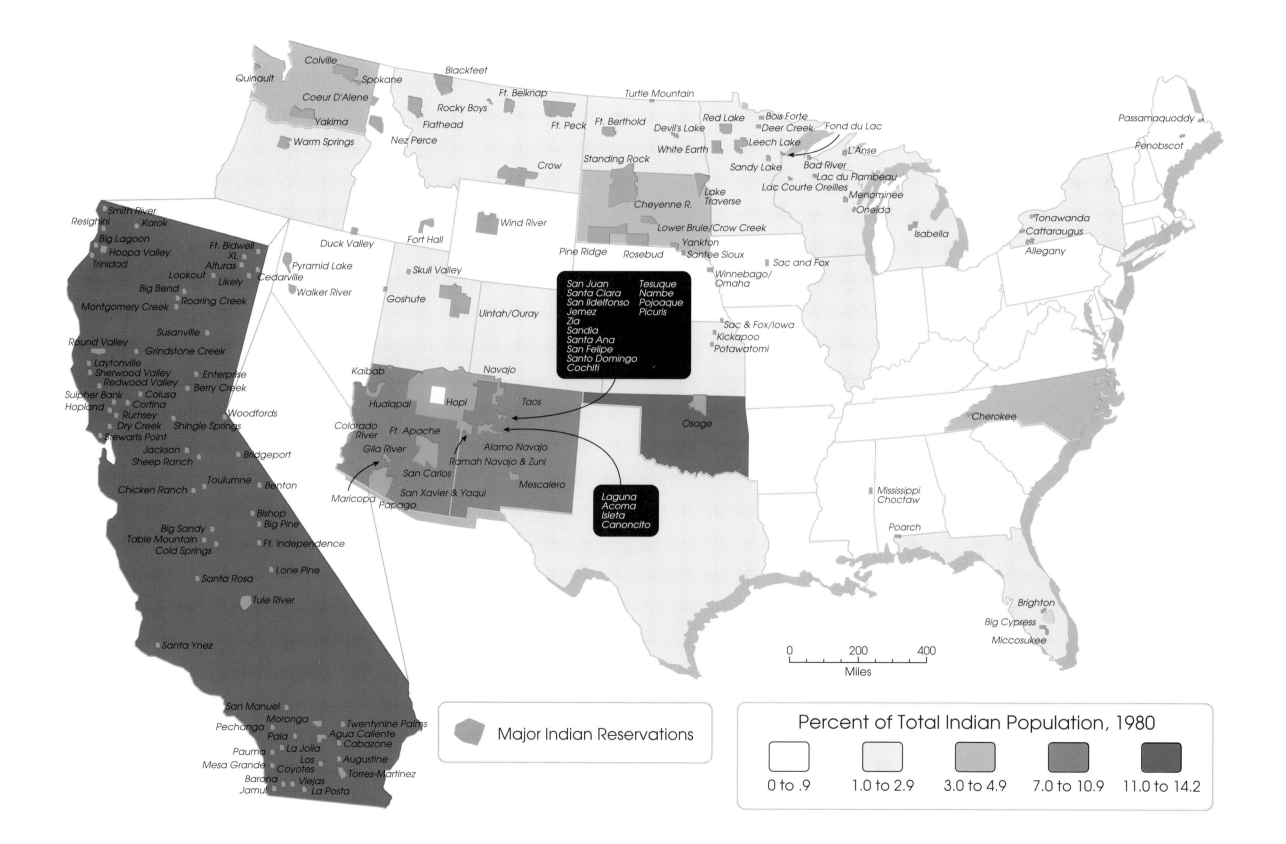

Quinault
Colville
Spokane
Blackfeet
Turtle Mountain
Passamaquoddy
Coeur D'Alene
Ft. Belknap
Red Lake
Bois Forte
Fond du Lac
Penobscot
Yakima
Rocky Boys
Ft. Peck
Ft. Berthold
Devil's Lake
Deer Creek
Leech Lake
L'Anse
Warm Springs
Flathead
Ft. Peck
White Earth
Sandy Lake
Bad River
Lac du Flambeau
Nez Perce
Crow
Standing Rock
Lac Courte Oreilles
Menominee
Oneida
Cheyenne R.
Lake Traverse
Isabella
Tonawanda
Smith River
Wind River
Lower Brule/Crow Creek
Cattaraugus
Resighini
Karok
Yankton
Sac and Fox
Allegany
Big Lagoon
Ft. Bidwell
Duck Valley
Fort Hall
Pine Ridge
Rosebud
Santee Sioux
Hoopa Valley
XL
Alturas
Winnebago/Omaha
Trinidad
Lookout
Cedarville
Likely
Skull Valley
Sac & Fox/Iowa
Big Bend
Pyramid Lake
Kickapoo
Roaring Creek
Walker River
Goshute
Potawatomi
Montgomery Creek

San Juan   Tesuque
Santa Clara   Nambe
San Ildelfonso Pojoaque
Jemez   Picuris
Zia
Sandia
Santa Ana
San Felipe
Santo Domingo
Cochiti

Susanville
Round Valley
Grindstone Creek
Kaibab
Navajo
Laytonville
Sherwood Valley
Enterprise
Redwood Valley
Berry Creek
Uintah/Ouray
Sulpher Bank
Colusa
Cherokee
Hopland
Cortina
Woodfords
Hualapai
Hopi
Taos
Osage
Rumsey
Dry Creek
Shingle Springs
Colorado River
Ft. Apache
Stewarts Point
Jackson
Bridgeport
Gila River
Alamo Navajo
Sheep Ranch
Ramah Navajo & Zuni
Chicken Ranch
Toulumne
Benton
San Carlos
Mescalero
Maricopa
San Xavier & Yaqui
Bishop
Papago
Big Sandy
Big Pine

Laguna
Acoma
Isleta
Canoncito

Table Mountain
Ft. Independence
Cold Springs
Lone Pine
Mississippi Choctaw
Santa Rosa
Poarch
Tule River
Santa Ynez
Brighton
Big Cypress
Miccosukee

San Manuel
Moronga
Pechanga
Twentynine Palms
Pala
Agua Caliente
Pauma
Cabazone
Mesa Grande
La Jolia
Los Coyotes
Augustine
Barona
Torres-Martinez
Jamul
Viejas
La Posta

Major Indian Reservations

Percent of Total Indian Population, 1980

0 to .9   1.0 to 2.9   3.0 to 4.9   7.0 to 10.9   11.0 to 14.2

0   200   400
Miles

There are several population trends in the United States. The population is aging as families grow smaller and Americans live longer. Since females live longer, they outnumber males in upper age categories as demonstrated in the population pyramids to the immediate right.

In each of the pyramids, population is compared for 1970 and 1980. The pyramid for the African-American population shows the same trends as those for the total population. Trends for other races are significantly different because they are heavily composed of migrants, i.e., men of working age.

The white population pyramid is larger because the numbers in this group are larger. Females outnumber males among this population more than any other (women outnumber men in upper age brackets in all developed countries). The life expectancy gender gap in the United States is greater than in almost any other country. American women live nine years longer, on average, than American men. The median age for females is also greater than that for males, being 33.3 years for females in 1987 compared with 30.9 for males.

The states of the traditional North American Manufacturing Belt, that is, the Northeastern states and those of the East North Central Region, have always been the nation's most densely populated. This is due to the presence of many large urban centers. As the center of the U.S. population has moved west and south, areas such as Florida and California have also become heavily populated and densely packed. Florida now ranks tenth in density and California ranks twelfth.

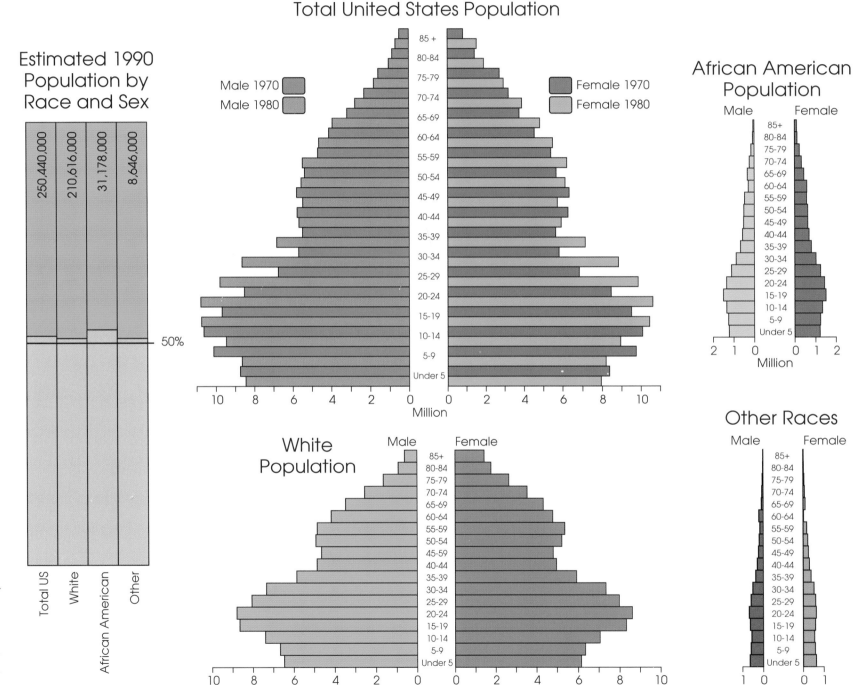

Estimated 1990 Population by Race and Sex

Total US 250,440,000
White 210,616,000
African American 31,178,000
Other 8,646,000

50%

Total United States Population

Male 1970
Male 1980
Female 1970
Female 1980

White Population

African American Population

Other Races

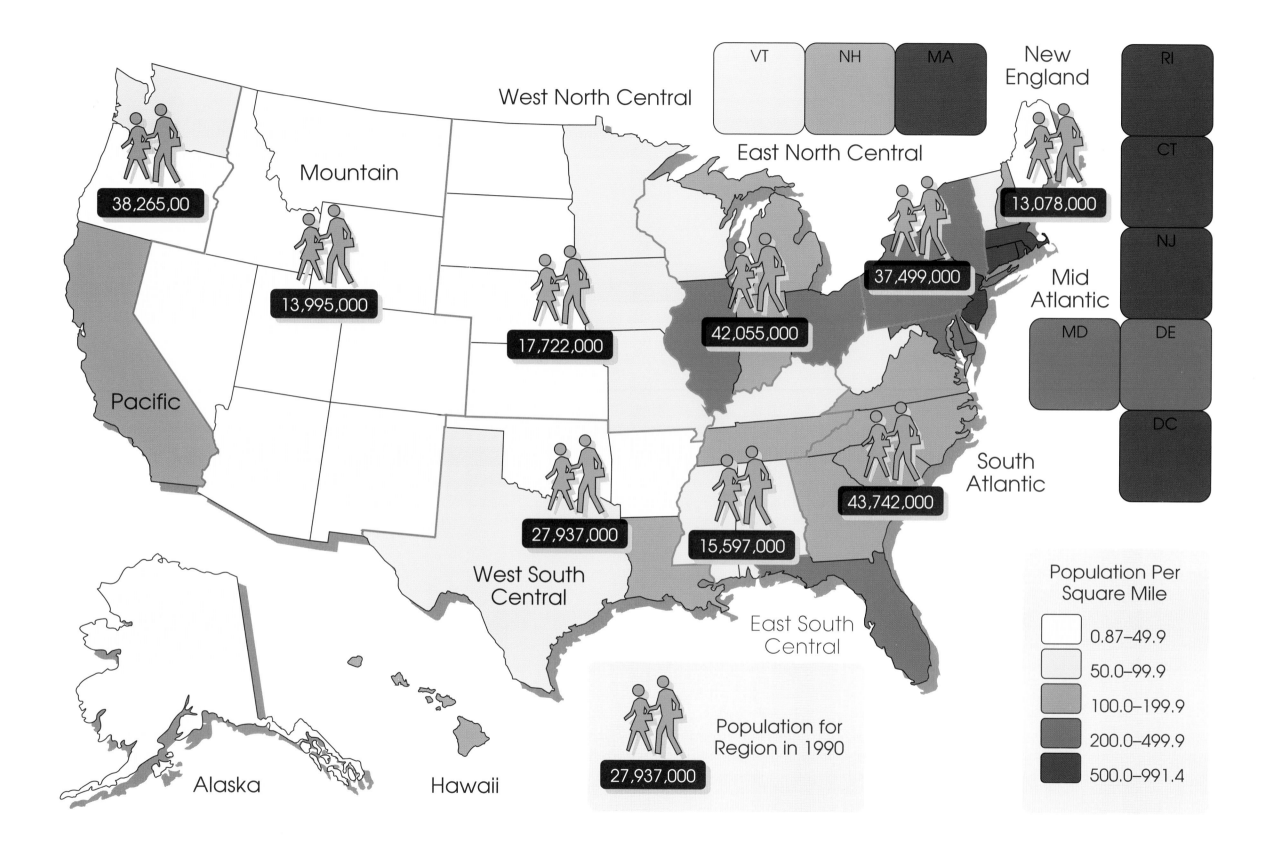

West North Central

Mountain

East North Central

New England

Pacific

38,265,00

13,995,000

17,722,000

42,055,000

37,499,000

13,078,000

Mid Atlantic

South Atlantic

27,937,000

15,597,000

43,742,000

West South Central

East South Central

Alaska

Hawaii

VT NH MA

RI

CT

NJ

MD DE

DC

Population for Region in 1990

27,937,000

Population Per Square Mile

0.87–49.9

50.0–99.9

100.0–199.9

200.0–499.9

500.0–991.4

There are now over 247 million Americans, making the United States the fourth most populous country in the world. Population is not distributed evenly over the country. Both the drier and mountainous regions of the western interior remain lightly populated, even though the population of some states there has grown rapidly in recent years. California is the most populated state with over 12 percent of the national total. Migration to the states of the West and South has changed the rank order of the states in recent times. New York remains the second most populated state, but other Eastern and Midwestern states have declined in relative population and importance. Texas and Florida have shown extremely rapid growth. Pennsylvania, another Eastern state, ranks fifth, followed by Illinois, Ohio, and Michigan, which contain the great urban centers of the Midwest and Lake States.

There have been significant changes in the ethnic composition of American population over the last 40 years. Migration from Europe has slowed significantly. Latin American and Asian countries now account for the overwhelming share of migrants. The proportion of Blacks in the populations has remained constant, while the proportion of Hispanics and Asians is increasing rapidly.

Because African-Americans were originally brought to the South as an involuntary labor force for Southern plantations, their number and degree of concentration was always greatest in that area. While there is still a strong concentration there, many have since migrated west and north throughout the country. White Americans dominate in every state, but particularly in those farthest away from the South and Southwest. As migration continues, the patterns will continue to reflect the availability of employment opportunities more than the regional origin of the moving population.

The Hispanic population, largely from Mexico, is concentrated in states bordering Mexico. Hispanics of Mexican background have migrated from that area to locations throughout the West. Hispanics east of the Mississippi are predominantly of Caribbean or Central American origin. They entered the country through New York or Miami within the last 40 years. Those of Puerto Rican origin dominate in the Northeast, while those of Cuban origin dominate in Florida. Puerto Ricans are American citizens and can migrate freely. Most others have entered on refugee status, fleeing violence and disruption in their homelands. Hispanics living in the East have had less time to diffuse to other locations though the process is well underway. Louisiana and Illinois are the meeting grounds of both currents of migration. Hispanic communities in those two states contain nearly equal proportions of Caribbean and Mexican Hispanics.

Migrants from Asia are concentrated in California and Hawaii. Asians of Chinese, Japanese, Indian, Pakistani, and Southeast Asian origin include large numbers of business people and professionals. This explains their higher than average numbers in New York and large metropolitan areas across the United States.

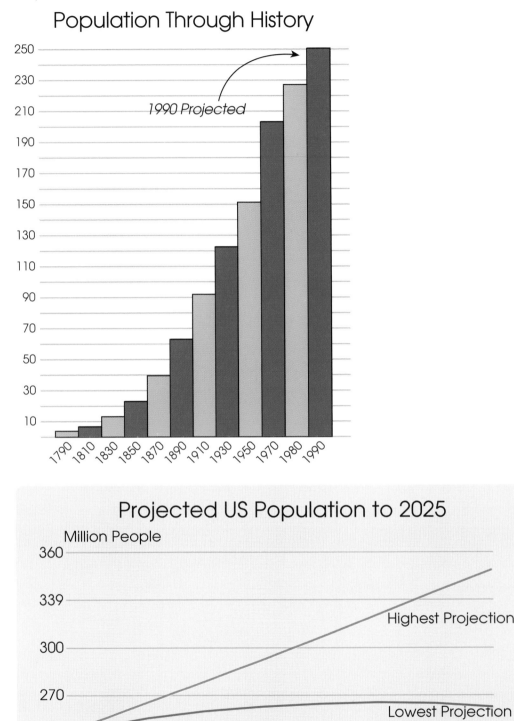

Population Through History

1990 Projected

Projected US Population to 2025

Million People

Highest Projection

Lowest Projection

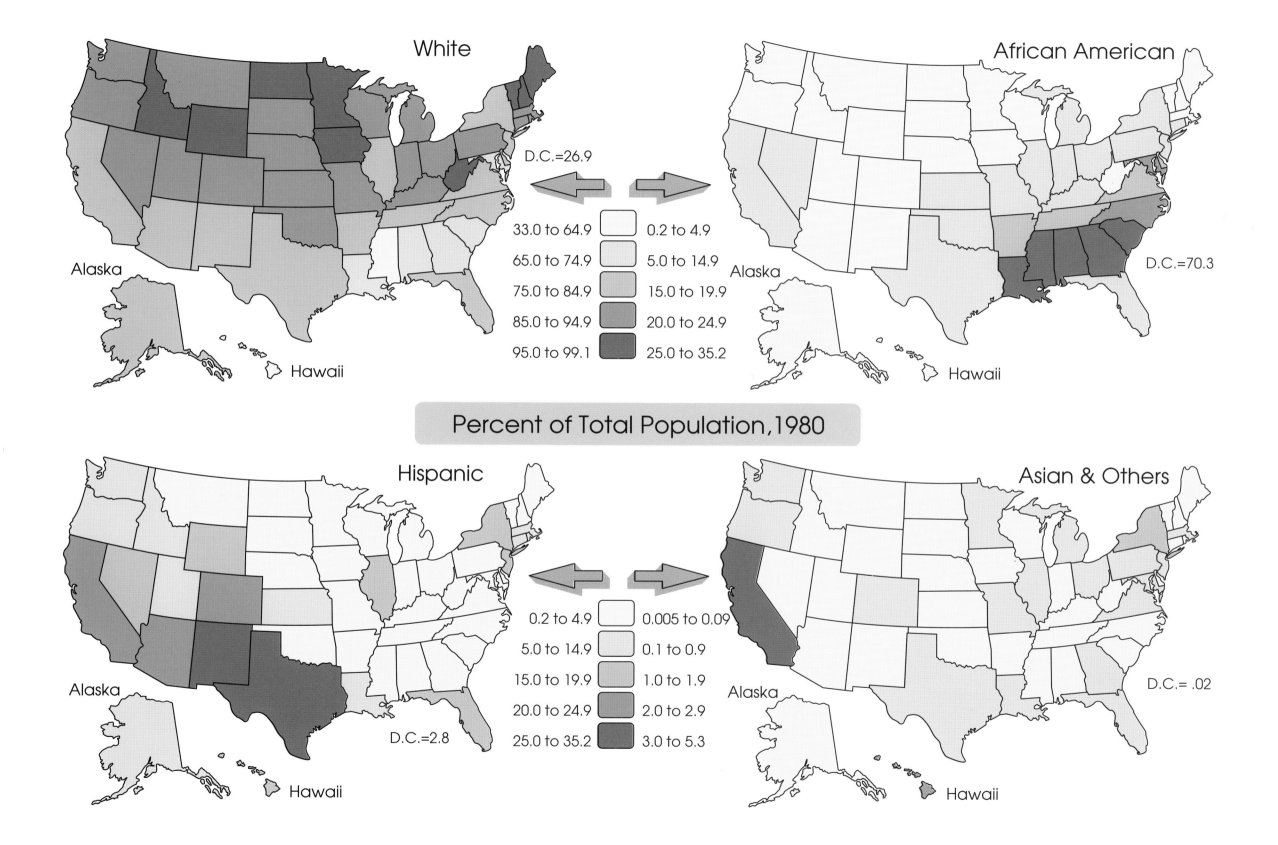

Percent of Total Population, 1980

White

D.C.=26.9

33.0 to 64.9	
65.0 to 74.9	
75.0 to 84.9	
85.0 to 94.9	
95.0 to 99.1	

Alaska

Hawaii

African American

0.2 to 4.9	
5.0 to 14.9	
15.0 to 19.9	
20.0 to 24.9	
25.0 to 35.2	

Alaska

D.C.=70.3

Hawaii

Hispanic

0.2 to 4.9	
5.0 to 14.9	
15.0 to 19.9	
20.0 to 24.9	
25.0 to 35.2	

Alaska

D.C.=2.8

Hawaii

Asian & Others

0.005 to 0.09	
0.1 to 0.9	
1.0 to 1.9	
2.0 to 2.9	
3.0 to 5.3	

Alaska

D.C.= .02

Hawaii

The age differences among the populations of the states is the result of migration at two ends of the scale. Large numbers of older people migrate at retirement age, while large numbers of young people migrate in search of education and employment. The ten states with the oldest populations represent desirable areas for retirement, limited employment opportunities or, in some cases, both.

The changing economy has modified the location of jobs. Declining employment opportunities in such areas as farming (Arkansas, Missouri, South Dakota, Nebraska), mining (Pennsylvania, West Virginia), and heavy industry (Pennsylvania) account for the steady outmigration of many young people. A similar decline in lumbering has affected Oregon. As manufacturing has declined in Massachusetts and Rhode Island, it has been replaced by technical and research employment that attracts somewhat older (over 30), highly educated people, while younger people without higher education leave.

The high percentage of senior citizens in Florida is the result of decades of retirement-age migration to that state's year-round warmth. Florida, however, is not the only target area for retirees. Texas, the Ozarks (Arkansas and Missouri), Kentucky, the mountains of Pennsylvania, Oregon, Nevada, and Arizona are all increasing their share of retirees. Thus, the factors of youth and old age operate in Pennsylvania, Missouri, Arkansas, and Oregon as reasonably-priced land, attractive scenery, and lower taxes play increasing roles in the migration decisions of retirees.

The states with the youngest populations are those in which job opportunities were best during the decade 1970–1980. Four of the eight states (Utah, Alaska, Louisiana, and Wyoming) were in the midst of energy booms during that decade. The tradition of large families among members of the Church of Jesus Christ of Latter Day Saints (Mormons) may explain why Utah's population is the youngest. The youth of Georgia is best explained by the influx of young people to booming Atlanta.

A comparison of the 1970 and 1987 pie charts highlights the aging of America. While the percentage of those over 65 has increased only a little, the proportion of those under 24 has declined significantly. Most importantly, the age group 25–44 has expanded rapidly. The United States experienced a great decline of births during the decade 1930–1940, because of the poor economic conditions experienced during the Great Depression. In the period 1946–1955, with unprecedented prosperity and the end of World War II, the country experienced the birth of an unusually large number of children. These factors account for the decrease in the 45–64 age group as well as the increase in the 25–44 age group between 1970 and 1987. The lower birth rates between 1968 and 1976 are reflected in the lower percentages of those under 18 in 1987.

Projections for the year 2010 show a continuation of these trends. The Depression era generation will have retired by then, as shown by the percentage of people in the over 65 category. The post World War II generation will have moved into the older worker category (ages 45–64). A decline in the youn-

ger worker category (ages 25–44) will be caused both by the aging "baby boom" generation and the low birth rates between 1968 and 1976. Between the years 2011 and 2021, the products of the post-war "baby boom" will have entered the over 65 age group, creating a record percentage of senior citizens and perhaps taxing social security retirement funds to the limit.

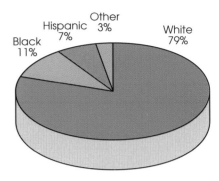

Population by Age

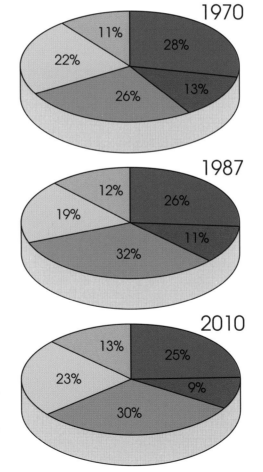

1970

1987

2010

0 to 17   45 to 64

18 to 24   Over 65

25 to 44

Youngest Aged States

	Percent Under 18
Utah	37.4
Alaska	32.6
Idaho	30.6
Wyoming	30.2
Mississippi	30.2
Texas	29.7
New Mexico	29.7
Louisiana	29.5
Georgia	27.9

Oldest Aged States

	Percent Over 65
Florida	17.8
Iowa	14.8
Pennsylvania	14.8
Rhode Island	14.7
Arkansas	14.6
South Dakota	14.0
West Virginia	13.9
Missouri	13.8
Nebraska	13.8

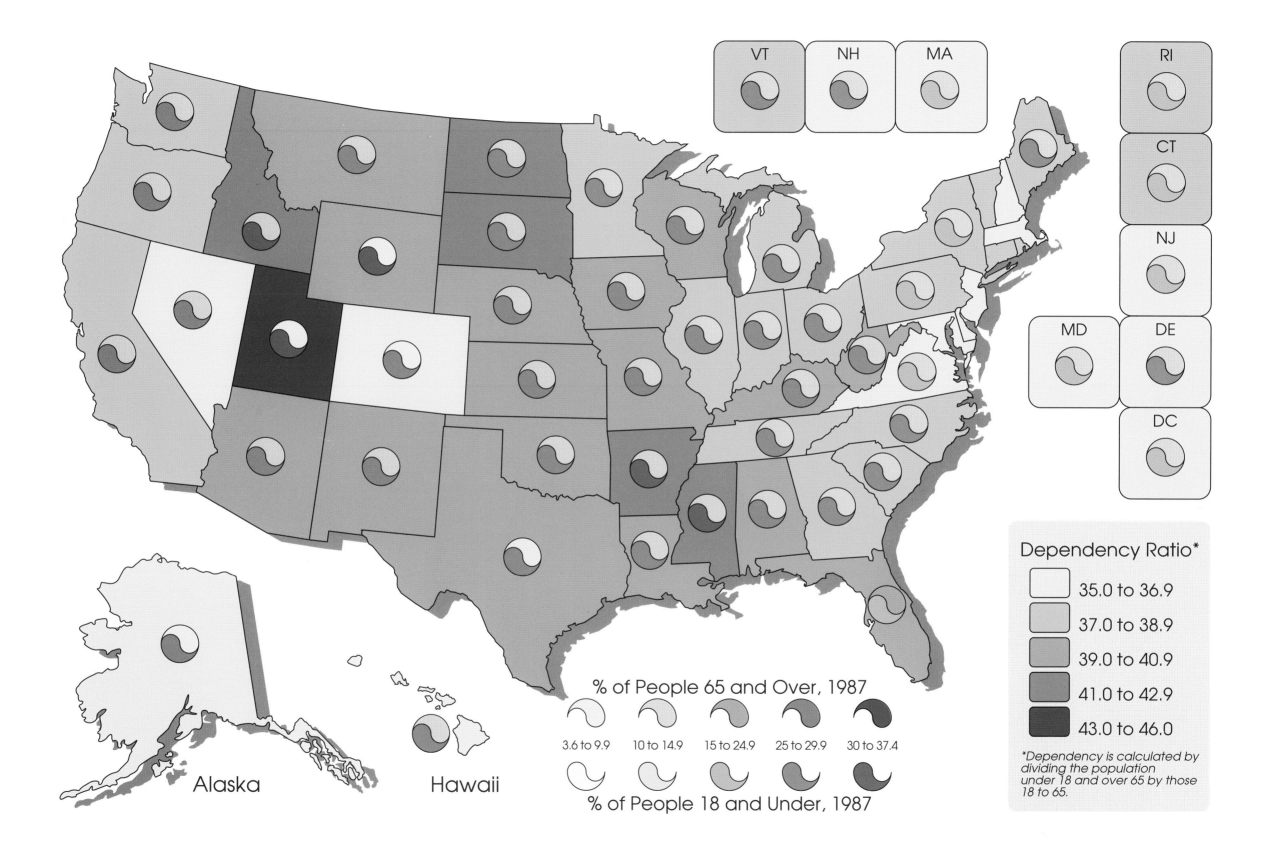

VT NH MA

RI CT NJ MD DE DC

% of People 65 and Over, 1987

3.6 to 9.9   10 to 14.9   15 to 24.9   25 to 29.9   30 to 37.4

% of People 18 and Under, 1987

Alaska

Hawaii

Dependency Ratio*

35.0 to 36.9
37.0 to 38.9
39.0 to 40.9
41.0 to 42.9
43.0 to 46.0

*Dependency is calculated by dividing the population under 18 and over 65 by those 18 to 65.

Roughly equal numbers live in three of the country's four major regions. While the South is clearly more populous, the U.S. population has shifted westward throughout history with changing opportunities and public preferences. From 1960 to 1970, greatest growth occurred in the West Coast and Gulf Coast states. In the following decade, the states of the mountain and desert West showed the greatest growth. Since 1980, growth has been most rapid in the Southwest and selected parts of the South. Arkansas, Florida, and parts of Texas increasingly attract retirees. Florida is the fastest growing state.

States losing population are those with declining industrial and mineral based economies. Washington, D.C., like almost all large cities, is suffering population decline. Relatively rapid growth in its Virginia and Maryland suburbs indicates that the metropolitan area, if not the city itself, is still growing.

Increasingly, Americans seek amenities or the good things of life. Space, pleasant climate, good wages, and a clean environment motivate people to move from cities to suburbs and from suburbs to rural surroundings.

The West remains a low density area due to the scarcity of water and job opportunities. The densely populated states of the Northeast are completely developed. Yet even in the Northeast, there are still vast empty areas away from the major metropolitan areas.

The population of the United States now increases at a slower rate than was the case in most of our history. Projections are estimates of future growth. They vary greatly but, in the short run, population projections are reasonably accurate.

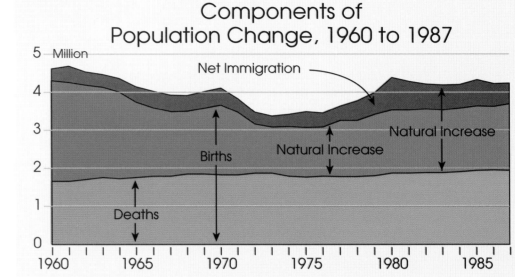

Components of Population Change, 1960 to 1987

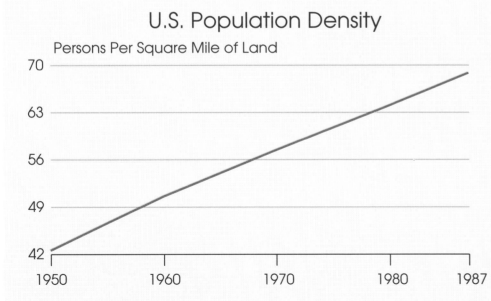

U.S. Population Density

Persons Per Square Mile of Land

Regional Population Density, 1987

	People per Square Mile
New England	203.8
Mid Atlantic	375.3
East North Central	171.8
West North Central	34.7
South Atlantic	156.2
East South Central	85.5
West South Central	63.0
Mountain	15.4
Pacific	40.8

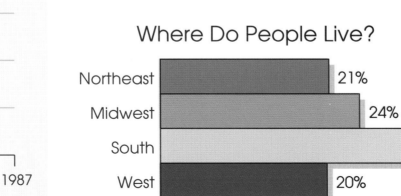

Where Do People Live?

Northeast 21%
Midwest 24%
South 34%
West 20%

States with Greatest Population Change 1980–1987

	Percent Gained
Arkansas	30.7
Nevada	25.8
Arizona	24.6
Florida	33.4
Texas	18.0
California	16.9
New Mexico	15.1
Utah	15.0
New Hampshire	14.8
Colorado	14.1

	Percent Lost
West Virginia	2.7
Dist. of Columbia	2.6
Iowa	2.7
Michigan	0.7
Ohio	0.1

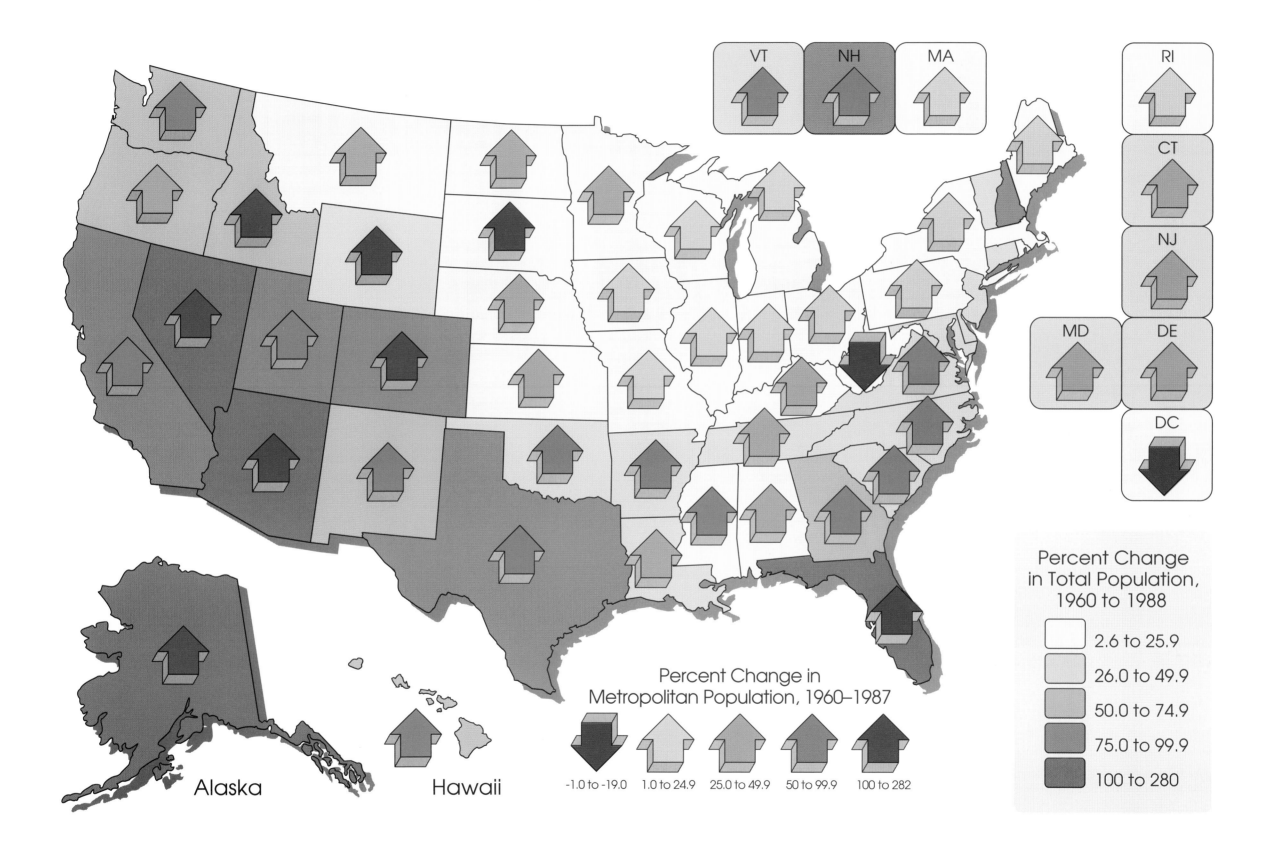

Percent Change in
Metropolitan Population, 1960–1987

-1.0 to -19.0 1.0 to 24.9 25.0 to 49.9 50 to 99.9 100 to 282

Percent Change
in Total Population,
1960 to 1988

2.6 to 25.9

26.0 to 49.9

50.0 to 74.9

75.0 to 99.9

100 to 280

Alaska   Hawaii

Americans' choices of where to live have changed a great deal in the last 60 years. Until the late 1920s, it was the goal of most Americans to live in one of the nation's big cities. By 1950, most major cities had reached their peak populations, and people flocked to the suburbs. Since 1970, Americans have been searching for even more space and privacy, and many have moved into areas far removed from major metropolitan areas. Of the country's 100 largest cities, 41 have lost population since 1980. Of the 120 largest metropolitan areas (cities plus their suburbs), 23 had declining populations. Fifty others grew at slow rates.

Of the country's largest cities, people are most tightly packed in New York and San Francisco. Urban growth is particularly significant in Texas, California, and Florida, where the network of cities and service centers is still evolving. In Florida, for example, urban settlement spreads in all directions, connecting large cities into a chain of solid urban development similar to what has come to be known as the Northeastern "megalopolis."

Population by Region, 1987

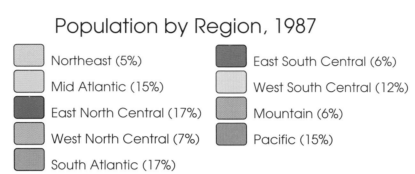

- Northeast (5%)
- Mid Atlantic (15%)
- East North Central (17%)
- West North Central (7%)
- South Atlantic (17%)
- East South Central (6%)
- West South Central (12%)
- Mountain (6%)
- Pacific (15%)

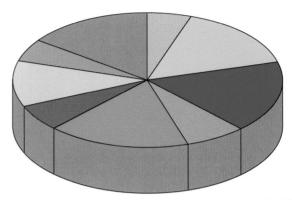

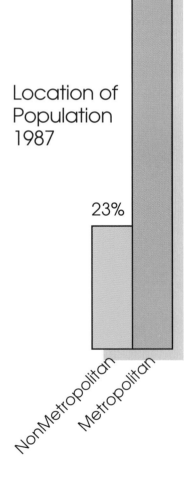

Location of Population 1987

77%

23%

NonMetropolitan   Metropolitan

Resident Population, 1988

Regions	Total	Per Square Mile
New England	12,966,000	203.8
Mid Atlantic	37,645,000	375.3
East North Central	42,149,000	171.8
West North Central	17,745,000	34.7
South Atlantic	42,601,000	156.2
East South Central	15,393,000	85.5
West South Central	26,884,000	63.0
Mountain	13,289,000	15.4
Pacific	37,135,000	40.8

Fifty Largest U.S. Cities, 1986

	Population in Thousands	Density Per Sq. Mile		Population in Thousands	Density Per Sq. Mile
1. New York, NY	7,263	24,089	26. Nashville-Davidson, TN	474	988
2. Los Angeles, CA	3,259	6,996	27. Austin, TX	467	2,011
3. Chicago, IL	3,010	13,194	28. Oklahoma City, OK	446	739
4. Houston, TX	1,729	3,019	29. Kansas City, MO	441	1,394
5. Philadelphia, PA	1,647	2,614	30. Fort Worth, TX	430	1,662
6. Detroit, MI	1,086	801	31. St. Louis, MO	426	6,943
7. San Diego, CA	1,015	3,086	32. Atlanta, GA	422	3,216
8. Dallas, TX	1,004	3,028	33. Long Beach, CA	396	7,957
9. San Antonio, TX	914	3,003	34. Portland, OR	388	3,405
10. Phoenix, AZ	894	2,384	35. Pittsburgh, PA	387	6,994
11. Baltimore, MD	753	9,375	36. Miami, FL	374	10,902
12. San Francisco, CA	749	16,142	37. Tulsa, OK	374	2,008
13. Indianapolis, IN	720	2,045	38. Honolulu, HI	372	4,280
14. San Jose, CA	712	4,209	39. Cincinnati, OH	370	4,740
15. Memphis, TN	653	2,471	40. Albuquerque, NM	367	2,883
16. Washington, DC	150	9,984	41. Tucson, AZ	359	2,862
17. Jacksonville, FL	610	803	42. Oakland, CA	357	6,623
18. Milwaukee, WI	605	6,316	43. Minneapolis, MN	357	6,476
19. Boston, MA	574	12,153	44. Charlotte, NC	352	2,315
20. Columbus, OH	566	3,030	45. Omaha, NE	349	3,517
21. New Orleans, LA	554	2,781	46. Toledo, OH	341	4,046
22. Cleveland, OH	536	6,783	47. Virginia Beach, VA	333	1,476
23. Denver, CO	505	4,728	48. Buffalo, NY	325	7,771
24. El Paso, TX	492	2,052	49. Sacramento, CA	324	3,325
25. Seattle, WA	486	5,816	50. Newark, NJ	316	13,122

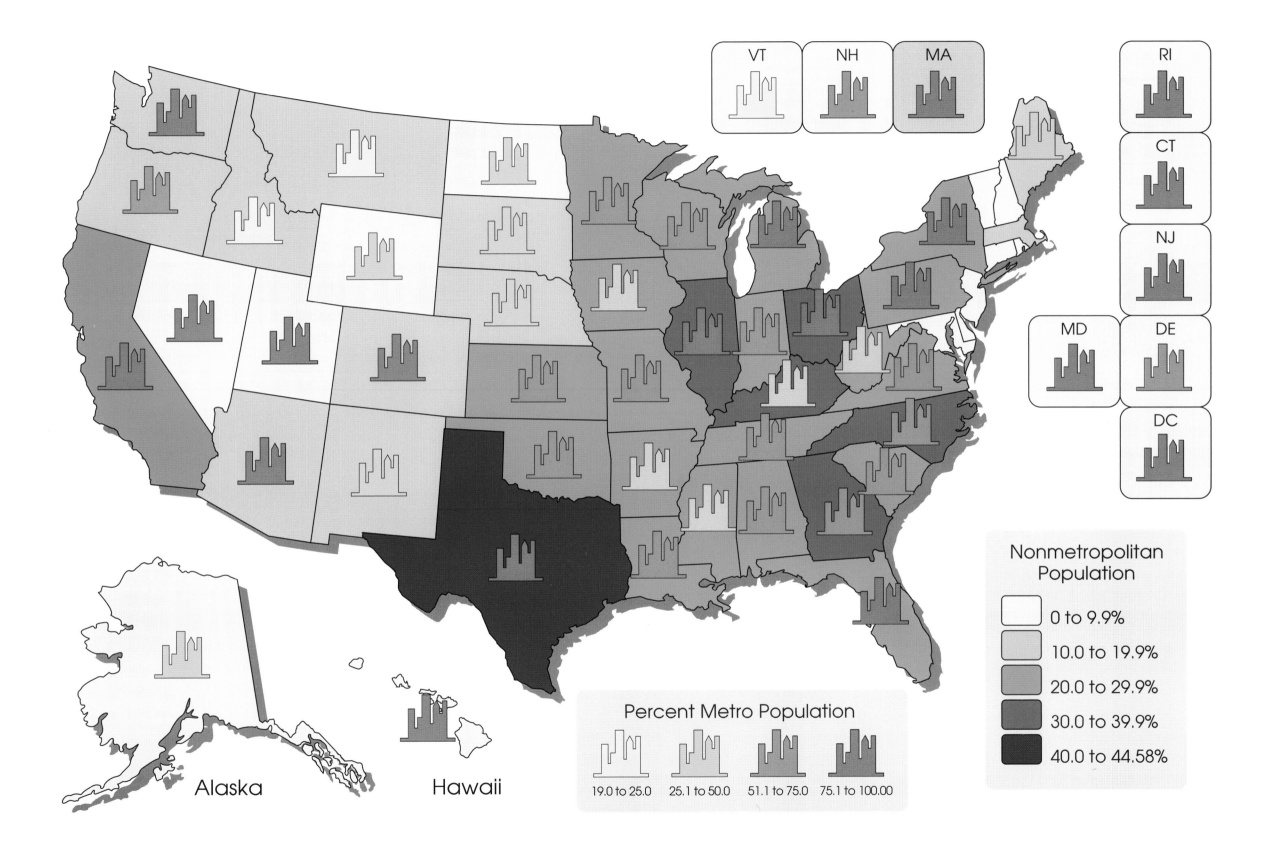

Nonmetropolitan
Population

0 to 9.9%
10.0 to 19.9%
20.0 to 29.9%
30.0 to 39.9%
40.0 to 44.58%

Percent Metro Population

19.0 to 25.0   25.1 to 50.0   51.1 to 75.0   75.1 to 100.00

Alaska   Hawaii

Comparing states with the highest percentage of people over 65 opens up a question. Are people retiring to those states or are the young simply moving out? Six states appear in the highest category in both 1970 and 1987. Where population growth has been consistently high, we can assume retirement; where growth is low, or decline has set in, we can assume out-migration of the young.

In Massachusetts, Rhode Island, and Pennsylvania, 30 years of slow growth implies the young have moved. Declining farm economies in Nebraska, Iowa and South Dakota allow for the same inference. West Virginia, with extremely high unemployment, falls into the same category. Missouri, Arkansas, and Oklahoma exhibit a combination of factors—the Ozark-Ouachita area shared by the three states attracts large numbers of retirees, while sluggish state economies cause the young to leave.

Florida, Maine, and Washington, while attracting retirees, also attract younger affluent individuals in search of rural amenities.

Consistently, the South and West attract migrants from other areas. Of the nine census regions, only four, two each in the South and West, have shown consistent growth. The Pacific and South Atlantic states are the most rapidly growing areas of the country.

Changing "Center of Population", 1790 to 1980

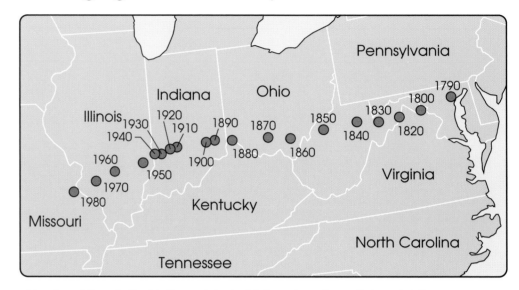

"Center of Population" is the point at which an imaginary flat, weightless, and rigid U.S. map would balance if identical weights were placed on it so that each weight represented the location of one person on the date of the census. A quick glance at the map above supports the notion that population has moved west and south from its origins in the northeast.

Resident Population

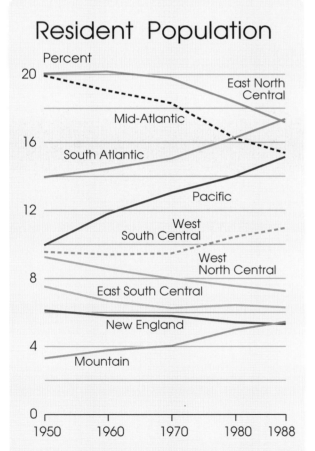

Population Dynamics, 1980 to 1986

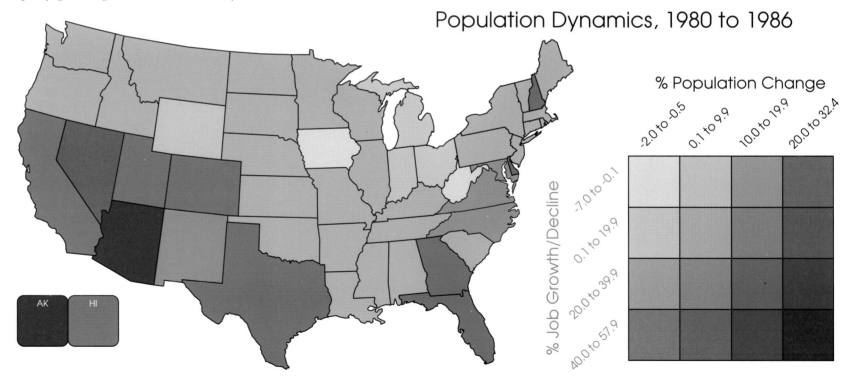

% Population Change

% Job Growth/Decline

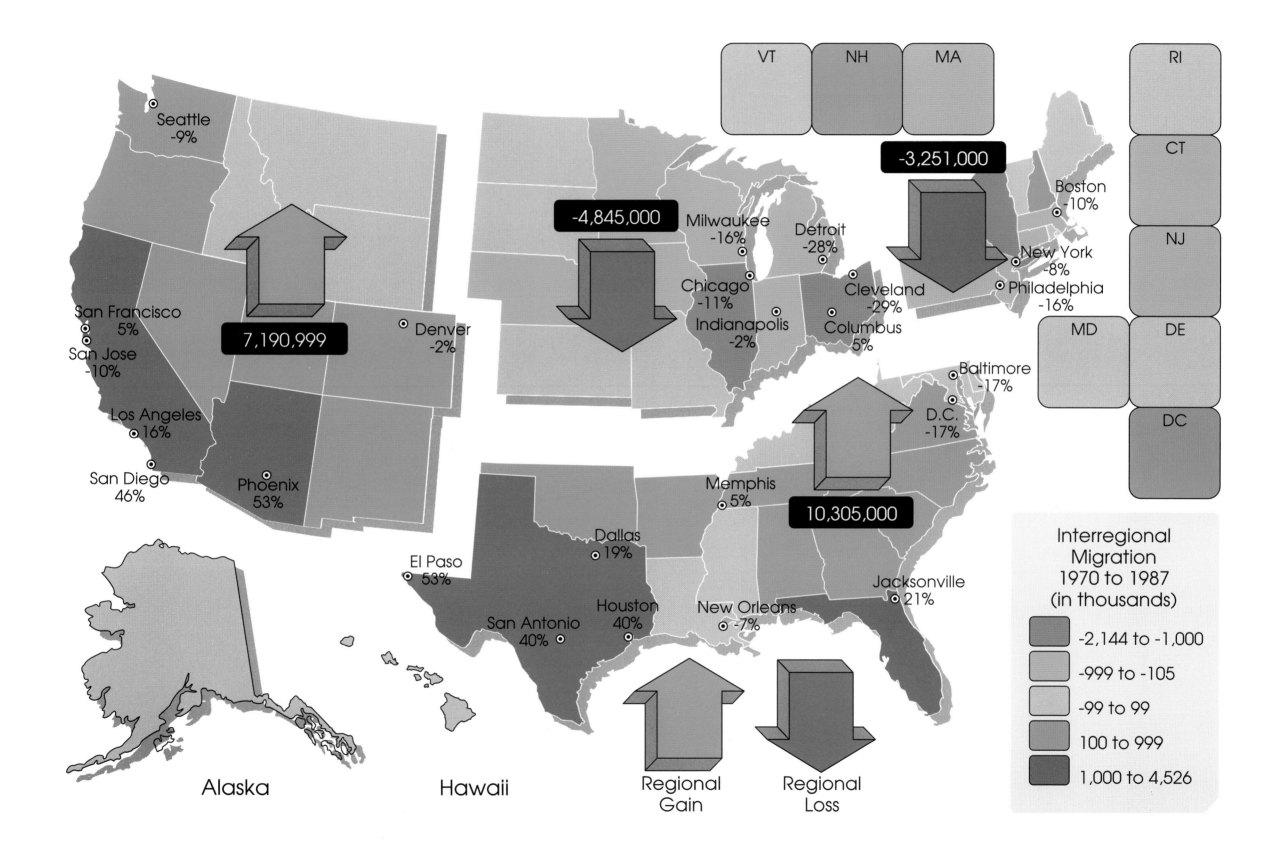

Seattle
-9%

San Francisco
5%

San Jose
-10%

Los Angeles
16%

San Diego
46%

Phoenix
53%

Denver
-2%

7,190,999

-4,845,000

Milwaukee
-16%

Detroit
-28%

Chicago
-11%

Indianapolis
-2%

Cleveland
-29%

Columbus
5%

VT

NH

MA

-3,251,000

Boston
-10%

New York
-8%

Philadelphia
-16%

Baltimore
-17%

D.C.
-17%

RI

CT

NJ

MD

DE

DC

El Paso
53%

Dallas
19%

San Antonio
40%

Houston
40%

New Orleans
-7%

Memphis
5%

10,305,000

Jacksonville
21%

Alaska

Hawaii

Regional
Gain

Regional
Loss

Interregional
Migration
1970 to 1987
(in thousands)

-2,144 to -1,000

-999 to -105

-99 to 99

100 to 999

1,000 to 4,526

America has welcomed millions of migrants to its shores. Europe has been the largest source of migrants—first, from the north and west of that continent, later from its eastern and southern portions. Originally, Britain and Ireland were the major sources of migrants, but Italy and Germany have sent more migrants to America than any other countries. Canada and Mexico have sent millions to the United States as well.

Since 1960, Asians and Latin Americans have been the chief sources of migrants to America. Central America, Mexico, and the Caribbean Islands, all technically part of North America, send far more migrants than South America.

The bulk of immigrants to America arrived in three great waves. Between 1820 and the Civil War, large numbers came to America as the result of war and starvation in Europe. The greatest wave occurred during the period 1880 through 1926. This movement paralleled rapid development and industrialization in America, bringing migrants in search of work. After 1921, immigration quotas limited the number of arrivals and parceled them out among countries in proportion to the various ethnic groups already here.

The third wave began in 1948 and continued through the early 1980s. It was composed primarily of refugees. In the aftermath of World War II, almost a million Europeans, liberated from concentration camps and work detention centers, entered the country under the Displaced Persons Act and other special laws. Upheavals elsewhere in the world resulted in further special admissions. Quotas were abolished in 1965.

Since 1960, over 1.5 million Mexicans, 500,000 Cubans, 400,000 Dominicans, 200,000 Haitians, and over 600,000 people from the smaller Caribbean islands have entered America legally. The number of illegal arrivals is anyone's guess. Over two million Asians have also migrated to the United States since 1960, primarily Chinese, Filipinos, Koreans, and Vietnamese. Recent migrants are not necessarily unskilled laborers; many have education and skills that were obtained in their country of origin.

The countries sending the most immigrants since 1986 are Mexico, the Philippines, Korea, Vietnam, Cuba, India, the Dominican Republic, Mainland China, Jamaica, and Iran. Many of these immigrants seek employment, but a vast number seek relief from political oppression in their native countries. The most recent wave of immigration to avoid political repression coincided with the end of the Vietnam War.

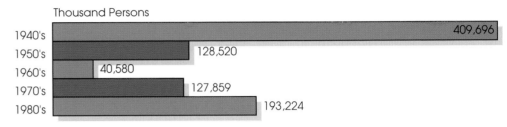

Immigrants Admitted Under Displaced Persons and Refugee Acts

Thousand Persons

Period	Persons
1940's	409,696
1950's	128,520
1960's	40,580
1970's	127,859
1980's	193,224

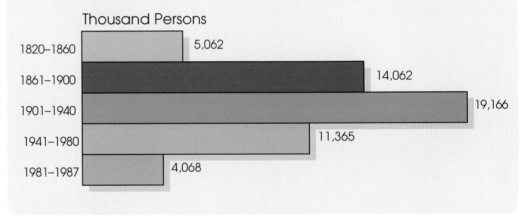

Total Immigration During Different Periods

Thousand Persons

Period	Persons
1820–1860	5,062
1861–1900	14,062
1901–1940	19,166
1941–1980	11,365
1981–1987	4,068

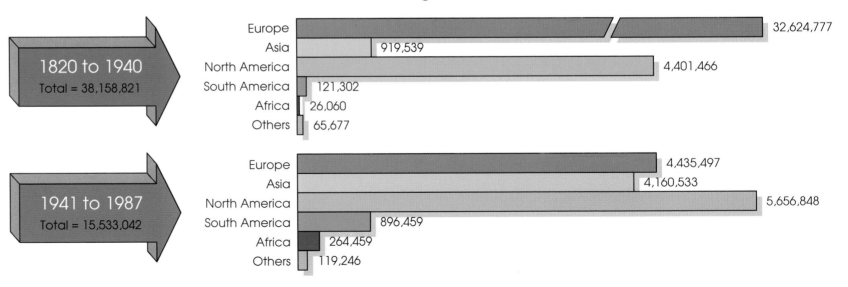

Immigration from Continent of Birth

1820 to 1940
Total = 38,158,821

Continent	Persons
Europe	32,624,777
Asia	919,539
North America	4,401,466
South America	121,302
Africa	26,060
Others	65,677

1941 to 1987
Total = 15,533,042

Continent	Persons
Europe	4,435,497
Asia	4,160,533
North America	5,656,848
South America	896,459
Africa	264,459
Others	119,246

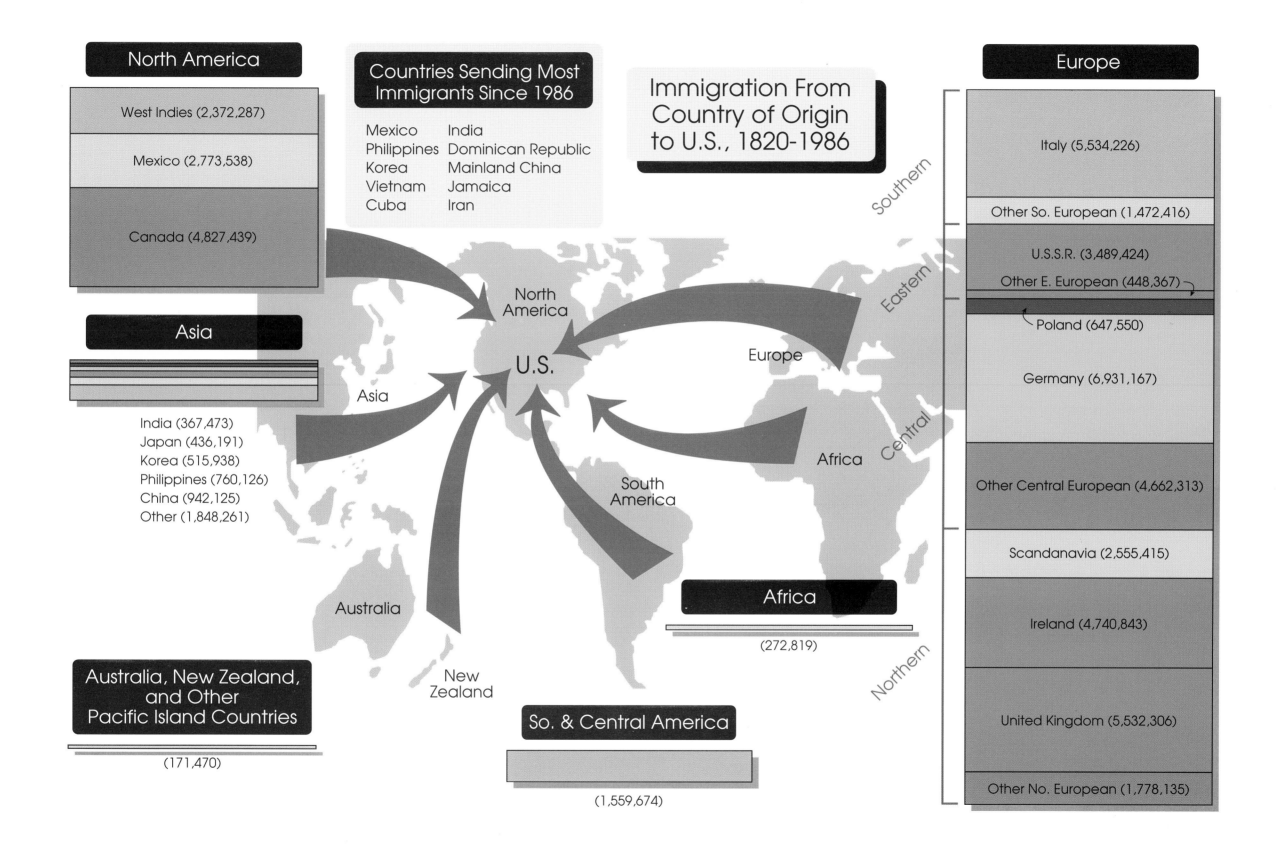

Immigration From Country of Origin to U.S., 1820-1986

North America
West Indies (2,372,287)
Mexico (2,773,538)
Canada (4,827,439)

Countries Sending Most Immigrants Since 1986
Mexico — India
Philippines — Dominican Republic
Korea — Mainland China
Vietnam — Jamaica
Cuba — Iran

Asia
India (367,473)
Japan (436,191)
Korea (515,938)
Philippines (760,126)
China (942,125)
Other (1,848,261)

Australia, New Zealand, and Other Pacific Island Countries
(171,470)

So. & Central America
(1,559,674)

Africa
(272,819)

Europe
Italy (5,534,226)
Other So. European (1,472,416)
U.S.S.R. (3,489,424)
Other E. European (448,367)
Poland (647,550)
Germany (6,931,167)
Other Central European (4,662,313)
Scandanavia (2,555,415)
Ireland (4,740,843)
United Kingdom (5,532,306)
Other No. European (1,778,135)

Southern

Eastern

Central

Northern

North America

Asia

Europe

Africa

South America

Australia

New Zealand

U.S.

During the last 20 to 30 years, the American family has grown smaller. The average household size in 1987 was 2.66 while it was 3.31 in 1962. Birth rates dropped from 23.7 per 1,000 population in 1960 to 15.6 in 1986. Divorce rates rose from 2.2 per 1,000 population in 1960 to 7.8 in 1987, and a larger number of people are living alone (10.9 million in 1970 compared to 21.1 million in 1987).

Almost half of all states fall into the middle map category of household size. Another 13 are in the category directly below. With such dominance in two categories, separated only by tenths of a person, regional patterns are difficult to identify.

Certainly the young, child-bearing populations of Texas, Alaska, and the mountain states lead to larger households. Florida's high percentage of older citizens has the reverse affect on that state's population.

Divorce rates are higher than average in the South and the West. And although there are no easy explanations for the patterns of divorce, it has been suggested that migration and job instability, common to these areas, are directly related to the disintegration of the traditional family unit.

The lowest divorce rates occur in the urban Northeast and the upper Midwest. A possible explanation for this variation is that both regions have large Catholic populations which are, in part, influenced by church doctrine against separation.

Marriage rates coincide quite well with age. States with younger populations have higher marriage rates. Though there are notable exceptions like Florida.

Marriage, in general, has declined. While 71.7 percent of the population was married in 1970 only 62.9 percent was married in 1987.

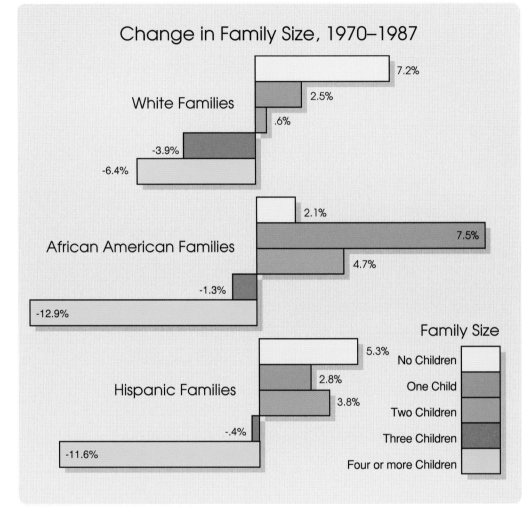

Change in Family Size, 1970–1987

White Families
- 7.2%
- 2.5%
- .6%
- -3.9%
- -6.4%

African American Families
- 2.1%
- 7.5%
- 4.7%
- -1.3%
- -12.9%

Hispanic Families
- 5.3%
- 2.8%
- 3.8%
- -.4%
- -11.6%

Family Size
- No Children
- One Child
- Two Children
- Three Children
- Four or more Children

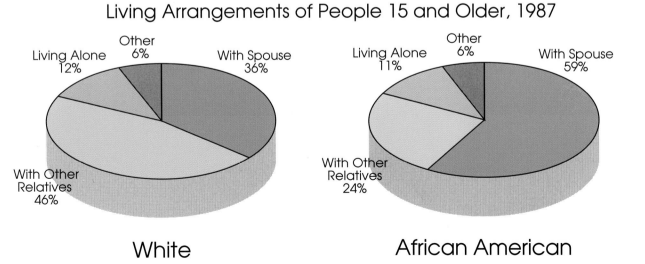

Living Arrangements of People 15 and Older, 1987

White
- Other 6%
- Living Alone 12%
- With Spouse 36%
- With Other Relatives 46%

African American
- Other 6%
- Living Alone 11%
- With Spouse 59%
- With Other Relatives 24%

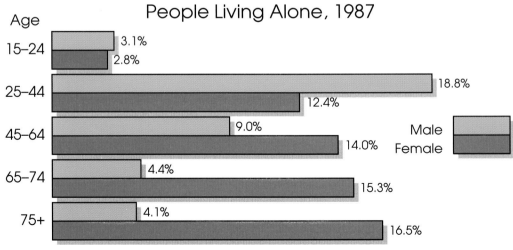

People Living Alone, 1987

Age
- 15–24: 3.1% / 2.8%
- 25–44: 18.8% / 12.4%
- 45–64: 9.0% / 14.0%
- 65–74: 4.4% / 15.3%
- 75+: 4.1% / 16.5%

Male / Female

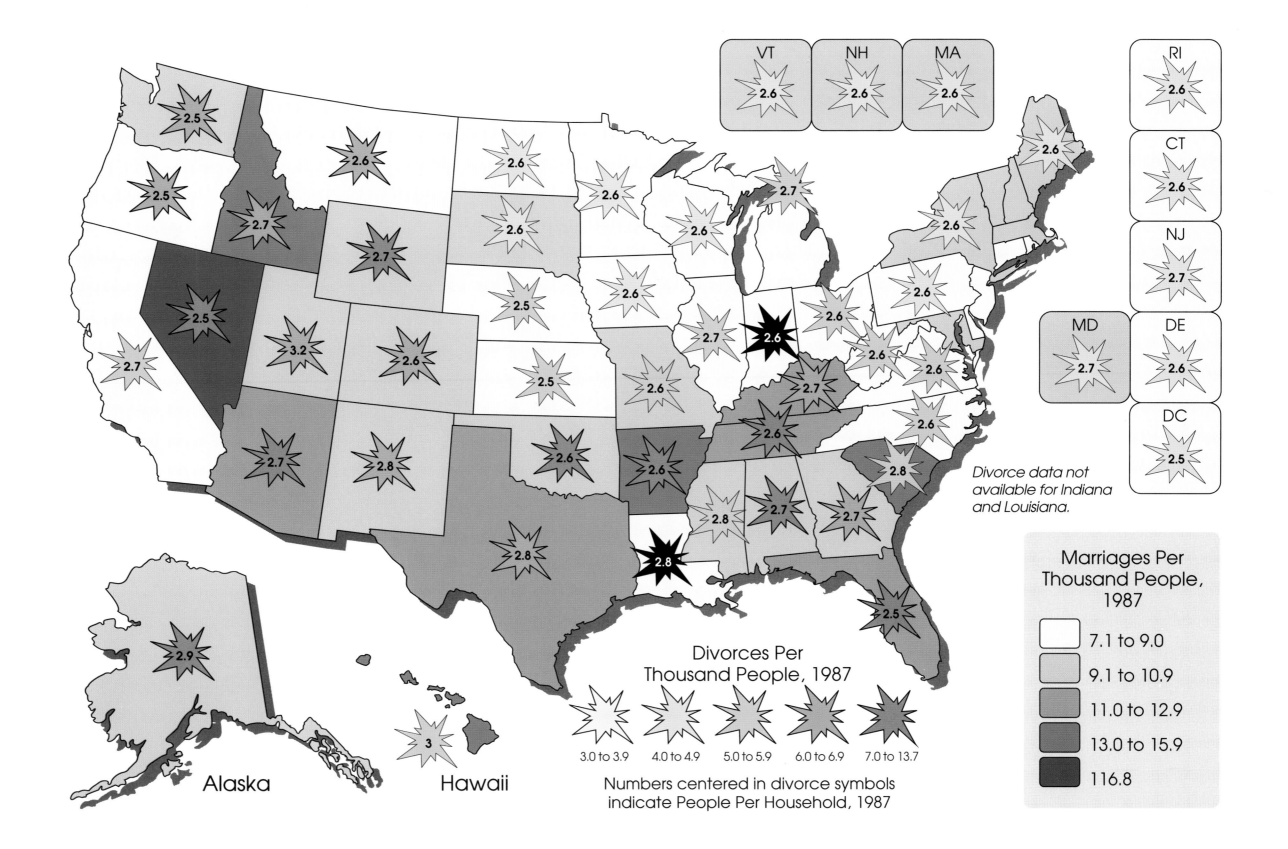

VT 2.6
NH 2.6
MA 2.6

RI 2.6
CT 2.6
NJ 2.7
MD 2.7
DE 2.6
DC 2.5

Divorce data not
available for Indiana
and Louisiana.

Divorces Per
Thousand People, 1987

3.0 to 3.9   4.0 to 4.9   5.0 to 5.9   6.0 to 6.9   7.0 to 13.7

Numbers centered in divorce symbols
indicate People Per Household, 1987

Alaska

Hawaii

Marriages Per
Thousand People,
1987

7.1 to 9.0
9.1 to 10.9
11.0 to 12.9
13.0 to 15.9
116.8

Considered by economists and social scientists to be an indicator of general national economic well-being, the word "housing" conjures up images as central to the American dream as liberty itself. Can Americans afford housing? Is such a simple birthright even available to all citizens?

There are more than 100 million housing units in the United States—a figure that has tripled since 1940. Prices for average single family homes in 1988 ranged from $191,800 in Washington, D.C. to $85,100 in New Mexico, reflecting a steady rise in housing costs in areas that have not suffered economic distress. With this rise, fewer families have been able to afford housing. In 1980, for example, 65 percent of American families owned homes. In 1988, the figure dropped to 57 percent.

The affordability of housing depends on the cost of a particular housing unit as well as its location. If an average family spends 30 percent of its income on housing it would have to earn $90,000 a year to own an average home in California. Metropolitan New York has the most expensive housing followed closely by San Francisco, Orange County, California, and Honolulu, Hawaii.

In some areas of the country the housing market is depressed. Oil-producing states, such as Texas, Louisiana, Oklahoma, and Colorado, and the agricultural states of the Great Plains have shown sharp drops in the costs of homes and the number of housing starts. Conversely, Eastern Great Lakes states, as well as those in eastern New England, have healthy housing markets due to the expansion of industry and the increase in high-tech jobs.

Renters pay more and a larger proportion of their incomes in the western United States. Average rents are $470 per month in the western states as compared to $334 in the South and $345 in the Midwest.

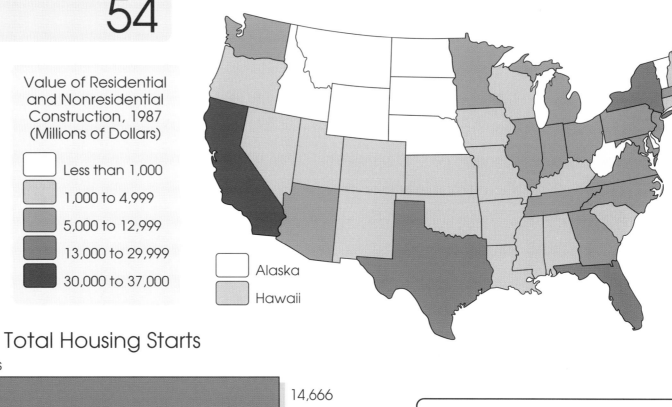

Value of Residential and Nonresidential Construction, 1987 (Millions of Dollars)

- Less than 1,000
- 1,000 to 4,999
- 5,000 to 12,999
- 13,000 to 29,999
- 30,000 to 37,000
- Alaska
- Hawaii

Total Housing Starts

Thousands

1950	14,666
1960	14,065
1970	17,676
1980	14,927

The Cost of Renting

Region	Annual Income (dollars)	Gross Rent (dollars)	Percent of Income
Northeast	17,400	420	29.0
Midwest	14,300	345	28.9
South	15,300	334	26.2
West	17,900	470	31.5

New Housing Units Started, 1987

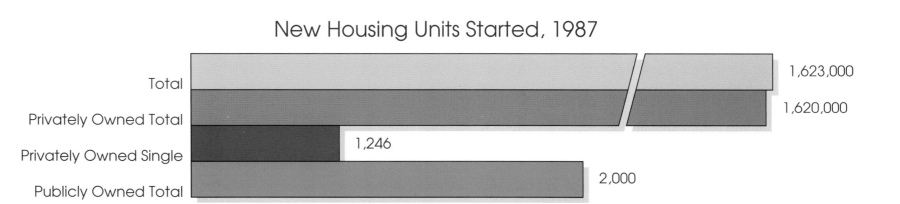

Total	1,623,000
Privately Owned Total	1,620,000
Privately Owned Single	1,246
Publicly Owned Total	2,000

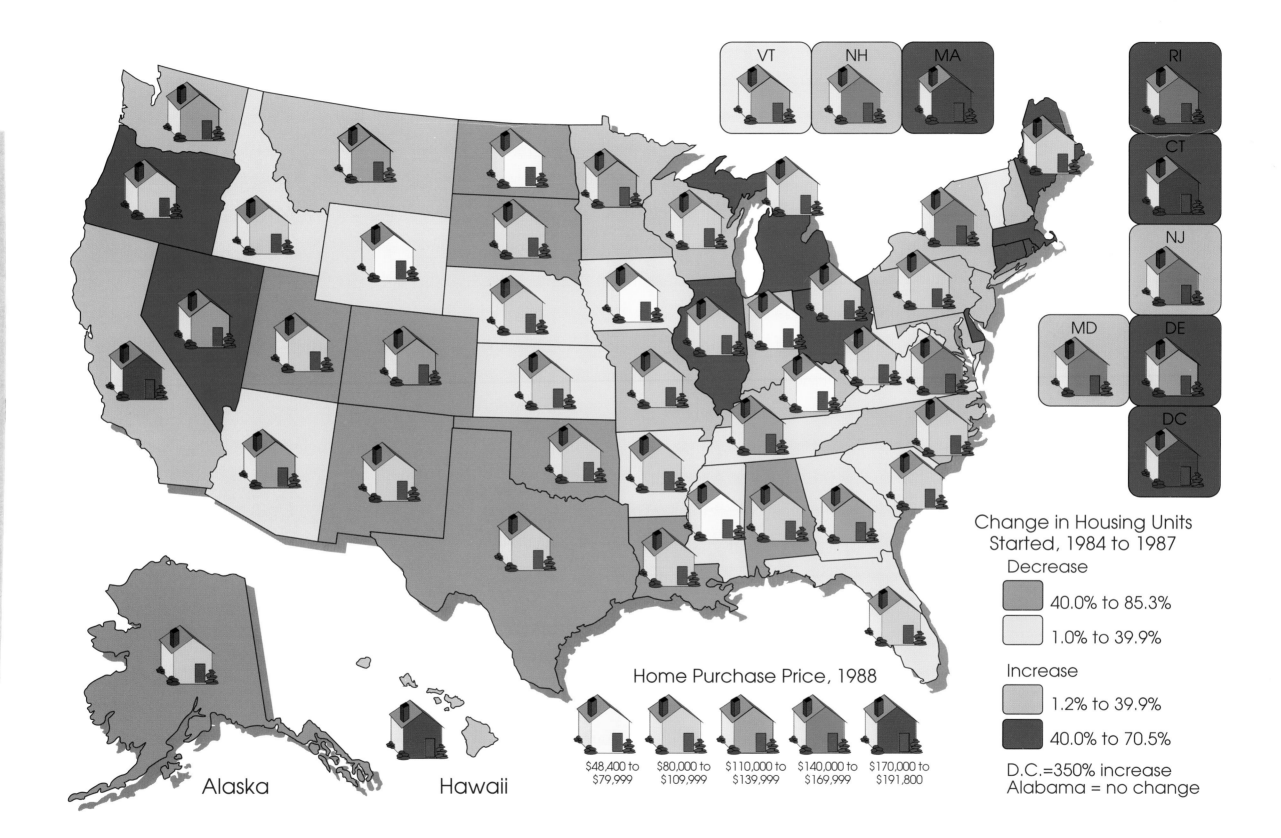

Change in Housing Units
Started, 1984 to 1987
Decrease

40.0% to 85.3%

1.0% to 39.9%

Increase

1.2% to 39.9%

40.0% to 70.5%

D.C.=350% increase
Alabama = no change

Home Purchase Price, 1988

| $48,400 to $79,999 | $80,000 to $109,999 | $110,000 to $139,999 | $140,000 to $169,999 | $170,000 to $191,800 |

Alaska

Hawaii

The income of American families rose sharply from 1946 to 1975. The increases have been fairly modest since. Americans have maintained their standard of living in the face of increasing costs by increasing both the number of hours worked and the number of people in the household working. Whereas 30 years ago, women stayed home to raise families, now many work outside the home to help keep pace with increased demands on family income.

Income per person differs widely from state to state. States with the highest personal income cluster in the Northeast, but also include Alaska and California. New Jersey and Connecticut are the country's richest states, at least in part because they contain wealthy suburbs of New York City. New England's high-tech industry and research functions and Maryland's concentration of comparatively well-paid federal government employees explain the high income levels in those states.

The South and the Mountain states remain the areas with the lowest per capita income. The legendary poverty of Appalachia and the rural South has not disappeared.

Income for Native Americans and Hispanic immigrants is staggeringly low, contributing to high poverty levels in South Dakota and New Mexico. As the map on the following page shows, poverty has become a significant problem in most parts of the country.

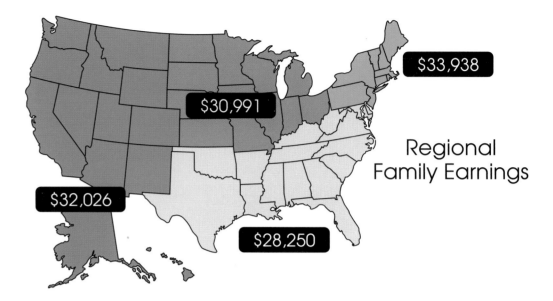

Regional Family Earnings

$33,938
$30,991
$32,026
$28,250

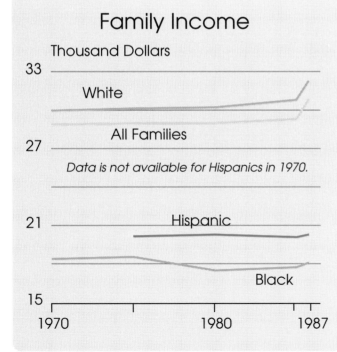

Family Income

Thousand Dollars

33 — White

All Families

27 —

Data is not available for Hispanics in 1970.

21 — Hispanic

Black

15 —

1970   1980   1987

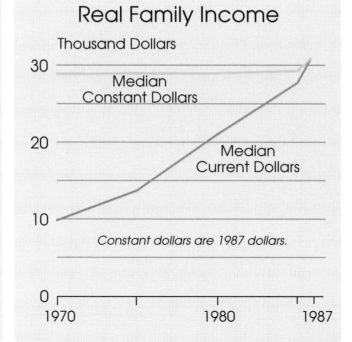

Real Family Income

Thousand Dollars

30 — Median Constant Dollars

20 — Median Current Dollars

10 —

Constant dollars are 1987 dollars.

0 —

1970   1980   1987

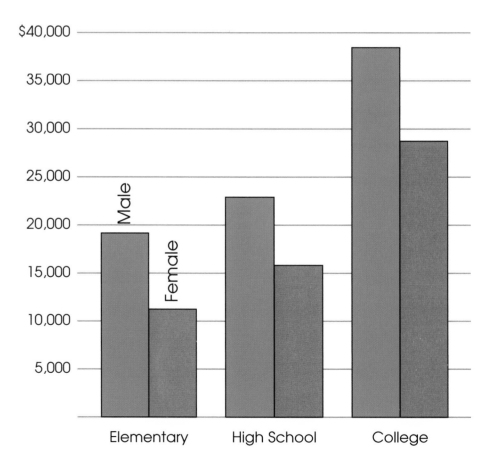

Earnings and Education, 1986

$40,000

35,000

30,000

25,000

20,000 Male

15,000 Female

10,000

5,000

Elementary   High School   College

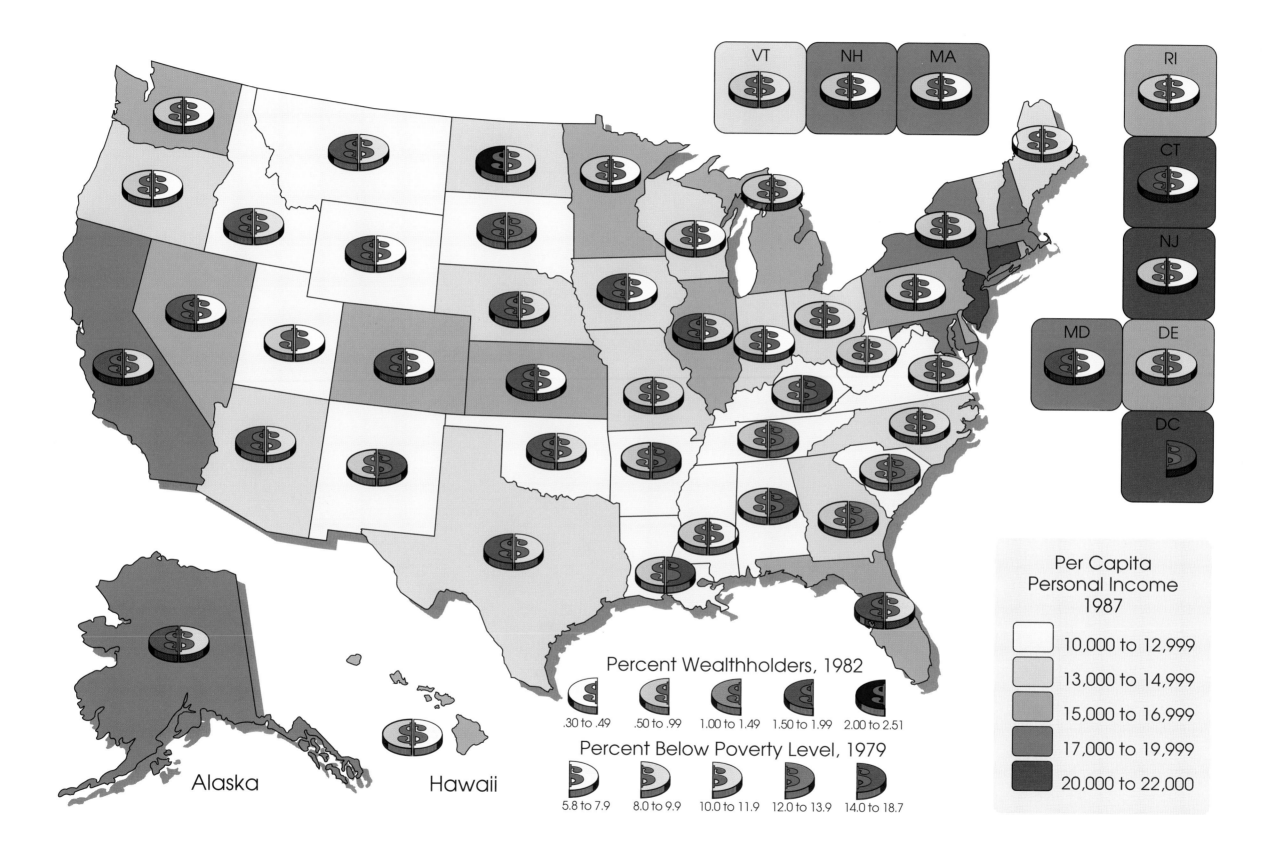

VT NH MA RI CT NJ MD DE DC

Per Capita
Personal Income
1987

10,000 to 12,999
13,000 to 14,999
15,000 to 16,999
17,000 to 19,999
20,000 to 22,000

Percent Wealthholders, 1982

.30 to .49   .50 to .99   1.00 to 1.49   1.50 to 1.99   2.00 to 2.51

Percent Below Poverty Level, 1979

5.8 to 7.9   8.0 to 9.9   10.0 to 11.9   12.0 to 13.9   14.0 to 18.7

Alaska   Hawaii

Issues of health in the United States are perplexing. While having more doctors, better equipment, and a health care budget that exceeds 600 billion dollars annually, medicine lags behind many industrialized nations in terms of availability and effectiveness. Problems like AIDS, teenage pregnancy, infant mortality, and drug use do not seem to go away despite a health budget that has increased from 7.4 percent of the gross national product in 1970 to 10.9 percent in 1986.

An example of this problem is the fact that among industrial nations the United States ranks 22d in infant mortality behind seemingly less sophisticated nations such as Singapore, Hong Kong, and Spain. And while miracle surgery is performed daily in U.S. hospitals, one of four women does not receive prenatal care during pregnancy, one of three poor children is not immunized against such simple and treatable diseases as measles, mumps, and rubella, and one of ten American children is not seen regularly by a physician.

Hospital payments have contributed largely to the rise in health costs. In 1970, a day in the hospital cost an average of $72.33. In 1986 the same stay cost $507.33. Of the 6,841 hospitals in the country in 1986, 35,200,000 patients spent at least part of the year occupying 1,283,000 beds while paying an average $3,533.00 per stay.

Physicians' fees have also increased dramatically. But doctors and dentists have been left with only modest net receipts after taxes, insurance, and office costs. The $200,300 average gross receipts for MDs translates into only $112,000 after expenses.

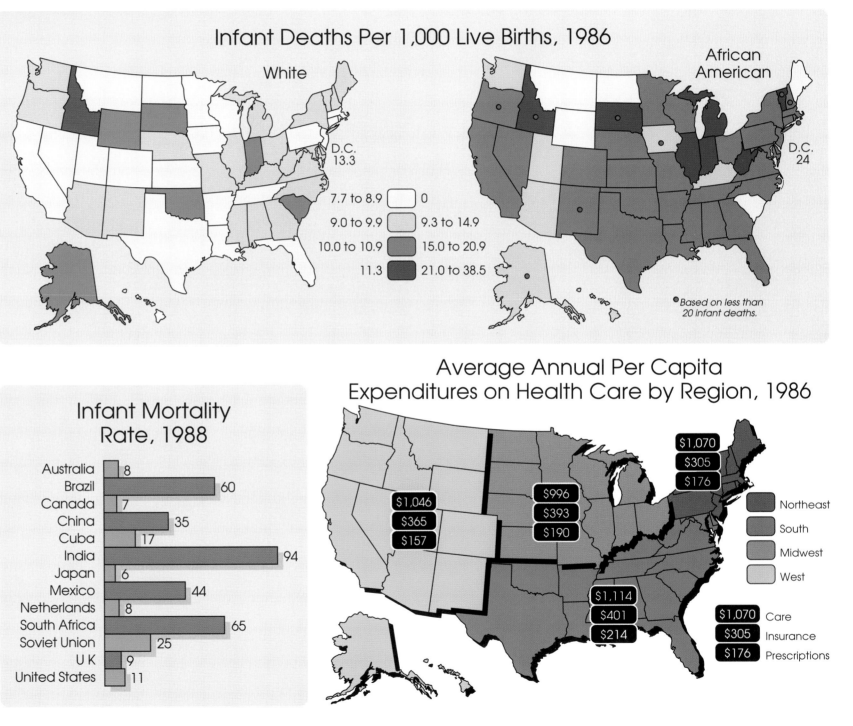

Infant Deaths Per 1,000 Live Births, 1986

White

D.C. 13.3

7.7 to 8.9	0
9.0 to 9.9	9.3 to 14.9
10.0 to 10.9	15.0 to 20.9
11.3	21.0 to 38.5

African American

D.C. 24

●Based on less than 20 infant deaths.

Infant Mortality Rate, 1988

Australia	8
Brazil	60
Canada	7
China	35
Cuba	17
India	94
Japan	6
Mexico	44
Netherlands	8
South Africa	65
Soviet Union	25
UK	9
United States	11

Average Annual Per Capita Expenditures on Health Care by Region, 1986

$1,070
$305
$176

$996
$393
$190

$1,046
$365
$157

$1,114
$401
$214

Northeast
South
Midwest
West

$1,070 Care
$305 Insurance
$176 Prescriptions

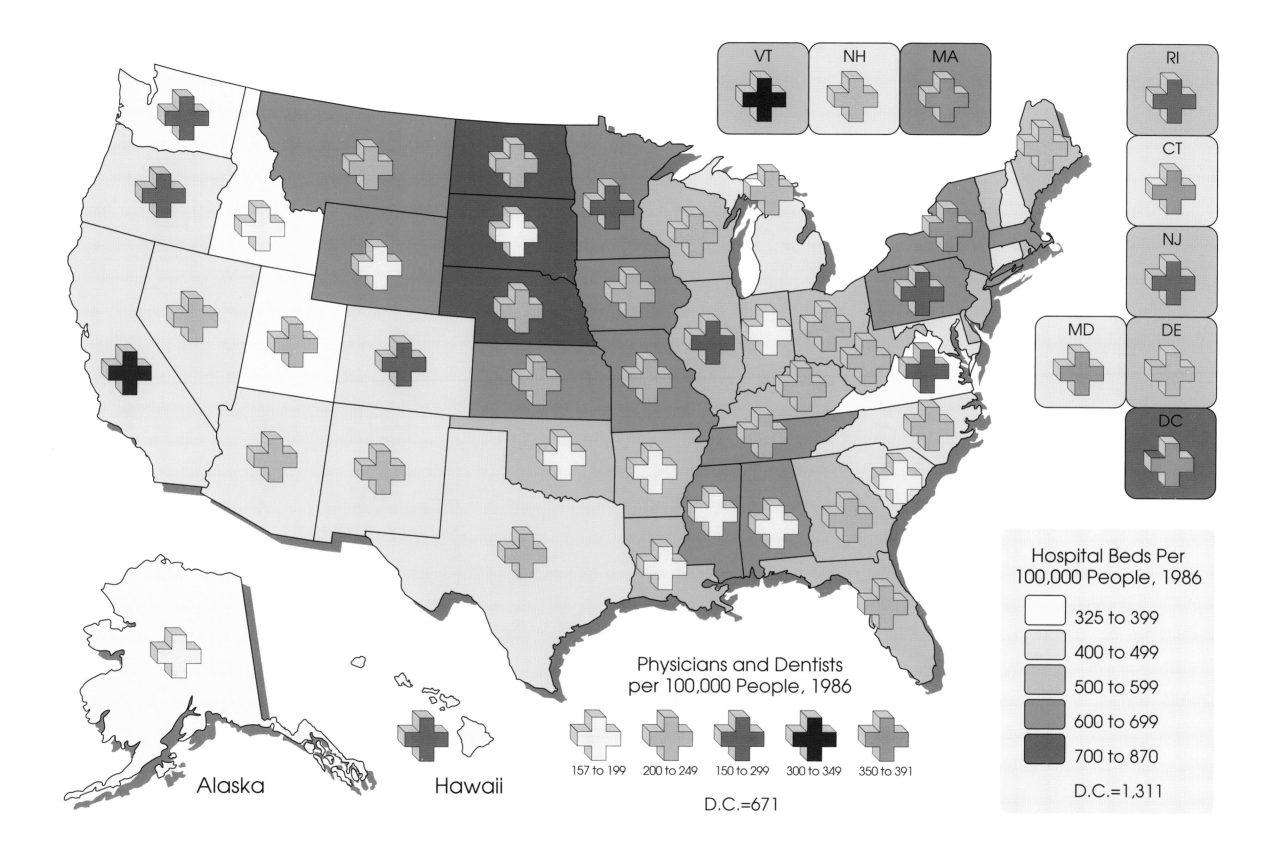

VT NH MA

RI CT NJ DE DC MD

Hospital Beds Per 100,000 People, 1986

325 to 399
400 to 499
500 to 599
600 to 699
700 to 870

D.C.=1,311

Alaska

Hawaii

Physicians and Dentists per 100,000 People, 1986

157 to 199   200 to 249   150 to 299   300 to 349   350 to 391

D.C.=671

Life expectancy for Americans depends on gender and ethnicity. Females live longer than males and whites longer than blacks. Disparity in life expectancy dependent on race is partially explained by the disproportionate number of infant deaths in the African-American and ethnic communities. Looking at the following maps one can see how infant mortality changes through the country. What is not shown is the number of blacks whose lives are shortened due to inner-city crime, a lack of health care, and diseases such as AIDS.

In general, Americans do not live as long as many others in the industrialized world. Countries such as Australia, Canada, Japan, the Netherlands, and the United Kingdom, which offer comprehensive health care packages, are places where citizens live longer lives.

Of the top killers of Americans, cardiovascular disease outranks all other causes for all racial groups. Malignancies and accidents follow as the nation's most potent killers.

Percent of Deaths Caused by Major Killers, 1986

	Male	Female	Black	White
Accidents/Adverse Effects	6	3	5	4
Cerebrovascular Diseases Chronic Obstructive	5	9	7	7
Chronic Liver Disease, Cirrhosis	2	.9	1	1
Diabetes Mellitus	1	2	3	2
Diseases of the Heart	35	37	31	37
Malignant Neoplasms	23	22	21	23
Pneumonia, Flu	3	4	3	3
Pulmonary Disease	4	3	2	.3
Suicide	2	.6	.7	2

Top Ten Killers, 1986

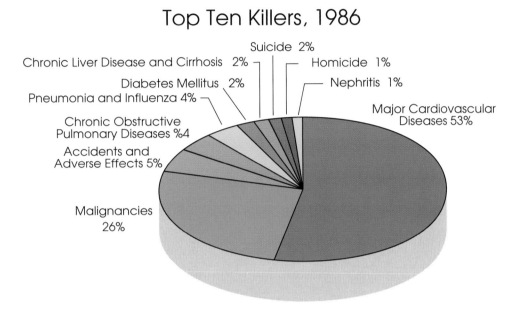

Suicide 2%
Chronic Liver Disease and Cirrhosis 2%
Homicide 1%
Diabetes Mellitus 2%
Nephritis 1%
Pneumonia and Influenza 4%
Major Cardiovascular Diseases 53%
Chronic Obstructive Pulmonary Diseases %4
Accidents and Adverse Effects 5%
Malignancies 26%

National Health Expenditures

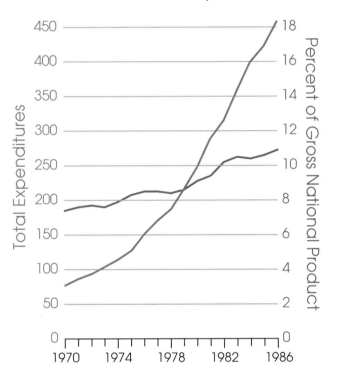

Life Expectancy at Birth, 1988

Australia	76.1
Brazil	67.0
Canada	77.1
China	68.8
Cuba	73.1
India	56.9
Japan	77.8
Mexico	69.7
Netherlands	77.1
South Africa	61.1
Soviet Union	68.9
U K	75.1
United States	75.3

Life Expectancy for Americans

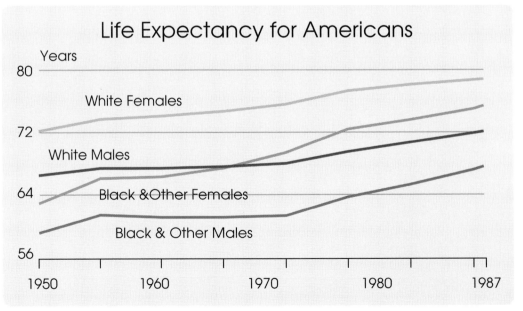

White Females
White Males
Black &Other Females
Black & Other Males

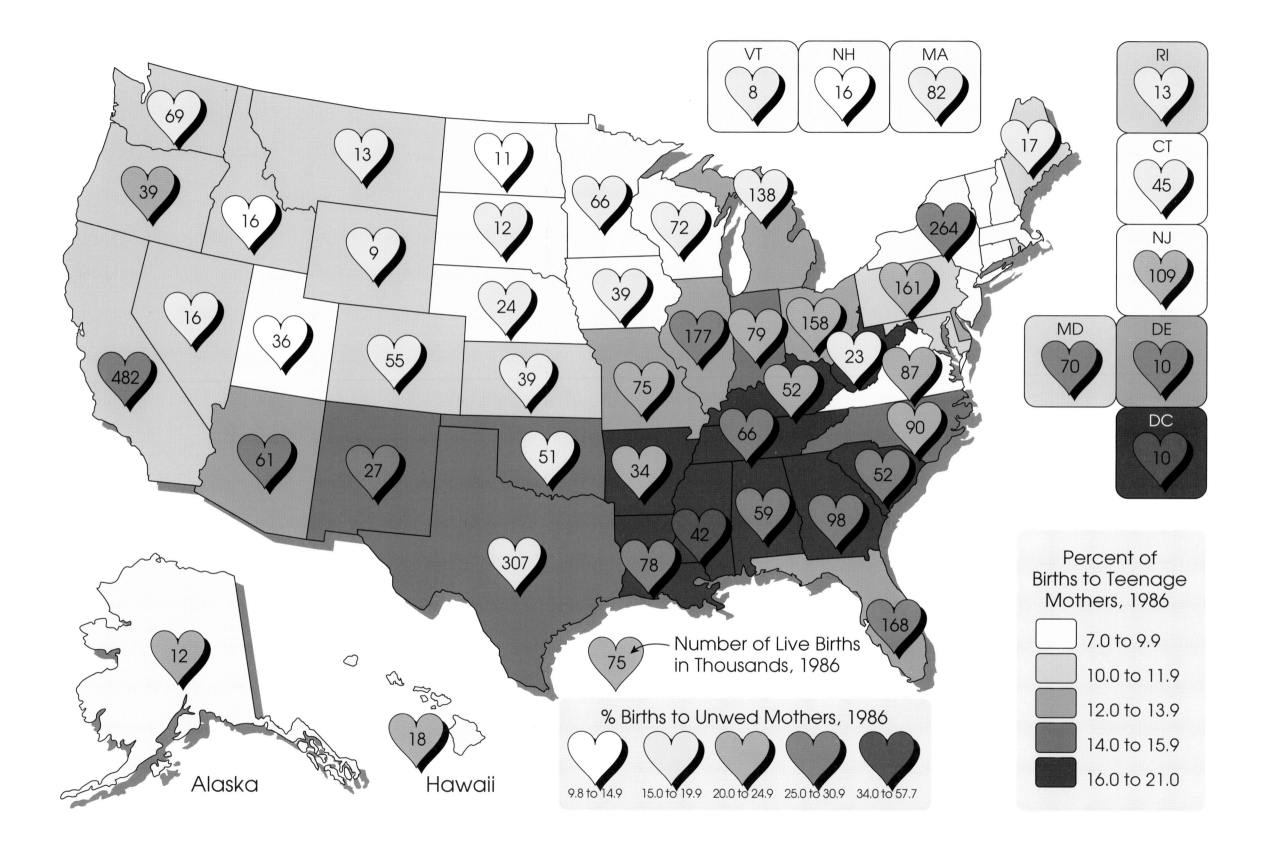

VT 8 — NH 16 — MA 82

RI 13 — CT 45 — NJ 109 — MD 70 — DE 10 — DC 10

Alaska 12 — Hawaii 18

75 ← Number of Live Births in Thousands, 1986

% Births to Unwed Mothers, 1986

9.8 to 14.9 — 15.0 to 19.9 — 20.0 to 24.9 — 25.0 to 30.9 — 34.0 to 57.7

Percent of Births to Teenage Mothers, 1986

7.0 to 9.9
10.0 to 11.9
12.0 to 13.9
14.0 to 15.9
16.0 to 21.0

AIDS 62

AIDS is a disease that breaks down the body's immune system, leaving it vulnerable to a variety of life-threatening illnesses. Since 1981, when AIDS was recognized as a disease, many government and health organizations have tracked its progression through socio-economic and demographic groups. After eight years, these groups conclude that AIDS is by far most common among homosexual or bisexual males and intravenous drug users and that males account for 89.4 percent of all cases.

Although reported cases of Caucasians with AIDS (43,423) through 1988 outnumber Blacks (19,692) and Hispanics (9,616), rates of infection reveal another pattern. Dividing reported cases by the population in each racial group, the rate of infection for Blacks is 65.0 per 100,000 population, 51.1 for Hispanics, and 20.9 for Whites.

Another interesting pattern shows that AIDS is a disease of young adults. While 1.8 percent of all reported cases affect those under 13 years and 3.4 percent those over 60, people 30 to 39 account for 46.3 percent. U.S. citizens between 14 and 29 account for 20.6 percent of all cases.

As there is a demography of AIDS, so also is there a geography. Starting out as a disease almost entirely concentrated in New York and California, AIDS has since steadily infected adjacent and interior states. In 1981, for example, New York and California accounted for nearly 70 percent of all cases while in 1988 they combined for only 41.5 percent.

Federal and state governments are working together in an effort to stop AIDS with 21 percent of a $946,935,000 budget going to education and 17 percent going toward AIDS research.

State Level Response to AIDS

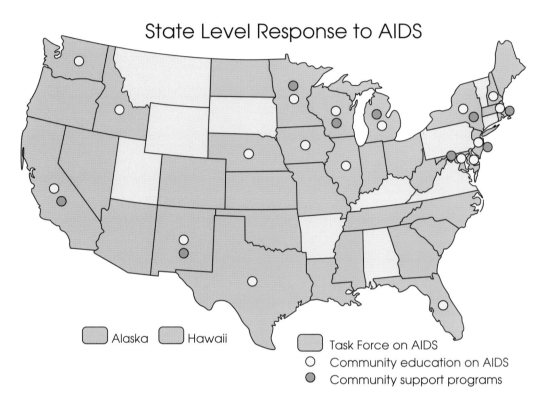

| | Alaska | | Hawaii | | Task Force on AIDS |
| ○ Community education on AIDS |
| ● Community support programs |

Ten States With the Most AIDS Cases Reported

	1981–1982	1988	Percent 1981–1982	Percent 1988
New York	461	6,992	53.7	22.3
California	134	6,005	15.6	19.2
Florida	67	2,606	7.8	8.3
New Jersey	64	2,620	7.5	8.5
Texas	20	2,233	2.3	7.1
Illinois	19	1,007	2.2	3.2
Pennsylvania	18	826	2.1	2.6
Georgia	11	729	1.3	2.3
Massachusetts	13	710	1.5	2.3
Maryland	5	548	.6	1.8

Source of AIDS Infection, May 1988

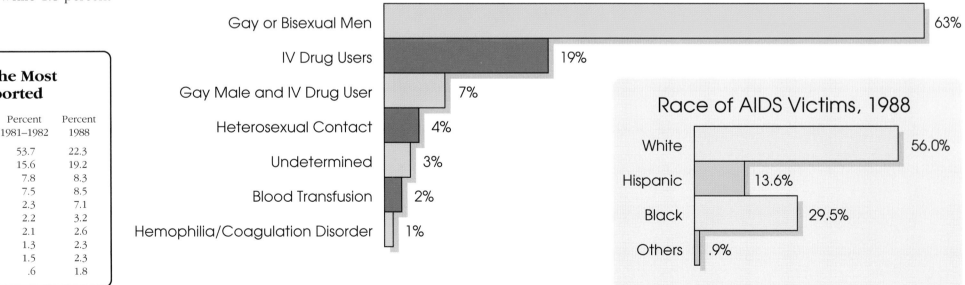

- Gay or Bisexual Men — 63%
- IV Drug Users — 19%
- Gay Male and IV Drug User — 7%
- Heterosexual Contact — 4%
- Undetermined — 3%
- Blood Transfusion — 2%
- Hemophilia/Coagulation Disorder — 1%

Race of AIDS Victims, 1988

- White — 56.0%
- Hispanic — 13.6%
- Black — 29.5%
- Others — .9%

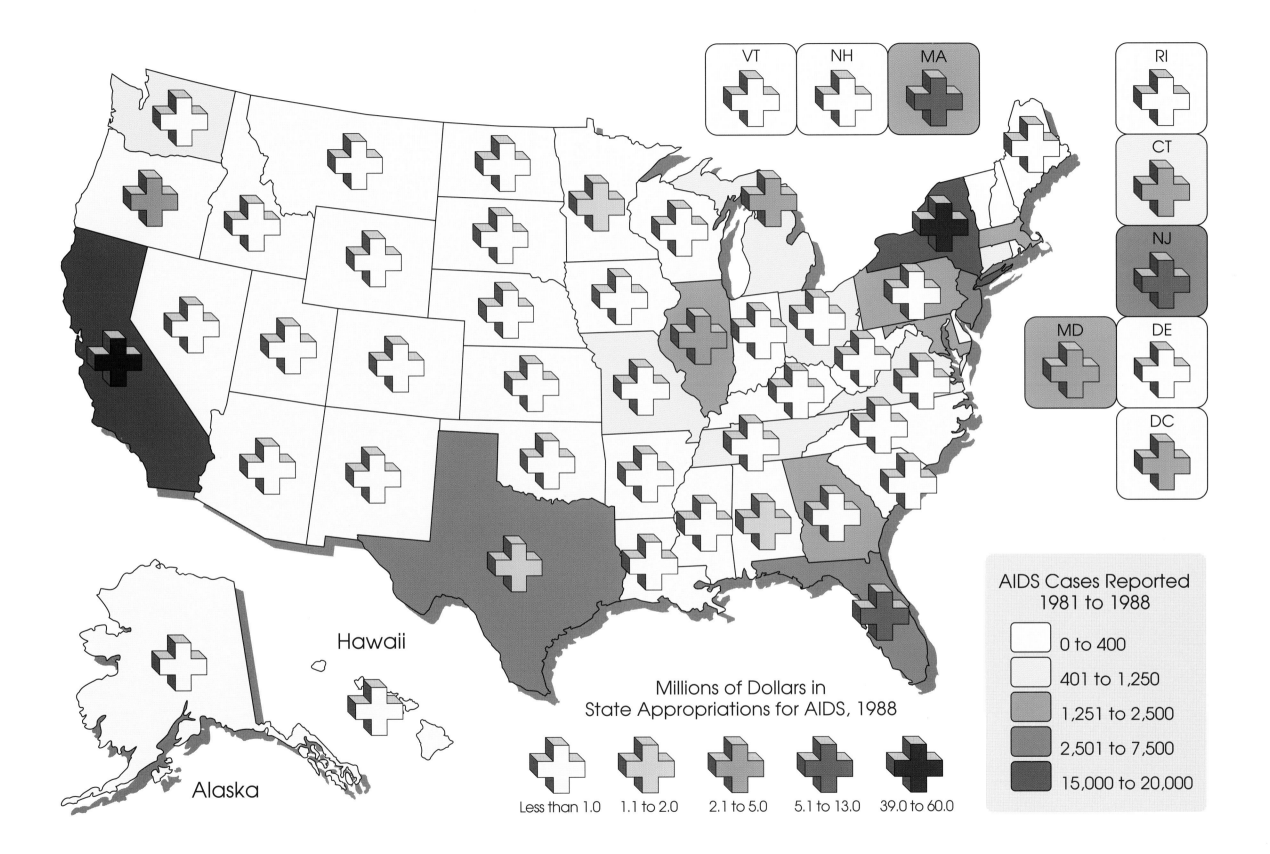

VT NH MA

RI

CT

NJ

MD DE

DC

Hawaii

Alaska

Millions of Dollars in
State Appropriations for AIDS, 1988

Less than 1.0   1.1 to 2.0   2.1 to 5.0   5.1 to 13.0   39.0 to 60.0

AIDS Cases Reported
1981 to 1988

0 to 400

401 to 1,250

1,251 to 2,500

2,501 to 7,500

15,000 to 20,000

School enrollments vary with changes in population and the expectations of society. Over the last 30 years, the educational requirements for Americans have increased greatly. More education is needed to obtain a job, and jobs that require greater amounts of education are increasing at a faster rate than those requiring less education. The current demand for better educated employees is reflected in the pie charts on this page.

In 1987, nearly one-quarter of all students were enrolled in college, an increase from 1965, when college enrollment accounted for 11 percent of the student population.

Lower birth rates in the 1970s meant fewer school age students, but higher birth rates in recent years have renewed the demand for teachers and schools. The dip for 1975 to 1985 on the graph showing *Total School Enrollment* reflects the lower birth rates, but the demand for education did not decrease as sharply because educational expectations continued to increase. By 1995, almost 55 million students will be enrolled in school. States with the lowest enrollment often have older populations and high private school attendance.

Although Whites had more education than Blacks or Hispanics in the past, the gap has narrowed in the years between 1970 and 1987, particularly among males.

Educational attainment also varies by state. The South is the most poorly educated. The highest percentage of people with high school diplomas occurs in the West and New England, where high-tech jobs dominate. The percentage is lower in the states where factory jobs have dominated employment opportunities.

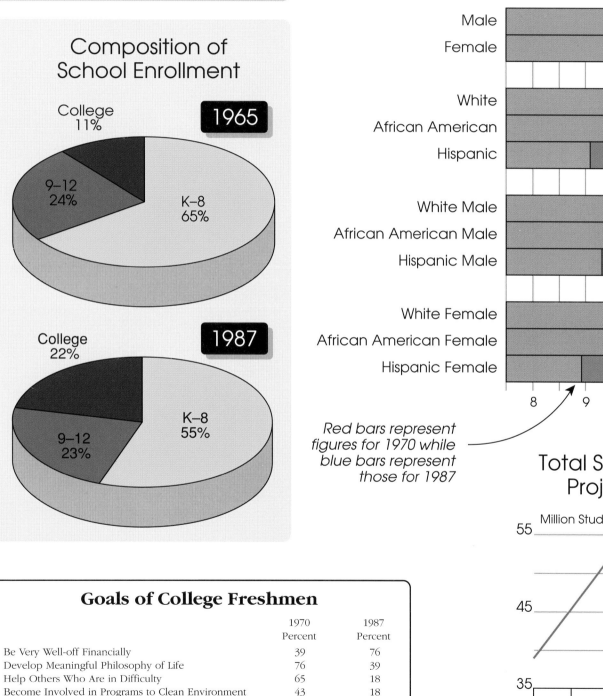

Composition of School Enrollment

1965

College 11%
9–12 24%
K–8 65%

1987

College 22%
9–12 23%
K–8 55%

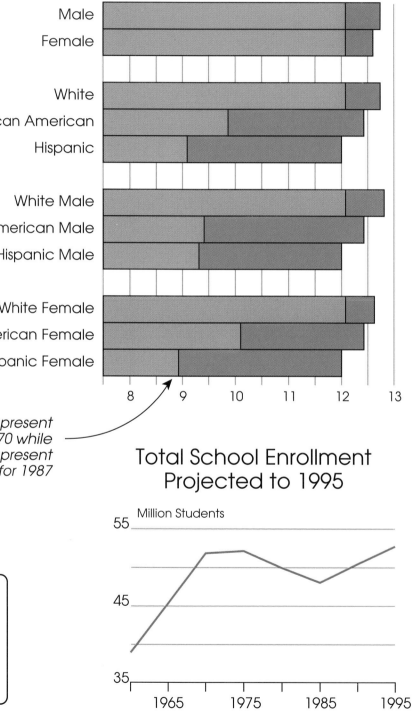

Median Years of School Completed 1970 and 1987

Male
Female

White
African American
Hispanic

White Male
African American Male
Hispanic Male

White Female
African American Female
Hispanic Female

8   9   10   11   12   13

Red bars represent figures for 1970 while blue bars represent those for 1987

Total School Enrollment Projected to 1995

Million Students

55

45

35

1965   1975   1985   1995

Goals of College Freshmen

	1970 Percent	1987 Percent
Be Very Well-off Financially	39	76
Develop Meaningful Philosophy of Life	76	39
Help Others Who Are in Difficulty	65	18
Become Involved in Programs to Clean Environment	43	18

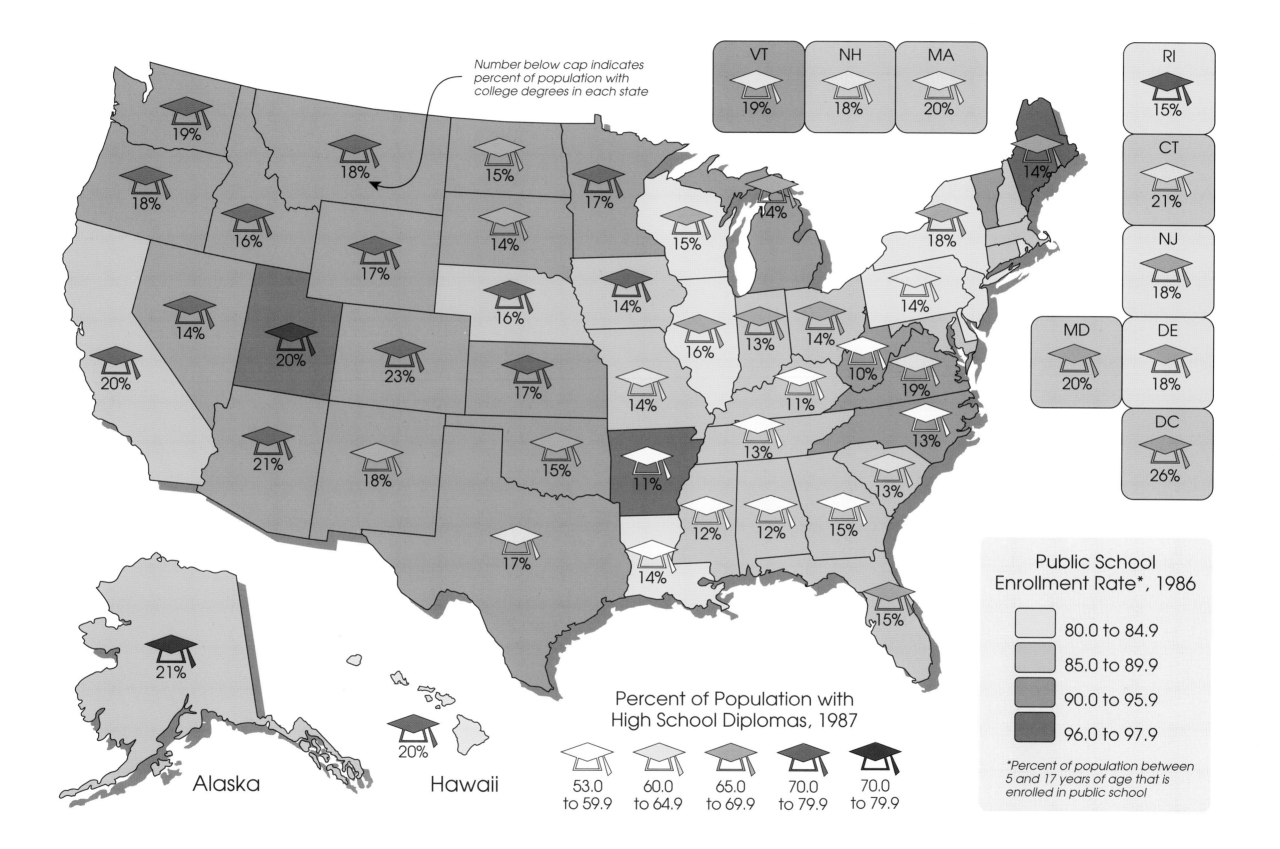

Number below cap indicates percent of population with college degrees in each state

Percent of Population with High School Diplomas, 1987

53.0 to 59.9   60.0 to 64.9   65.0 to 69.9   70.0 to 79.9   70.0 to 79.9

Public School Enrollment Rate*, 1986

80.0 to 84.9
85.0 to 89.9
90.0 to 95.9
96.0 to 97.9

*Percent of population between 5 and 17 years of age that is enrolled in public school

Alaska   Hawaii

The cost of educating public school students varies from a low of $2,400 to over $7,000 per pupil. The size of individual classes, money spent on maintenance and construction of schools, the purchase of equipment and supplies, and teachers' salaries are reflected in this dollar figure. With some notable exceptions, education costs are highest in the Northeast and lowest in the South, the western desert states, and the states of the Great Plains. State and local taxes fund the greatest share of school costs.

The series of maps shown here helps to measure some of the costs of education. The number of students per teacher is smallest in rural farm states where populations are widely scattered, and in the Northeast where public education is often highly specialized. Classes are largest in the rapidly growing western states, in Michigan, and in states of the Upper South. Teachers' salaries show no regional patterns. High salaries reflect a teacher shortage, in some cases. In others it shows a strong commitment to improve education.

Circulation of books by American public libraries is quite low overall when compared to similar figures for Western Europe, Japan, and the Soviet Union. In the Northeast, the low circulation figure reflects the high incidence of private libraries and, in some cases, large in-school libraries. Until recently, the level of investment in libraries was very low in the South. This is still reflected in the national pattern.

Microcomputers for Public School Students, 1987

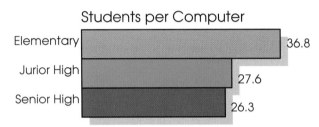

Students per Computer

Elementary	36.8
Jurior High	27.6
Senior High	26.3

Source of Finances for Education

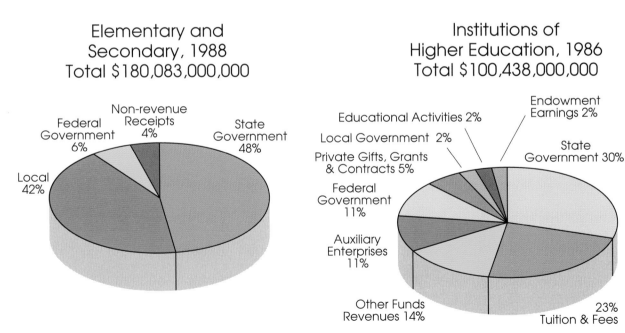

Elementary and Secondary, 1988
Total $180,083,000,000

- Non-revenue Receipts 4%
- Federal Government 6%
- State Government 48%
- Local 42%

Institutions of Higher Education, 1986
Total $100,438,000,000

- Educational Activities 2%
- Endowment Earnings 2%
- Local Government 2%
- Private Gifts, Grants & Contracts 5%
- State Government 30%
- Federal Government 11%
- Auxiliary Enterprises 11%
- Other Funds Revenues 14%
- Tuition & Fees 23%

Higher Education, 1986

	Number of Institutions		Number of Institutions
Alabama	79	Montana	17
Arizona	32	Nebraska	33
Arkansas	34	Nevada	9
Alaska	15	New Hampshire	28
California	299	New Jersey	61
Colorado	52	New Mexico	21
Connecticut	49	New York	308
Delaware	10	North Carolina	125
D.C.	18	North Dakota	19
Florida	89	Ohio	142
Georgia	81	Oklahoma	47
Hawaii	14	Oregon	45
Idaho	10	Pennsylvania	212
Illinois	163	Rhode Island	13
Indiana	76	South Carolina	62
Iowa	61	South Dakota	18
Kansas	52	Tennessee	82
Kentucky	56	Texas	163
Louisiana	32	Utah	14
Maine	31	Vermont	22
Maryland	56	Virginia	75
Massachusetts	121	Washington	52
Michigan	91	West Virginia	29
Minnesota	73	Wisconsin	62
Mississippi	42	Wyoming	9I
Missouri	92		

Cost of Elementary and Seconday Education, 1988

	Dollars Spent per Pupil	Rank by Money Spent
Alabama	2,752	49
Alaska	7,038	1
Arizona	3,265	40
Arkansas	2,410	51
California	3,994	26
Colorado	4,359	17
Connecticut	6,141	5
Delaware	4,994	10
D.C.	5,643	6
Florida	4,389	16
Georgia	2,939	46
Hawaii	3,894	30
Idaho	2,814	47
Illinois	4,217	20
Indiana	3,616	35
Iowa	3,846	32
Kansas	4,262	19
Kentucky	3,355	38
Louisiana	3,211	41
Maine	4,276	18
Maryland	4,871	13
Massachusetts	5,396	8
Michigan	4,122	22
Minnesota	4,513	15
Mississippi	2,760	48
Missouri	3,566	36
Montana	4,061	24
Nebraska	3,641	34
Nevada	3,829	33
New Hampshire	3,990	27
New Jersey	6,910	2
New Mexico	3,880	31
New York	6,864	4
North Carolina	3,911	28
North Dakota	3,353	39
Ohio	4,019	25
Oklahoma	3,051	45
Oregon	4,574	14
Pennsylvania	5,063	9
Rhode Island	5,456	7
South Carolina	3,075	44
South Dakota	3,159	43
Tennessee	3,189	42
Texas	3,462	37
Utah	2,658	50
Vermont	4,949	12
Virginia	4,145	21
Washington	4,083	23
West Virginia	3,895	29
Wisconsin	4,991	11
Wyoming	6,885	3

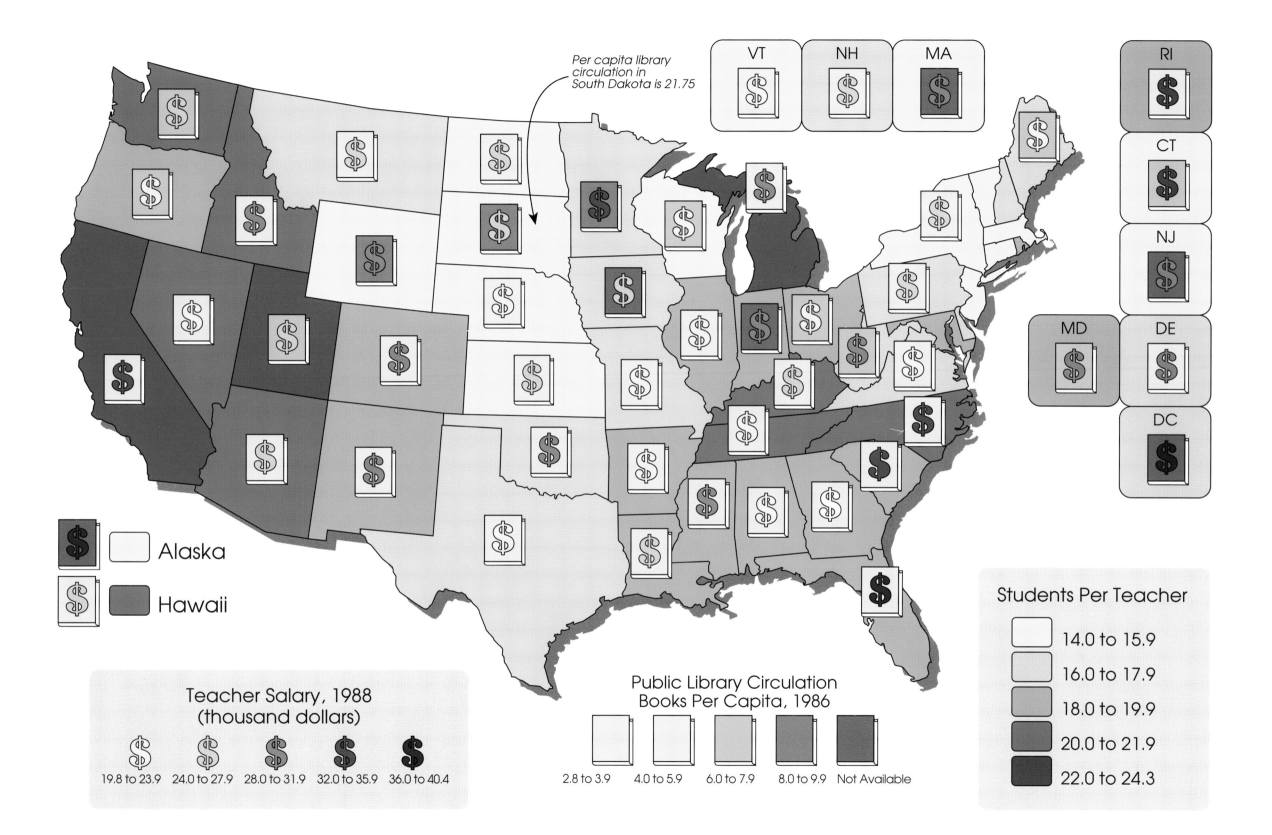

Per capita library circulation in South Dakota is 21.75

VT NH MA

RI CT NJ MD DE DC

$ Alaska

$ Hawaii

Teacher Salary, 1988 (thousand dollars)

$ 19.8 to 23.9 $ 24.0 to 27.9 $ 28.0 to 31.9 $ 32.0 to 35.9 $ 36.0 to 40.4

Public Library Circulation Books Per Capita, 1986

2.8 to 3.9   4.0 to 5.9   6.0 to 7.9   8.0 to 9.9   Not Available

Students Per Teacher

14.0 to 15.9
16.0 to 17.9
18.0 to 19.9
20.0 to 21.9
22.0 to 24.3

Each year, an average American spends $1,226 on entertainment. Almost half of that amount goes toward electronics, toys, and sporting goods and equipment.

In 1988, manufacturers shipped 11,270,000 audio and 12,738,000 video units valued at 2.1 and 4.8 billion dollars, respectively. Pre-recorded video tape sales accounted for 2.4 billion dollars in the sale of 69.2 million units.

Entertainment spending is greatest in the Northeast and the West and among Americans 35 to 44 years old who spend two dollars for every dollar spent by groups under 25 and over 65. Individuals with incomes of more than $40,000 spend more than all other groups at a rate of $2,282 per year.

Although reading is not high on the list of entertainment priorities, accounting for only 11 percent of the entertainment dollar, it is a 26-billion-dollar-a-year industry catering primarily to those with higher incomes and more education. Males read less than females, and readership decreases with age.

State appropriations in support of the arts are highest in the Northeast, Florida, and Alaska. Hawaii's contributions include state support of Hawaiian ethnic cultural activities, native dance, art, and music.

Per Capita Expenditures for Entertainment & Reading, 1986

Equipment/Services	$405
Television, Radios, & Sound Equipment	$373
Fees/Admissions	$308
Reading	$140

State Appropriations for the Arts, 1988

State Spending for Parks and Recreation (dollars per capita)

$0.65 to 4.99
$5.00 to 8.99
$9.00 to 12.99
$13.00 to 16.99
$17.00 to 36.48

Below National Average   Above National Average

National yearly average is $0.92 per resident

Dividing the Recreation & Entertainment Dollar, 1986

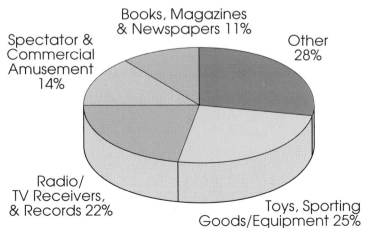

Books, Magazines & Newspapers 11%
Other 28%
Spectator & Commercial Amusement 14%
Radio/ TV Receivers, & Records 22%
Toys, Sporting Goods/Equipment 25%

Americans are enthusiastic about sports. Whether it means watching football on television with a bowl of popcorn or playing Little League in Cedar Rapids, Iowa, a national preoccupation has turned into a multi-billion dollar industry.

Since 1980, sports sales have sky-rocketed toward 40 billion dollars annually. Athletic shoe sales, which can be used as a simple example of this economic growth, are expected to reach 100 million dollars in 1990. Since 1980, these and other sales show an average annual growth rate of 11.5 percent.

Attendance at sporting events has also increased. Surprisingly, horseracing is the most watched professional sporting event, followed by baseball and greyhound racing.

Franchises for Major League sports are almost invariably found in large metropolitan areas where a crowd can be guaranteed for almost any event. The largest number of franchises are found in the largest cities: New York/Northern New Jersey has nine; Los Angeles/Orange County has six; Philadelphia, Detroit, Chicago, Boston, and the San Francisco Bay area have four each. Hockey is found over-whelmingly in northern areas where conditions favor winter sports.

Intercollegiate competition, once a manifestation of "school spirit" and a "love for the game," has also become big business. Universities with recognized programs in Division I football and basketball not only command huge profits at the gates, but also capitalize on their reputations in sports as advertisements for incoming students.

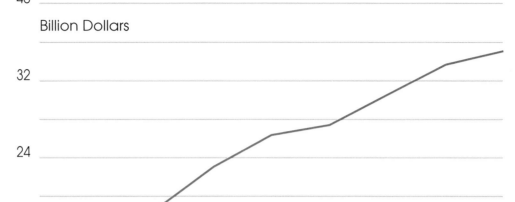

Total Sales of Sporting Goods Products

Billion Dollars

Sneaker Sales
1980 Projected to 1990*

1980	43,275,000
1985	65,250,000
1990	89,275,000

*Sales of all athletic shoes calculated at an average cost of $40 per pair

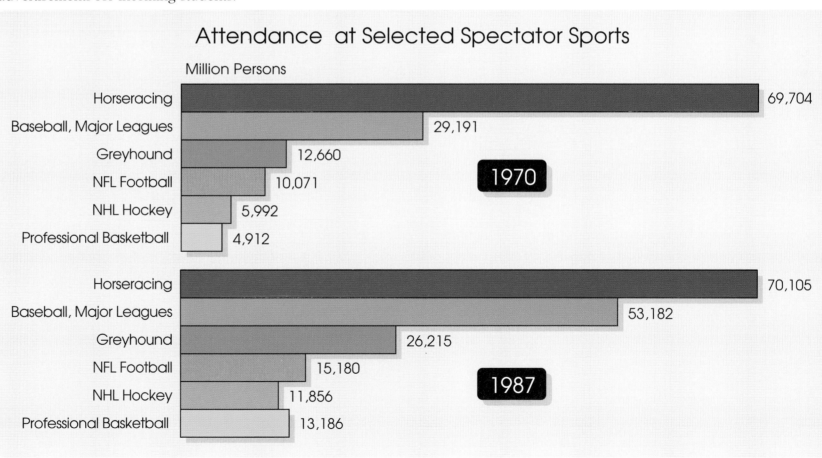

Attendance at Selected Spectator Sports

Million Persons

1970

Horseracing	69,704
Baseball, Major Leagues	29,191
Greyhound	12,660
NFL Football	10,071
NHL Hockey	5,992
Professional Basketball	4,912

1987

Horseracing	70,105
Baseball, Major Leagues	53,182
Greyhound	26,215
NFL Football	15,180
NHL Hockey	11,856
Professional Basketball	13,186

Americans have a strong tradition of participation in sports. As the first country to attain the 40-hour work week, Americans devote more time to recreation than people in any other society. In addition, Americans "invented" baseball, football, basketball, and volleyball, and have assimilated hockey and lacrosse from other cultures.

Sports have always been a part of American education. Such proverbs as "a sound mind in a sound body" were taken quite seriously, and children and young adults were encouraged to participate in school. The great variety of sports in which Americans participate reflects a rich ethnic heritage, a varied climate, and a landscape replete with breathtaking scenery.

Americans, in general, are active in sports in all parts of the country. Differences in regional participation are probably not significant. Those who hunt or fish have increased in number to over 50 million in 1988.

Involvement in sports is a function of age and income. Individuals earning less than $15,000 a year are most active. Americans also are more active as they get older, reflecting a trend toward recreational cycling and walking.

In collegiate sports, the size of an institution plays a significant role in the success of its sports programs. National Collegiate Championships are almost always awarded to big schools whose participating students come from a national pool of competing athletes. The prevalence of such awards in any one region, for this reason, is a bit deceiving. Titles awarded to Southern Cal, for example, could very easily have been won by athletes from points as far east as North Carolina.

Participation in Sports, 1987

Men	Million	Women	Million
Swimming	36	Swimming	37
Fishing	35	Bicycling	29
Bicycling	24	Aerobics	22
Pool	23	Bowling	21
Basketball	22	Hiking	19
Weights	22	Fishing	18
Softball	21	Camping	17
Camping	20	Calisthenics	16
Hiking	20	Jogging, Running	14
Bowling	19	Volleyball	14
		Weights	14

Regional Participation in Sports

West, Midwest, South, Northeast

Participation in Sports by Age and Income, 1987

Thousands $
- Under 15.0
- 15.0 to 24.9
- 25.0 to 34.9
- 35.0 to 49.9
- Over 50.0

Age
- 7 to 11
- 12 to 17
- 18 to 24
- 25 to 34
- 35 to 54
- Over 55

Millions of Participants

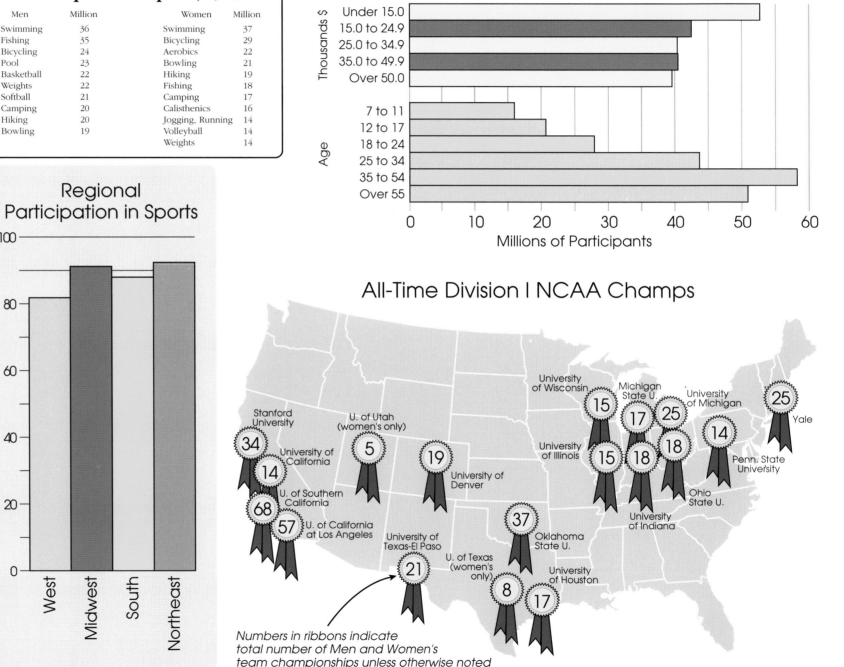

All-Time Division I NCAA Champs

University of Wisconsin — 15
Michigan State U. — 17
University of Michigan — 25
Stanford University — 34
U. of Utah (women's only) — 5
University of California — 14
University of Illinois — 15
U. of Denver — 19
U. of Southern California — 68
U. of California at Los Angeles — 57
University of Indiana — 18
Ohio State U. — 18
University of Michigan — 14
Yale — 25
Penn. State University
University of Texas-El Paso — 21
U. of Texas (women's only) — 8
Oklahoma State U. — 37
University of Houston — 17

Numbers in ribbons indicate total number of Men and Women's team championships unless otherwise noted

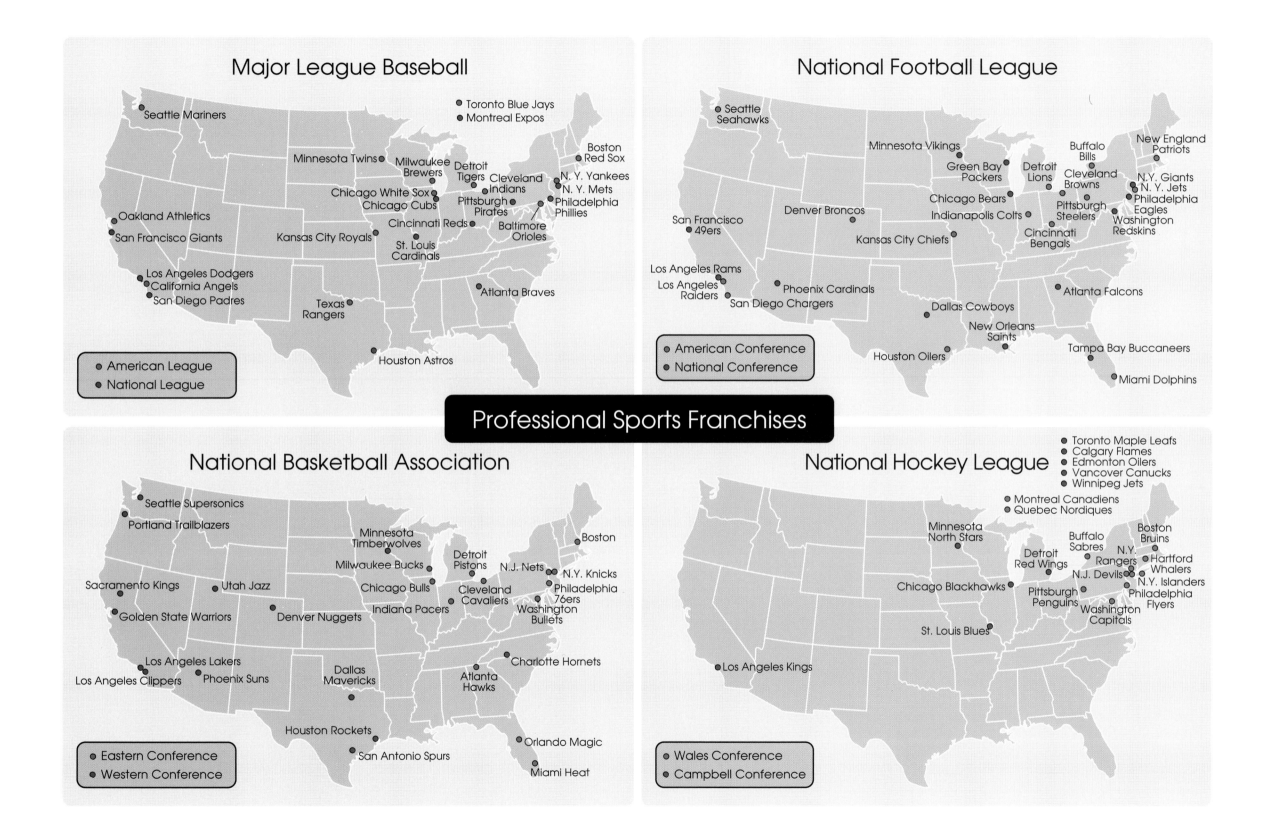

Professional Sports Franchises

Major League Baseball

Seattle Mariners
Toronto Blue Jays
Montreal Expos
Boston Red Sox
Minnesota Twins
Milwaukee Brewers
Detroit Tigers
Cleveland Indians
N. Y. Yankees
N. Y. Mets
Chicago White Sox
Chicago Cubs
Pittsburgh Pirates
Philadelphia Phillies
Oakland Athletics
San Francisco Giants
Cincinnati Reds
Baltimore Orioles
Kansas City Royals
St. Louis Cardinals
Los Angeles Dodgers
California Angels
San Diego Padres
Texas Rangers
Atlanta Braves
Houston Astros

● American League
● National League

National Football League

Seattle Seahawks
Minnesota Vikings
Buffalo Bills
New England Patriots
Green Bay Packers
Detroit Lions
Cleveland Browns
N. Y. Giants
N. Y. Jets
Philadelphia Eagles
Chicago Bears
Pittsburgh Steelers
San Francisco 49ers
Denver Broncos
Indianapolis Colts
Cincinnati Bengals
Washington Redskins
Kansas City Chiefs
Los Angeles Rams
Los Angeles Raiders
Phoenix Cardinals
San Diego Chargers
Atlanta Falcons
Dallas Cowboys
New Orleans Saints
Tampa Bay Buccaneers
Houston Oilers
Miami Dolphins

● American Conference
● National Conference

National Basketball Association

Seattle Supersonics
Portland Trailblazers
Minnesota Timberwolves
Boston
Milwaukee Bucks
Detroit Pistons
N.J. Nets
N.Y. Knicks
Sacramento Kings
Utah Jazz
Chicago Bulls
Cleveland Cavaliers
Philadelphia 76ers
Golden State Warriors
Denver Nuggets
Indiana Pacers
Washington Bullets
Los Angeles Lakers
Phoenix Suns
Charlotte Hornets
Los Angeles Clippers
Dallas Mavericks
Atlanta Hawks
Houston Rockets
Orlando Magic
San Antonio Spurs
Miami Heat

● Eastern Conference
● Western Conference

National Hockey League

Toronto Maple Leafs
Calgary Flames
Edmonton Oilers
Vancover Canucks
Winnipeg Jets
Montreal Canadiens
Quebec Nordiques
Minnesota North Stars
Buffalo Sabres
Boston Bruins
N.Y. Rangers
Detroit Red Wings
Hartford Whalers
N.J. Devils
N.Y. Islanders
Chicago Blackhawks
Pittsburgh Penguins
Philadelphia Flyers
Washington Capitals
St. Louis Blues
Los Angeles Kings

● Wales Conference
● Campbell Conference

Americans are placing greater and greater demands on the nation's recreational resources. Workers, confined to office buildings during the week, are heading for the countryside and seashores in ever-increasing numbers on the weekends. This recreation surge has led state, local, and federal governments to increase both funding and the amount of available space for recreational activities.

One of the most widely used components of America's recreational infrastructure is the National Park System, which began with Yellowstone National Park in 1872. Comprised of 75,863,000 acres that are broken into 49 parks, 26 historical sites, 77 national monuments, and countless military, historic, and recreation areas, the system has nearly tripled in size since 1970 and is now entertaining a record-high 364,600,000 yearly visitors since 1986 with a budget of just over one billion federal dollars. Visits to the National Park System have increased from 172 million in 1970 to 364 million in 1986 and the annual budget has increased from $174,600,000 to $1,634,400,000 for the same time period.

Additionally, there are parks at the state, county, and local municipal level. New York's Central Park and Philadelphia's Fairmount Park are examples of how big industrial cities made communities more livable at the turn of the century in what has come to be known as the "city beautiful movement."

The state park movement has no definite beginning, but New York state early established protected areas in the Adirondacks and Catskills to insure a supply of pure water for New York City. During the Great Depression of the 1930s, the federal government set up work camps for the unemployed, providing jobs and training in conservation. Many state parks and forests date from that time, as states took over management of these camps and converted them to public parks.

Most states have developed sizable park systems. Today, state parks include 13,752,000 acres that service 694,432,000 visitors yearly.

Population, in part, explains differences in visits on a state level. The Northeast and the Pacific Coast have large populations that generate many daytime visitors. Number and accessibility of state parks are also important. Pennsylvania and West Virginia have developed at least one state park in almost every county. Ohio has established several state parks within an hour of nearly all its cities.

Composition of America's Recreational Book Readers 1983

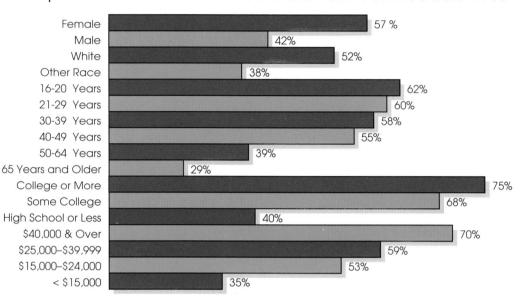

Female	57%
Male	42%
White	52%
Other Race	38%
16-20 Years	62%
21-29 Years	60%
30-39 Years	58%
40-49 Years	55%
50-64 Years	39%
65 Years and Older	29%
College or More	75%
Some College	68%
High School or Less	40%
$40,000 & Over	70%
$25,000–$39,999	59%
$15,000–$24,000	53%
< $15,000	35%

National Park Visits, 1986

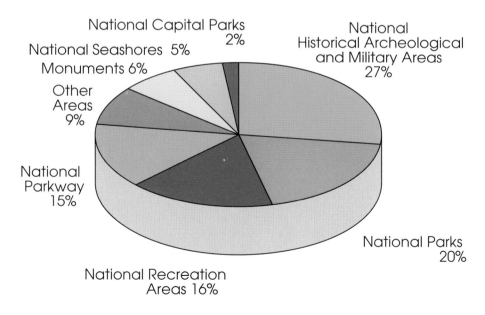

National Capital Parks 2%
National Historical Archeological and Military Areas 27%
National Seashores 5%
Monuments 6%
Other Areas 9%
National Parkway 15%
National Parks 20%
National Recreation Areas 16%

Visits to National Parks & National Park Growth

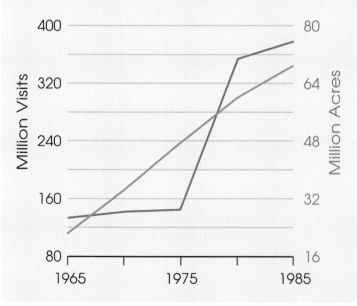

Million Visits
Million Acres

400 — 80
320 — 64
240 — 48
160 — 32
80 — 16

1965   1975   1985

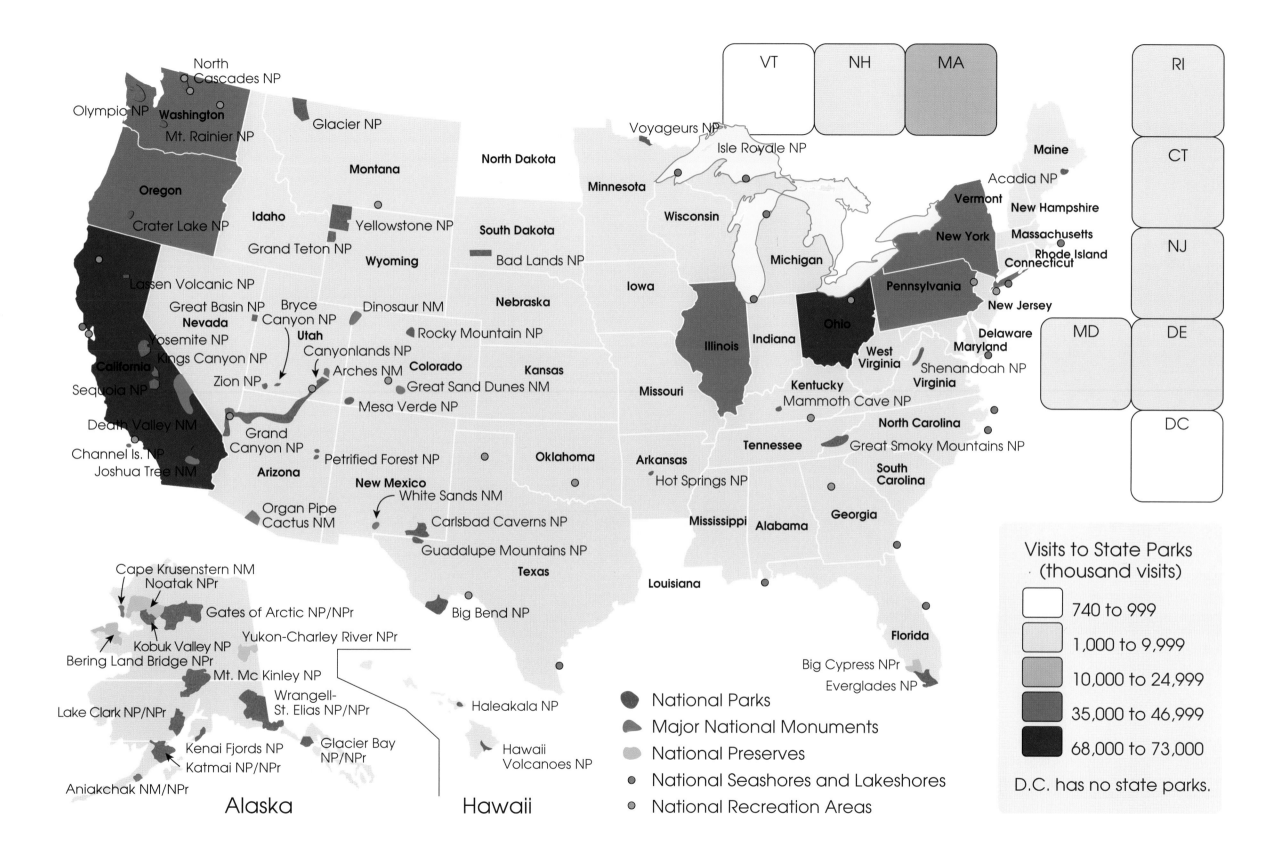

North Cascades NP
Olympic NP
Washington
Mt. Rainier NP
Oregon
Crater Lake NP
Lassen Volcanic NP
Great Basin NP
Bryce Canyon NP
Nevada
Yosemite NP
Kings Canyon NP
Utah
Zion NP
California
Sequoia NP
Death Valley NM
Channel Is. NP
Joshua Tree NM
Canyonlands NP
Arches NM
Colorado
Great Sand Dunes NM
Mesa Verde NP
Grand Canyon NP
Petrified Forest NP
Arizona
New Mexico
Organ Pipe Cactus NM
White Sands NM
Carlsbad Caverns NP
Guadalupe Mountains NP
Texas
Big Bend NP
Louisiana
Florida
Big Cypress NPr
Everglades NP

Glacier NP
Montana
North Dakota
Yellowstone NP
Idaho
Grand Teton NP
Wyoming
South Dakota
Bad Lands NP
Dinosaur NM
Rocky Mountain NP
Nebraska
Iowa
Kansas
Missouri
Oklahoma
Arkansas
Hot Springs NP
Mississippi
Alabama
Georgia

Voyageurs NP
Isle Royale NP
Minnesota
Wisconsin
Michigan
Illinois
Indiana
Ohio
Kentucky
Mammoth Cave NP
Tennessee
North Carolina
Great Smoky Mountains NP
South Carolina

VT | NH | MA
Maine
Acadia NP
Vermont
New Hampshire
New York
Massachusetts
Rhode Island
Connecticut
Pennsylvania
New Jersey
Delaware
Maryland
Shenandoah NP
West Virginia
Virginia

RI
CT
NJ
MD | DE
DC

Cape Krusenstern NM
Noatak NPr
Gates of Arctic NP/NPr
Kobuk Valley NP
Yukon-Charley River NPr
Bering Land Bridge NPr
Mt. Mc Kinley NP
Wrangell-St. Elias NP/NPr
Lake Clark NP/NPr
Kenai Fjords NP
Glacier Bay NP/NPr
Katmai NP/NPr
Aniakchak NM/NPr
Alaska

Haleakala NP
Hawaii Volcanoes NP
Hawaii

National Parks
Major National Monuments
National Preserves
National Seashores and Lakeshores
National Recreation Areas

Visits to State Parks (thousand visits)

	740 to 999
	1,000 to 9,999
	10,000 to 24,999
	35,000 to 46,999
	68,000 to 73,000

D.C. has no state parks.

Crime is defined as an act for which society provides a sanctioned punishment. Under a simple classification scheme, crimes of property outnumbered crimes of violence nine to one.

Property crime occurs with such frequency that 99 percent of all Americans will be victims at sometime in their lives. Violent crime, which has dropped 8 percent since 1976, still took 5,822,000 Americans as victims in 1985 and can be shown to be most common in the West, the South, the industrialized Northeast, and in Florida. Trends show that all crimes are more prevalent in metropolitan areas and in states with large urban centers. In 1987, Dallas and Detroit were the most crime-ridden cities, ranking in the top five for virtually every crime classification. Florida can be considered the most violent state, having eleven of the nation's most violent cities within its borders.

Statistics about crime show that criminals are those who have been left out of the American Dream. Crime is committed by minorities in disproportionate numbers.

Serious crime is highest among those 16 to 18 years old and is committed by black males in numbers that are disproportionate to their presence in the overall population. While blacks made up only 12 percent of the U.S population, they committed 47 percent of all violent crimes and accounted for 27 percent of all arrests in 1985. Speaking to the endless cycle of desperation and hopelessness of the urban ghetto, blacks are six times more likely to go to jail in their lifetime than whites.

Drug use also plays a large part in criminal activity. Seventy-eight percent of all prisoners reported that they were drug users prior to incarceration. Studies have also shown that many criminals, especially those who have committed violent crimes, have themselves been victims of child abuse.

Most Americans would agree that not enough is being done to stop or punish criminals. Despite regional yearly per capita expenditures of as much as $270, prison overcrowding and court backlogs result in criminals being turned back to the street. A possible solution lies in increased expenditures for police and judicial services. Currently, 48.5 billion dollars is being spent yearly for crime compared to 288.7 for national defense, 205.9 for education, and 172.7 for interest on the national debt.

Incidents of Crime Per 100,000 Metropolitan Residents, 1987

Violent Crime

Aggravated Assault 446
Robbery 315
Forcible Rape 46
Murder 10.2

Property Crime

Motor Vehicle Theft 3,968
Larceny-theft 1,602
Burglary 709

Likelihood of Being the Victim of Crime in One's Lifetime

Personal Theft 99%
Violent Crimes* 83%
Assault 74%
Robbery 30%
Rape 8%
Injury During Robbery/Assault 40%

Violent crimes include assault, robbery, and rape.

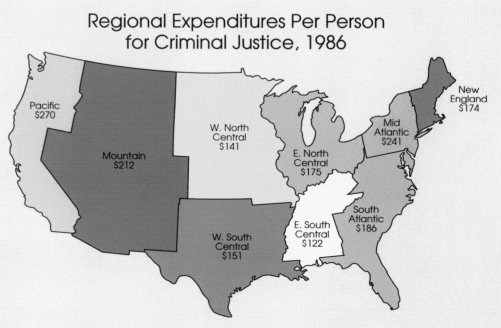

Regional Expenditures Per Person for Criminal Justice, 1986

Pacific $270
Mountain $212
W. North Central $141
E. North Central $175
New England $174
Mid Atlantic $241
South Atlantic $186
W. South Central $151
E. South Central $122

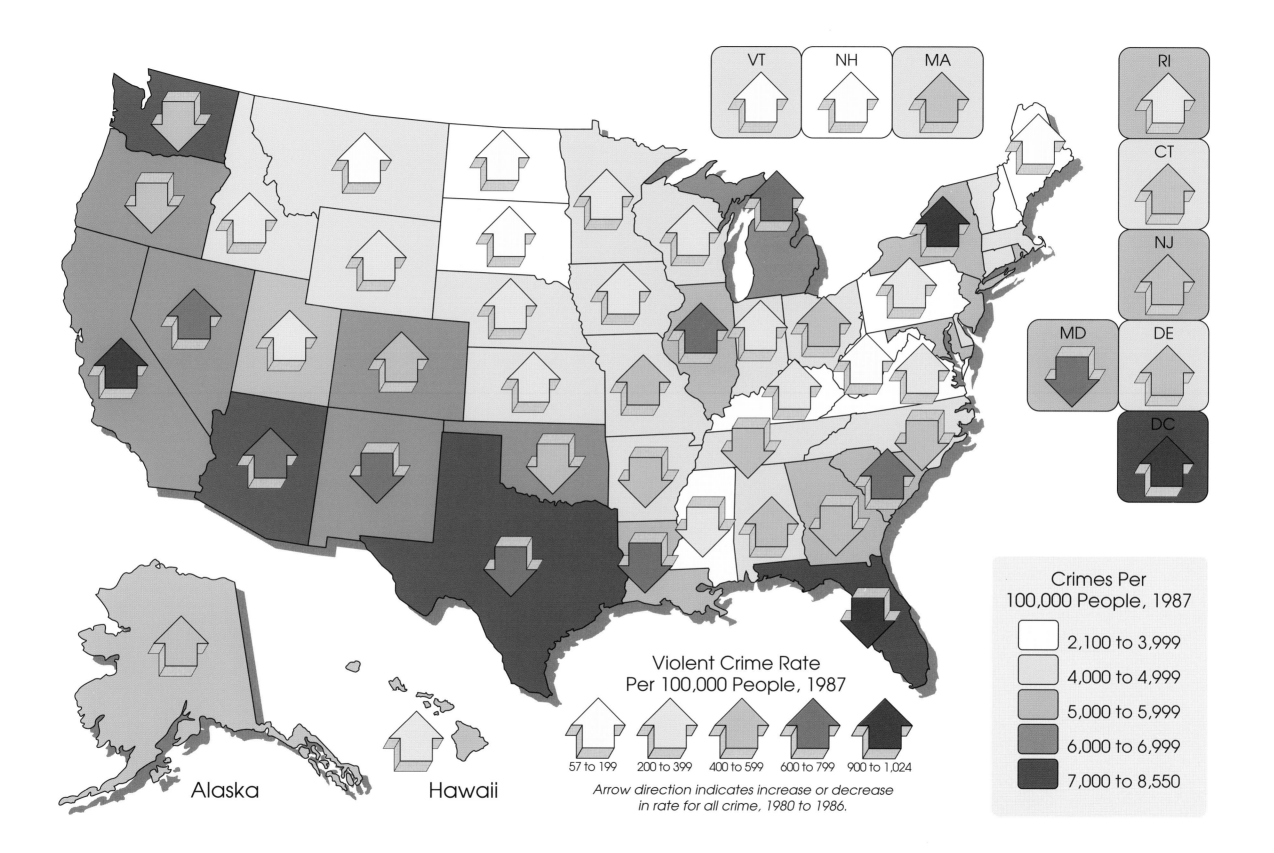

VT **NH** **MA**

RI **CT** **NJ** **MD** **DE** **DC**

Alaska

Hawaii

Violent Crime Rate
Per 100,000 People, 1987

| 57 to 199 | 200 to 399 | 400 to 599 | 600 to 799 | 900 to 1,024 |

*Arrow direction indicates increase or decrease
in rate for all crime, 1980 to 1986.*

Crimes Per
100,000 People, 1987

	2,100 to 3,999
	4,000 to 4,999
	5,000 to 5,999
	6,000 to 6,999
	7,000 to 8,550

Drug use is one of America's biggest problems, causing crime and violence in street battles over the control of drug sales. But who uses drugs and where do they come from?

The use of drugs in the United States has increased steadily since 1970. Marijuana, cocaine, and stimulant users have been joined by a crop of "designer drug" users that has reached at least 144,000,000 strong. Among this staggering number of Americans who use or at least have tried drugs, males aged 25 to 44 are the greatest offenders.

Drugs not produced in the United States travel across U.S. borders from several primary sources. Most of the marijuana consumed by Americans originates in Mexico, Central America, Jamaica, and the northern part of South America. These shipments are joined by a particularly strong variety grown in Thailand which is imported through Hong Kong to the West Coast. Coca—grown throughout South America and, in particular, Peru—is processed to form cocaine in Ecuador and Columbia for shipment through Mexico to the southwestern United States. Shipments from Brazil, Paraguay, Uruguay, Venezuela, and Bolivia reach markets in New York and the East Coast. Opiates, which are derived from poppy flowers, are produced in the Far East, Iran, Afghanistan, and Pakistan and join hashish shipments moving west through Africa and Southern Europe.

Law enforcement alone does not seem to be able to stop the flow of incoming drugs. Although seizures at U.S. borders have risen dramatically since 1970, drugs continue to enter the country at record rates.

Narcotics Seizures at US Borders

Million Dollars

(Line graph with y-axis values: 600, 480, 360, 240, 120, 0; x-axis values: 1970, 1980, 1987)

U.S. District Court Drug Convictions

Convictions

(Line graph with y-axis values: 8,000, 6,400, 4,800, 3,200, 1,600, 0; x-axis values: 1980, 1987, 1987)

Prison Sentences for Drug Abuse

Months

(Line graph with y-axis values: 87, 72, 56, 40; x-axis values: 1980, 1985, 1987)

— Marijuana
— Drugs
— Controlled Substances/ Prescribed Drugs

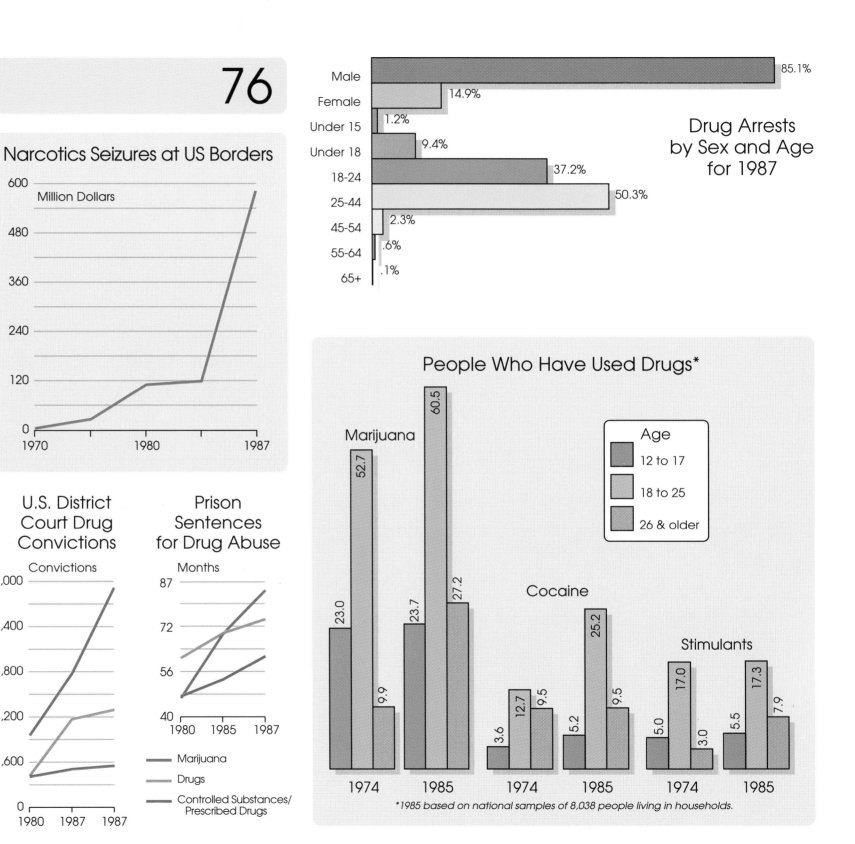

Drug Arrests by Sex and Age for 1987

Male 85.1%
Female 14.9%
Under 15 1.2%
Under 18 9.4%
18-24 37.2%
25-44 50.3%
45-54 2.3%
55-64 .6%
65+ .1%

People Who Have Used Drugs*

Age
12 to 17
18 to 25
26 & older

Marijuana
23.0   52.7   9.9   23.7   60.5   27.2

Cocaine
3.6   12.7   9.5   5.2   25.2   9.5

Stimulants
5.0   17.0   3.0   5.5   17.3   7.9

1974   1985   1974   1985   1974   1985

*1985 based on national samples of 8,038 people living in households.

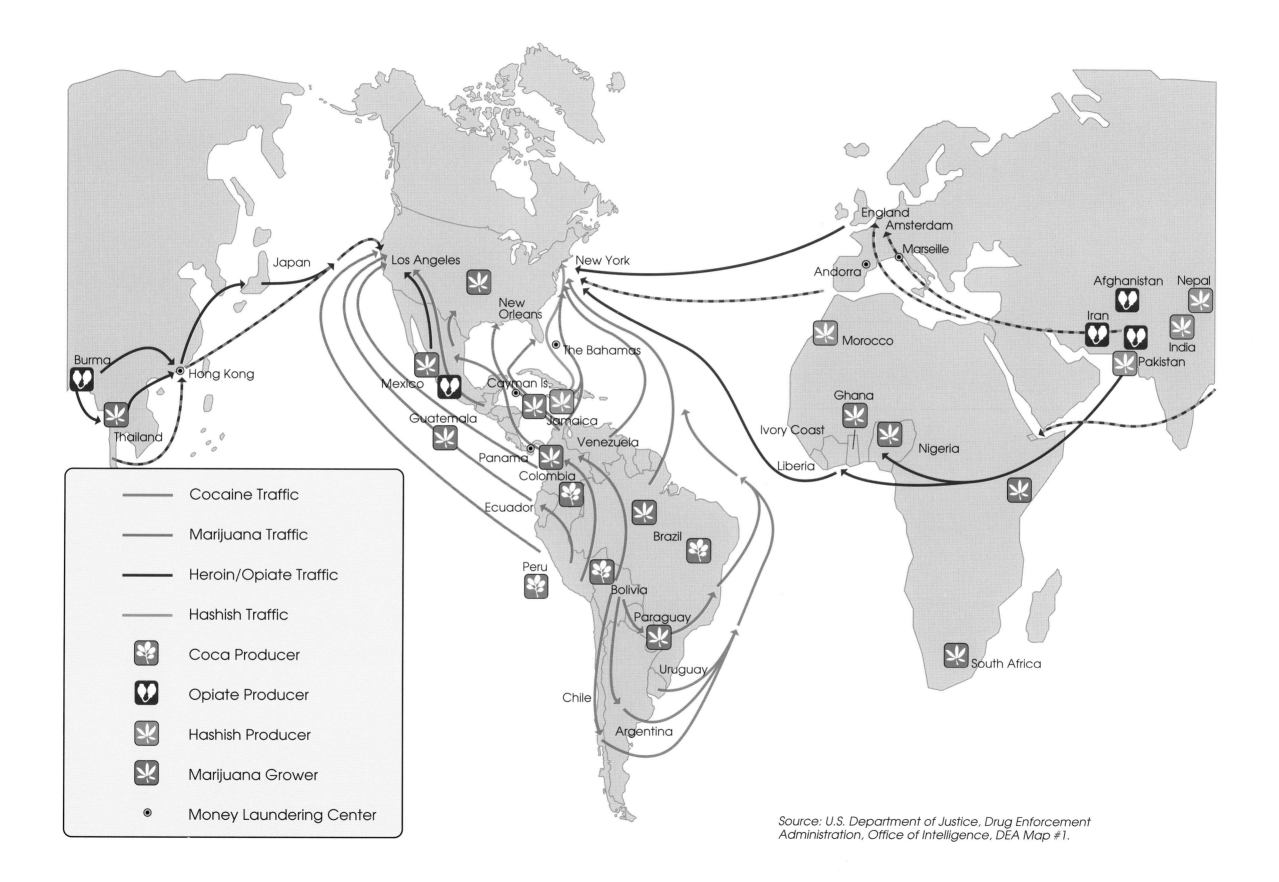

England
Amsterdam
Marseille
Andorra
Afghanistan
Nepal
Iran
India
Pakistan
Burma
Japan
Los Angeles
New York
Hong Kong
New Orleans
Morocco
Thailand
Mexico
The Bahamas
Ghana
Guatemala
Cayman Is.
Jamaica
Ivory Coast
Nigeria
Panama
Venezuela
Liberia
Colombia
Ecuador
Peru
Brazil
Bolivia
Paraguay
South Africa
Uruguay
Chile
Argentina

Cocaine Traffic

Marijuana Traffic

Heroin/Opiate Traffic

Hashish Traffic

🌿 Coca Producer

Opiate Producer

Hashish Producer

Marijuana Grower

⊙ Money Laundering Center

Source: U.S. Department of Justice, Drug Enforcement Administration, Office of Intelligence, DEA Map #1.

THE ECONOMY   79

In an effort to remain competitive in the world market, American farms have grown larger. Many small farmers are forced out of business with this trend towards fewer and larger farm units. Farms are largest in the mountain and desert areas of the West and in the Great Plains, and are devoted to the cultivation of grain. In those areas, a large percentage of farmland is simply rangeland suitable for grazing sheep and cattle.

California is America's leading agricultural state in the value of crops produced. The two largest grain and livestock producing areas are the states of the Great Plains (Kansas, Nebraska, Minnesota, and a part of Texas) and the states of the prairies (Ohio, Indiana, Iowa, and Illinois). The South is next in importance as an agricultural producer.

The major crop for each state varies greatly across the country. In some cases, such as tobacco or citrus, a rather small acreage can produce a great deal of income. Hay, corn, and wheat are the country's most prominent crops. Crops that can be used as both live-stock feed and as industrial raw materials, such as peanuts (in the South) and soybeans, are becoming increasingly important.

The states of the Midwest frequently refer to themselves as "America's Heartland." These states are level, fertile, and well-watered. Most of that region's states are in the top two prime cropland classes on the map on page 81. Ten of the 13 North Central states are classed as Agricultural Heartland states, and only four other states, all in the South, are included in this category of agriculturally rich states.

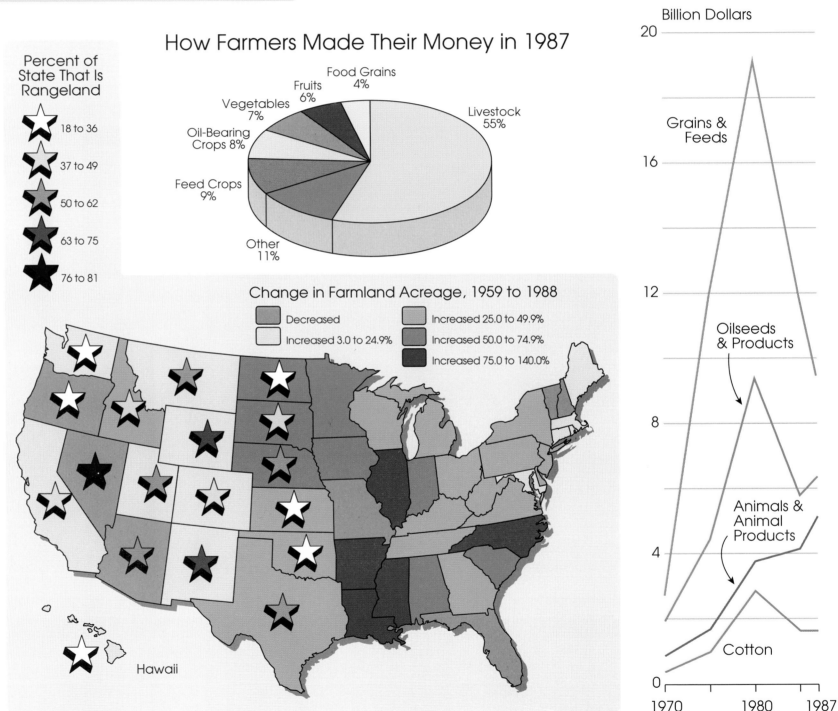

Percent of State That Is Rangeland

- 18 to 36
- 37 to 49
- 50 to 62
- 63 to 75
- 76 to 81

How Farmers Made Their Money in 1987

- Food Grains 4%
- Fruits 6%
- Vegetables 7%
- Oil-Bearing Crops 8%
- Feed Crops 9%
- Other 11%
- Livestock 55%

Change in Farmland Acreage, 1959 to 1988

- Decreased
- Increased 3.0 to 24.9%
- Increased 25.0 to 49.9%
- Increased 50.0 to 74.9%
- Increased 75.0 to 140.0%

Hawaii

Export of Farm Products

Billion Dollars

Grains & Feeds

Oilseeds & Products

Animals & Animal Products

Cotton

20

16

12

8

4

0

1970 1980 1987

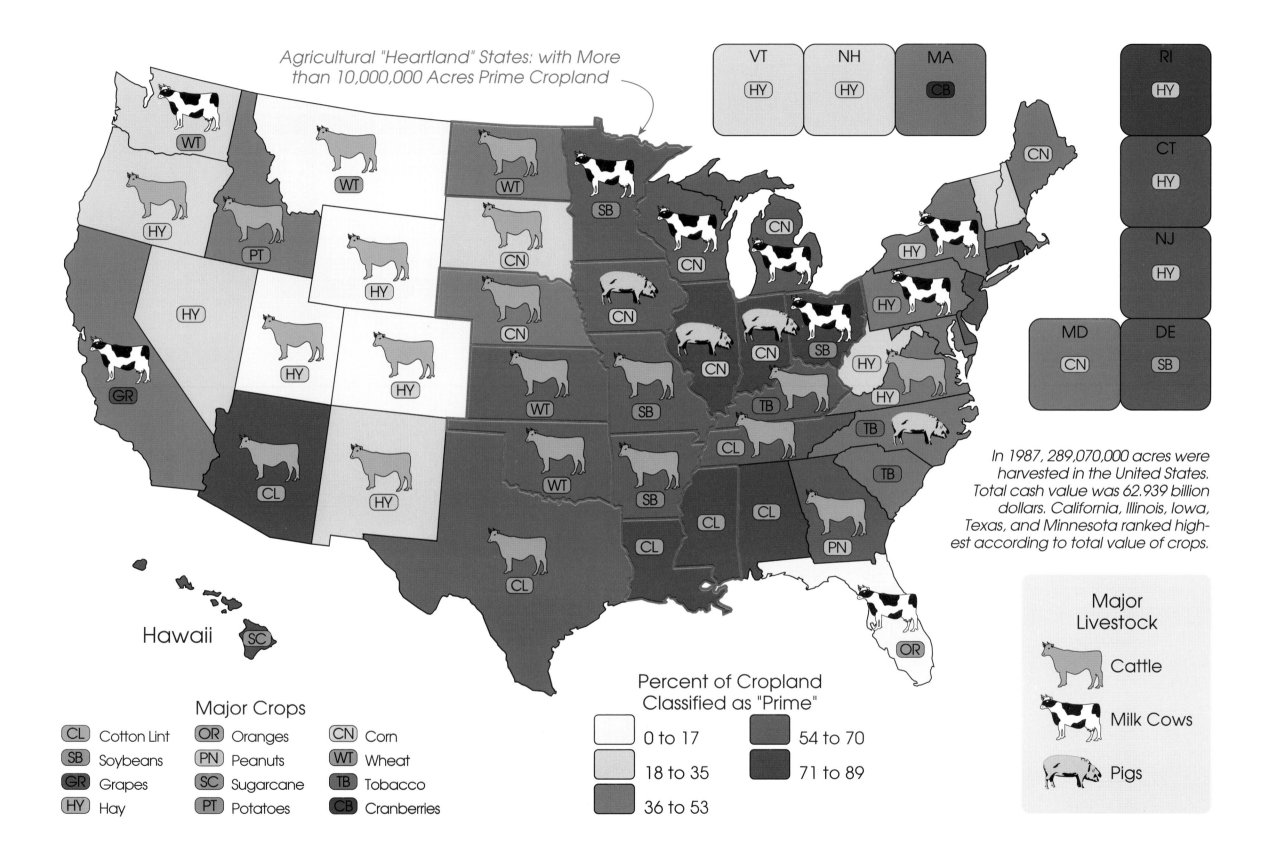

Agricultural "Heartland" States: with More than 10,000,000 Acres Prime Cropland

In 1987, 289,070,000 acres were harvested in the United States. Total cash value was 62.939 billion dollars. California, Illinois, Iowa, Texas, and Minnesota ranked highest according to total value of crops.

Hawaii

Major Crops

CL Cotton Lint   OR Oranges   CN Corn
SB Soybeans   PN Peanuts   WT Wheat
GR Grapes   SC Sugarcane   TB Tobacco
HY Hay   PT Potatoes   CB Cranberries

Percent of Cropland Classified as "Prime"

0 to 17   54 to 70
18 to 35   71 to 89
36 to 53

Major Livestock

Cattle

Milk Cows

Pigs

Even though pioneers cleared much of America's native forest for their farms, 35 percent of the country is still forested. Since the first decade of the 20th century, the federal government has set standards for the conservation and management of this important resource. Throughout most of the country, the annual amount of new growth exceeds the amount of timber cut. This has been accomplished through a combination of scientific forestry and ever-increasing import of lumber.

The country's forest reserves are unevenly distributed. The nation's agricultural heartland, located in the Great Plains and in the southern states of the North Central region, has a very limited area of forest. The Northeast and Great Lakes areas of the North Central states were so heavily cut before 1910, that their forested area, while quite large, often consists of poorer grades of timber and younger trees. The states of the South and the Pacific states (except Hawaii) contain most of the nation's commercially valuable timber.

There are two categories of timber: hardwoods, used primarily in furniture production; and softwoods, used in making pulp and paper, and in housing construction. Most of the nation's softwoods come from Alaska, the Pacific Northwest, California, and the northern Rockies. The total for these regions accounts for nearly half of all U.S. production. The South, which produces most of the nation's hardwood (as well as considerable softwood), produces one-third of the total.

America's national forests are divided among areas of current heavy production, those areas where the resource was largely destroyed in the lumber boom of 1870–1910, and the drylands of the southern Rockies and the desert Southwest. The only area of the country where cutting exceeds growth is the Pacific Northwest, making conservation in this area a national concern.

Yellow pine is the most common softwood produced in the South, Douglas fir in the Pacific States, and ponderosa pine in the Rockies. Oak is the dominant hardwood variety produced, but softwood production far outweighs hardwood in importance. Of the 44.9 billion board feet produced in 1987, only 20 percent was hardwood.

Hardwoods
797,289,000,000
Board Feet

Softwoods
2,025,957,000,000
Board Feet

U.S. Total=2,823 billion

Leaders in Lumbering, 1987

	Total Timber (thousand acres)	Timber Production (million board feet)	Growing Stock: Reserves (million cubic feet)
1. Oregon	21,749	372,612	64,930
2. Washington	16,849	333,954	61,620
3. California	16,712	311,966	53,771
4. Alaska	15,763	176,144	41,260
5. Idaho	14,534	140,566	32,592
6. Montana	14,737	92,962	28,016
7. Georgia	23,384	92,311	30,694
8. North Carolina	18,358	91,881	28,952
9. Louisiana	13,872	70,735	18,992
10. Mississippi	16,674	68,567	19,185

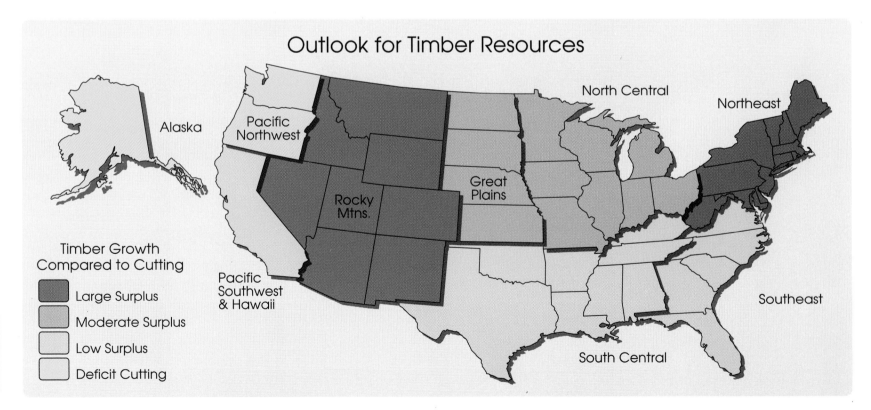

Outlook for Timber Resources

Alaska

Pacific Northwest

North Central

Northeast

Great Plains

Rocky Mtns.

Pacific Southwest & Hawaii

Southeast

South Central

Timber Growth Compared to Cutting

- Large Surplus
- Moderate Surplus
- Low Surplus
- Deficit Cutting

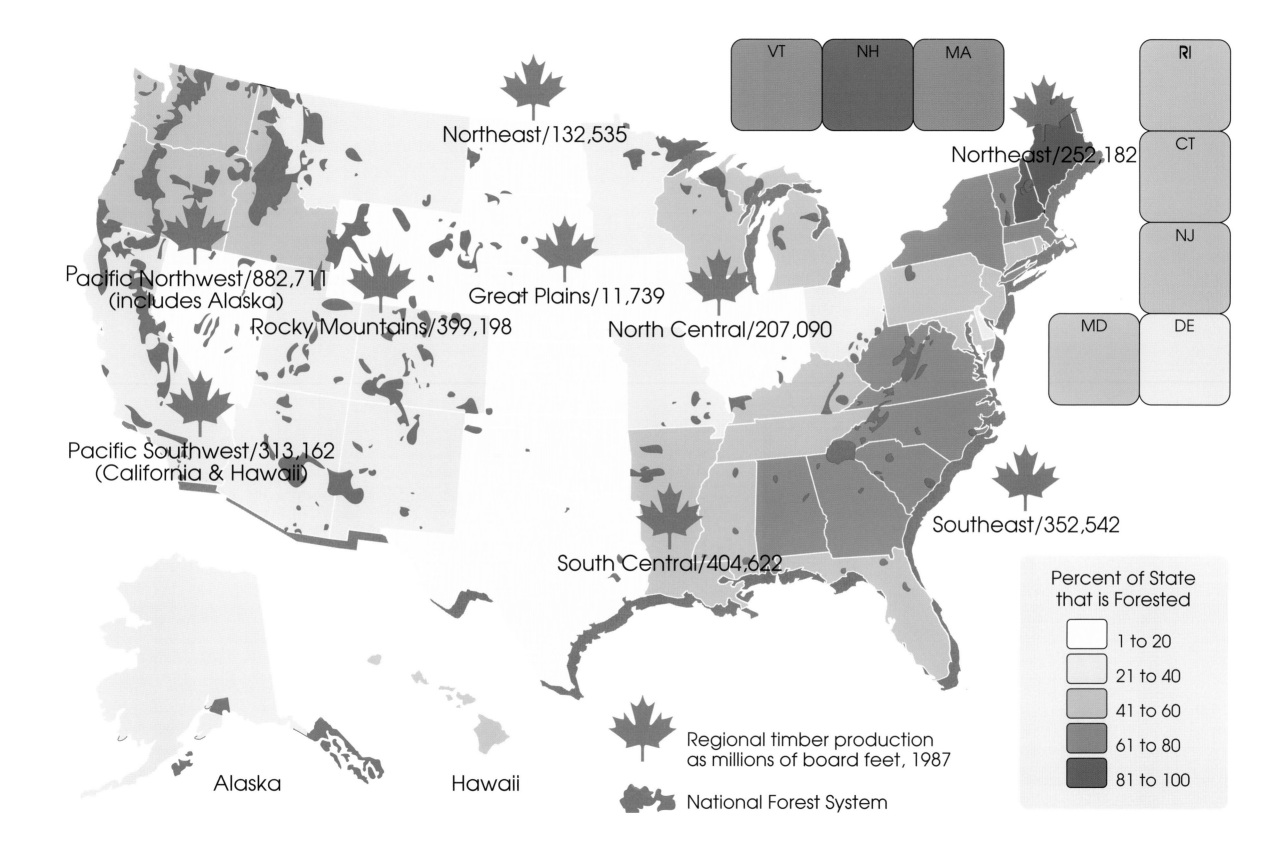

Northeast/132,535

Pacific Northwest/882,711
(includes Alaska)

Rocky Mountains/399,198

Great Plains/11,739

North Central/207,090

Northeast/252,182

Pacific Southwest/313,162
(California & Hawaii)

Southeast/352,542

South Central/404,622

Alaska

Hawaii

VT   NH   MA

RI

CT

NJ

MD   DE

Regional timber production
as millions of board feet, 1987

National Forest System

Percent of State
that is Forested

1 to 20

21 to 40

41 to 60

61 to 80

81 to 100

While mining employment usually plays a small part in any economy, minerals are the basic raw materials for many important industries. America's top mineral producing states include Alaska, California, Louisiana, and Oklahoma, all of which produce primarily oil and natural gas. Traditional coal-producing states such as Pennsylvania, West Virginia, and Kentucky also play an important role in the U.S. mining industry.

Fuel minerals account for the most important segment of both American mineral production and mineral imports. Thirty to forty percent of all oil is imported.

Most metal imports are for minerals used in defense and high-tech industry. The United States is dependent on countries such as Canada, Mexico, South Africa, and China for these strategic materials.

Internally, coal is America's most abundant fuel resource. Even at increased rates of production, it is estimated that the United States can meet fuel needs with its own coal for at least 1,000 years. Coal reserves are found mainly west of the Mississippi River while markets are found mainly to the east.

Mining equals 1.9% GNP. Total equal 117.5 billion 1982 constant dollars.

Composition of Mining In America

Oil & Gas 79%
Coal 14%
Nonmetallic Minerals 5%
Metal 2%

Imported Key Minerals

Percent Imported

Mineral	Percent	Source Countries
Arsenic	100%	Sweden, Canada, Mexico
Columbium	100%	Brazil, Canada, Thailand, Nigeria
Graphite	100%	Mexico, China, Brazil, Madagascar
Manganese	100%	Republic of South Africa, France, Gabon, Brazil
Mica (sheet)	100%	India, Belgium, Japan, France
Strontium	100%	Mexico, Spain, China
Yttrium	100%	Australia
Gem Stones	99%	Bel-Lux, Israel, India, Republic of South Africa
Bauxite & Alumina	97%	Australia, Guinea, Jamaica, Suriname
Tantalum	92%	Thailand, Brazil, Australia, Canada
Diamond (industrial)	89%	Republic of South Africa, UK, Ireland, Bel.-Lux.
Fluorspar	88%	Mexico, Republic of South Africa, Spain, Italy, China
PT-Group Metals	88%	Republic of South Africa, UK, U.S.S.R.
Cobalt	86%	Zaire, Zambia, Canada, Norway
Tungsten	80%	China, Canada, Bolivia, Portugal
Chromium	75%	Republic of South Africa, Zimbabwe, Turkey, Yugo.
Nickel	74%	Canada, Australia, Norway, Botswana
Tin	73%	Brazil, Thailand, Indonesia, Bolivia
Potash	72%	Canada, Israel, German Dem. Rep., U.S.S.R.
Zinc	69%	Canada, Mexico, Peru, Australia
Cadmium	66%	Canada, Australia, Mexico, Fed. Rep. of Germany
Barite	63%	China, Morocco, India
Silver	57%	China, Mexico, UK, Peru
Asbestos	51%	Canada, Republic of South Africa
Gypsum	37%	Canada, Mexico, Spain
Silicon	33%	Brazil, Canada, Norway, Venezuela
Iron Ore	28%	Canada, Brazil, Venezuela, Liberia
Copper	25%	Canada, Chile, Peru, Zaire, Zambia, Mexico
Aluminum	24%	Canada, Japan, Venezuela, Brazil

Thousands Employed In U.S. Mining, 1958 to 1982

Year	Thousands
1958	734
1963	616
1967	567
1972	595
1977	799
1982	1,114

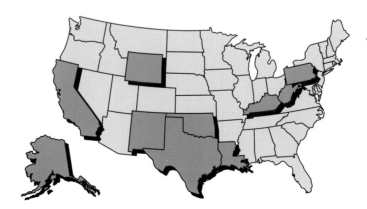

Ten Leading Mineral Producing States

#1 Texas
#2 Alaska
#3 Louisiana
#4 California
#5 Oklahoma
#6 West Virginia
#7 Kentucky
#8 Wyoming
#9 New Mexico
#10 Pennsylvania

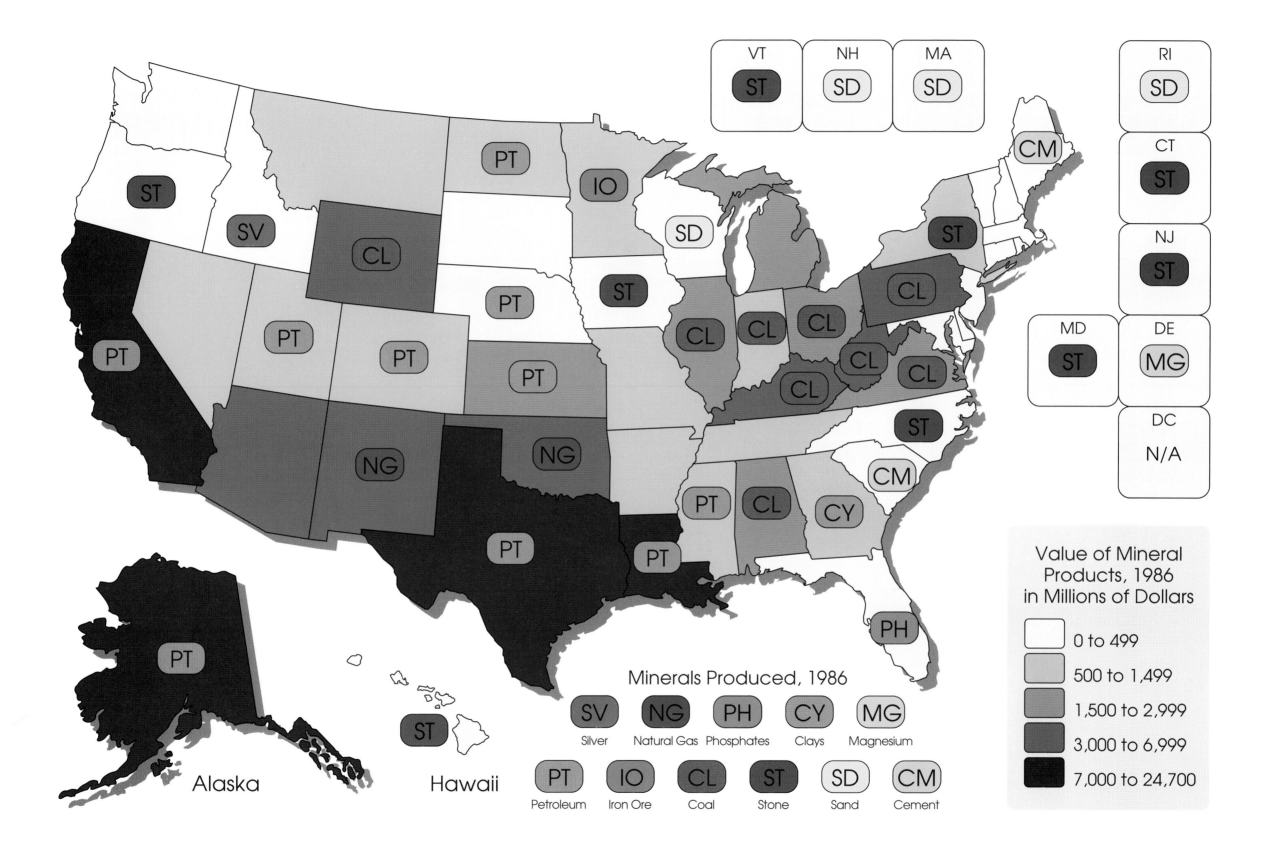

VT: ST
NH: SD
MA: SD
RI: SD
CT: ST
NJ: ST
MD: ST
DE: MG
DC: N/A

Value of Mineral Products, 1986 in Millions of Dollars

	0 to 499
	500 to 1,499
	1,500 to 2,999
	3,000 to 6,999
	7,000 to 24,700

Alaska

Hawaii

Minerals Produced, 1986

SV — Silver
NG — Natural Gas
PH — Phosphates
CY — Clays
MG — Magnesium
PT — Petroleum
IO — Iron Ore
CL — Coal
ST — Stone
SD — Sand
CM — Cement

Three fossil fuels provide America with nearly all of its energy. The most widely-used is oil, followed by natural gas and coal. While the United States lays claim to as much as 30 percent of the world's coal reserves, oil and gas are increasingly expensive to recover and difficult to find on American soil.

Currently, America imports about 35 percent of its oil. About half of this comes from non-Arab members of OPEC. Some 20 percent of imported oil (10 percent of total consumption) comes from Arab states. Oil from within the United States comes primarily from the Gulf Coast with Texas being the largest producer. Texas, Louisiana, and Oklahoma are the country's largest producers of natural gas.

Coal has often been suggested as an alternative to America's dependence on foreign oil. Although two-thirds of U.S. coal reserves are in the west, coal production centers mainly in Pennsylvania, Kentucky, West Virginia, and several other states east of the Mississippi River.

Whether coal becomes America's number one energy fuel depends more on environmental perception than on availability or cost. While coal is much cheaper to produce and more readily available than oil or gas, it is considered dirty by many consumers who envision huge smokestacks belching black soot into urban industrial environments. In reality, coal by-products are no more dangerous than those from oil and natural gas. One legitimate concern does exist, however, and that revolves around the environmental damage that is caused by mining processes that literally denude entire landscapes.

The Nations of OPEC

Algeria	Libya
Ecuador	Nigeria
Gabon	Qatar
Indonesia	Saudi Arabia
Iran	Venezuela
Iraq	United Arab
Kuwait	Emirates

Largest Foreign Oil Suppliers

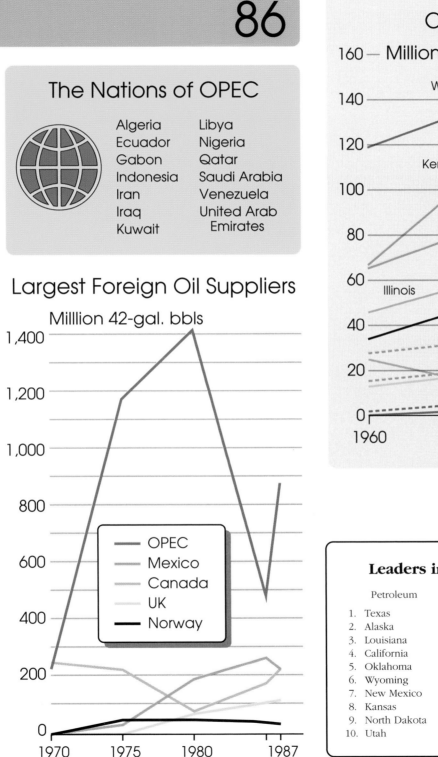

Million 42-gal. bbls

— OPEC
— Mexico
— Canada
— UK
— Norway

Coal States & Their Production

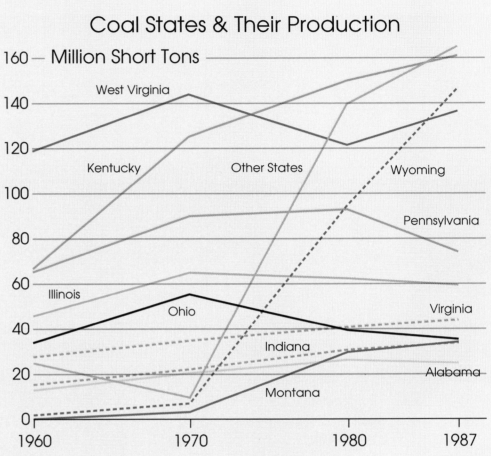

160 — Million Short Tons

West Virginia
Kentucky
Other States
Wyoming
Illinois
Ohio
Pennsylvania
Virginia
Indiana
Montana
Alabama

1960   1970   1980   1987

Leaders in Production, 1987

	Petroleum	Natural Gas	Coal
1.	Texas	Texas	Kentucky
2.	Alaska	Louisiana	Wyoming
3.	Louisiana	Oklahoma	West Virginia
4.	California	New Mexico	Pennsylvania
5.	Oklahoma	Wyoming	Illinois
6.	Wyoming	California	Virginia
7.	New Mexico	Alaska	Ohio
8.	Kansas	Colorado	Montana
9.	North Dakota	Michigan	Indiana
10.	Utah	Mississippi	Alabama

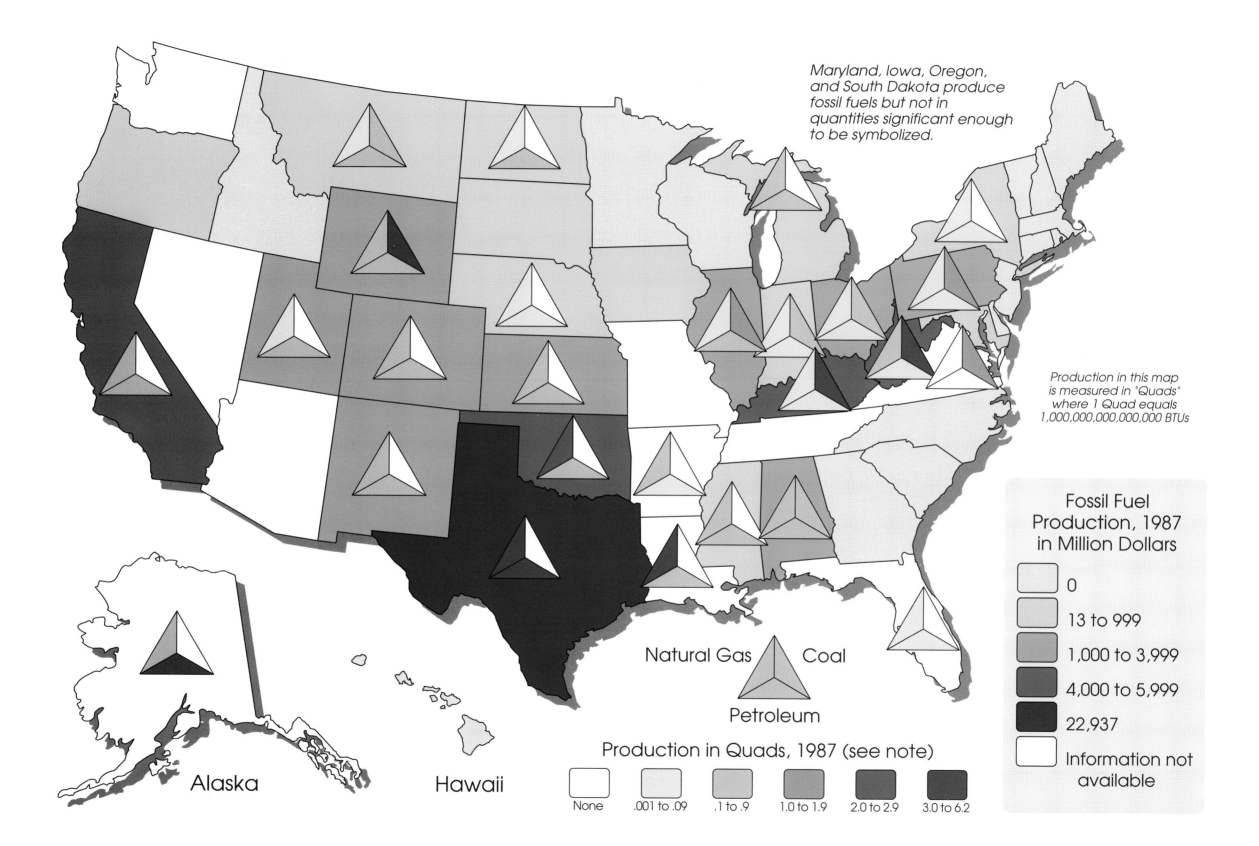

Maryland, Iowa, Oregon, and South Dakota produce fossil fuels but not in quantities significant enough to be symbolized.

Production in this map is measured in "Quads" where 1 Quad equals 1,000,000,000,000,000 BTUs

Natural Gas   Coal

Petroleum

Production in Quads, 1987 (see note)

None   .001 to .09   .1 to .9   1.0 to 1.9   2.0 to 2.9   3.0 to 6.2

Alaska   Hawaii

Fossil Fuel Production, 1987 in Million Dollars

0

13 to 999

1,000 to 3,999

4,000 to 5,999

22,937

Information not available

The concentration of both people and industry in the Middle Atlantic and Central states leads to a high level of energy consumption in those areas. Energy consumption in the West South Central region is much greater than its share of population because of industry.

The mix of fuels used varies regionally. Hydro-electric power is particularly important in the Pacific Northwest. The giant Tennessee Valley Authority project, with its multiple dams, accounts for the importance of hydro-power in the South Atlantic region. Coal, while most important in the Central and Middle Atlantic states, has increased in importance in most regions. The relative decline of natural gas almost everywhere reflects the scarcity of gas reserves. Nuclear energy is currently the least important of all energy sources. Its share had increased steadily until the Three Mile Island disaster in 1979.

The map of per capita energy consumption more closely resembles the pattern of energy production than that of population. Such densely populated areas as California, Florida, or the North Central and Northeast regions show a low overall rate of energy consumption. Large oil producing states like Alaska, Texas, Louisiana, and Wyoming have the highest rates of consumption per capita.

Although industry is the largest consumer of energy (36 percent), the heavy concentrations of manufacturing industry in the Northeast, Midwest, and South seem to have little bearing on per capita energy consumption. It is not the amount but the type industry that is important. Energy producing states often have concentrations of energy-using industries such as petroleum refining, chemicals, and fertilizer production. Attracted by cheap and plentiful fuel in the past, many other fuel-consuming industries are located in areas of surplus oil and gas production as well.

Of the 74,255 trillion Btu's of energy used in 1986 nationwide, 20 percent of all energy was used residentially, 16 percent commercially, and 36 percent industrially. The remaining 28 percent was used for transportation.

U.S. Energy Regions

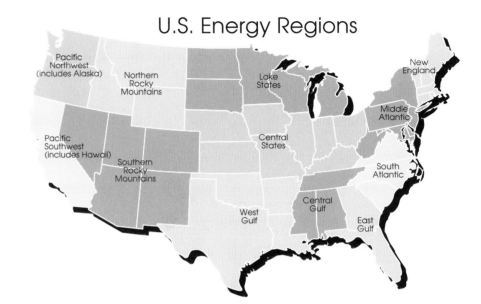

Regional Energy Consumption (trillion BTUs)

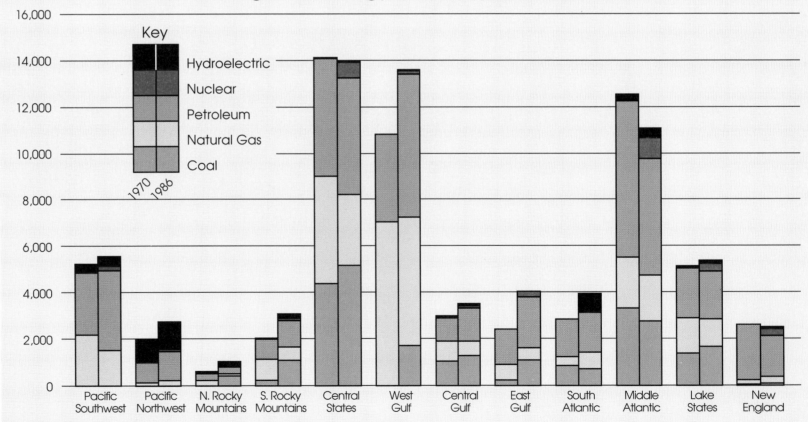

Key

Hydroelectric
Nuclear
Petroleum
Natural Gas
Coal

1970 1986

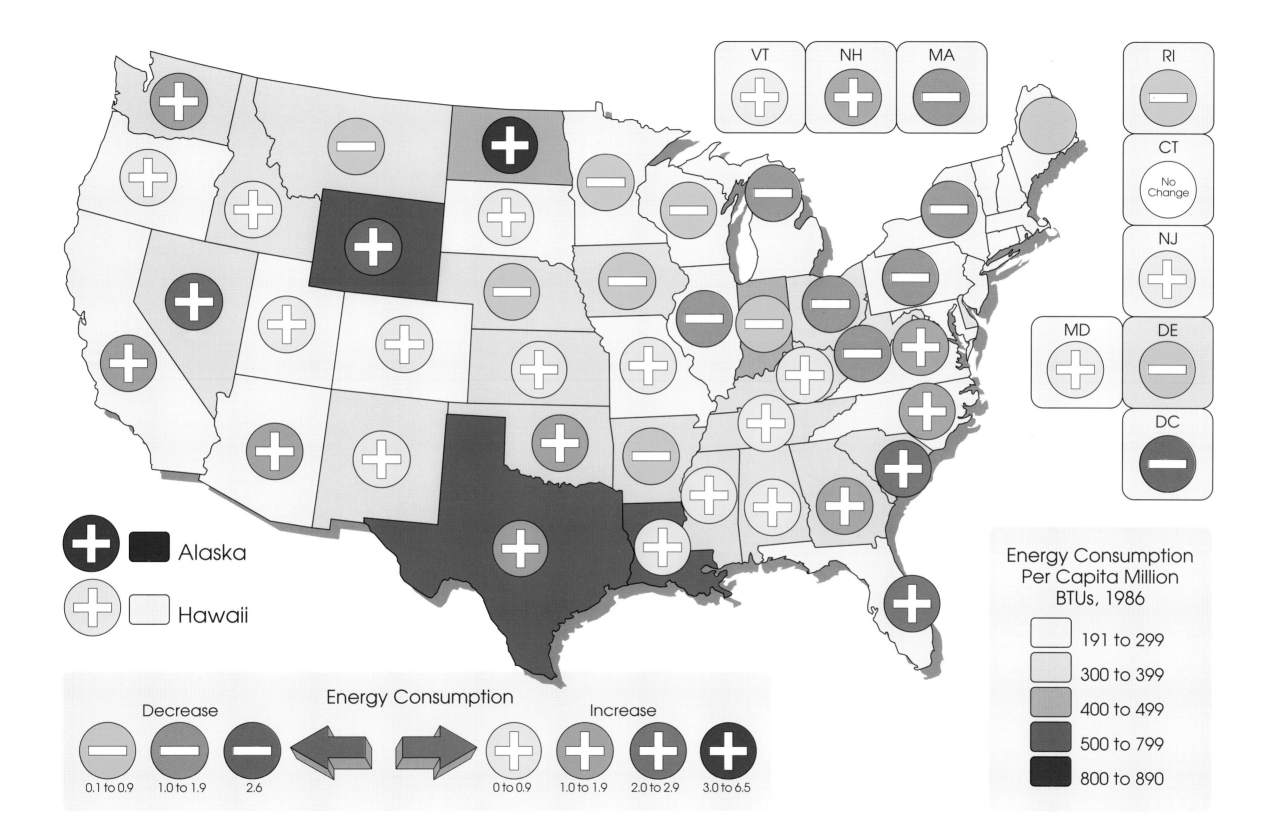

VT NH MA RI CT No Change NJ MD DE DC

Alaska
Hawaii

Energy Consumption
Per Capita Million
BTUs, 1986

191 to 299
300 to 399
400 to 499
500 to 799
800 to 890

Energy Consumption

Decrease
0.1 to 0.9   1.0 to 1.9   2.6

Increase
0 to 0.9   1.0 to 1.9   2.0 to 2.9   3.0 to 6.5

The seven states with the largest populations generate the most electricity. Six of these seven states (California, Texas, Illinois, Ohio, Pennsylvania, and New York) are also the country's largest manufacturing states.

The energy mineral most widely consumed in the United States is petroleum. The energy resource available in the most plentiful supply is coal.

Three things changed America from being a coal-dominated to a petroleum-dominated society after 1950: the increase in automobile ownership, the ease and convenience of shipping and burning oil, and the availability of large supplies of cheap imported oil.

During the energy crisis of the 1970s, many states sought to diversify their energy production by substituting other fuels and technologies for petroleum. Many electrical generating stations switched to coal, new nuclear generating units were planned, new technologies (like solar energy) were tried, and many Americans reverted to wood-burning stoves for heat. As of 1988, 22.9 percent of all Americans burned wood for home heat.

Despite these changes, petroleum remains the dominant energy source in 34 states. Hydropower dominates only in the Pacific Northwest, where huge dams and plentiful water make this type of energy generation practical. Coal dominates in many of the traditional coal producing states east of the Mississippi and in a few Western states where it is cheaply produced in giant strip mines. Louisiana and Oklahoma rely on natural gas produced within their borders.

Nuclear energy has specific patterns of production and use across the American landscape. Because nuclear generating stations require large amounts of water for cooling most are concentrated in wetter parts of the country. The South, which produces 37.3 percent of the nation's nuclear power, dominates. The West produces the least at 12.5 percent.

While the United States leads the world in nuclear generation of electricity, nuclear energy is not the dominant energy source as it is in some European nations such as France, Sweden, and Switzerland. Even though there are nuclear plants in many U.S. states, nuclear energy is the predominant source of energy only in South Carolina.

Use of Nuclear Power, 1987

	Electrical Generation (billion kWh)		Number of Reactors
1. United States	480.9	United States	108
2. France	265.5	France	53
3. Japan	186.2	Great Britain	38
4. West Germany	130.5	Japan	36
5. Canada	80.6	West Germany	19
6. Sweden	67.2	Canada	18
7. Great Britain	56.2	Sweden	12
8. Belgium	42.0	Spain	8
9. Spain	41.2	South Korea	7
10. South Korea	37.8	Belgium	7
11. Taiwan	33.0	India	6
12. Switzerland	23.0	Taiwan	6
13. Finland	19.4	Switzerland	5
14. South Africa	6.6	Finland	4
15. Argentina	6.5	Italy	2
16. India	5.5	Argentina	2
17. Yugoslavia	4.5	Brazil	1
18. Netherlands	3.6	Netherlands	1
19. Pakistan	.3	Pakistan	1
20. Italy	.2	South Africa	1
21. Brazil	.1	Yugoslavia	1

Predominant Energy Source Used in 1986

Petroleum   Coal   Nuclear
Hydro Power   Natural Gas

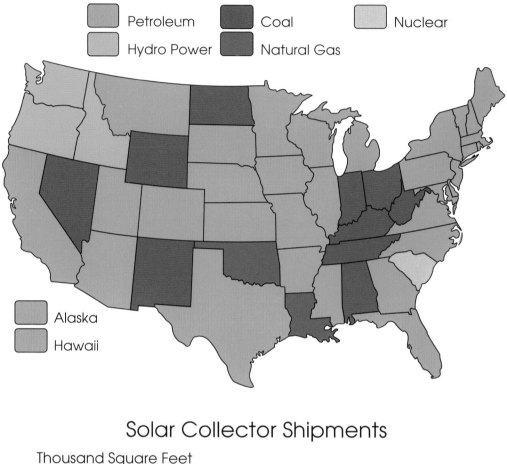

Alaska
Hawaii

Solar Collector Shipments

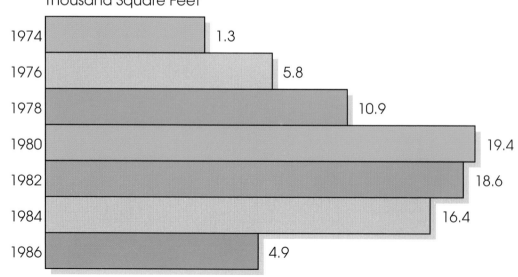

Thousand Square Feet

Year	Thousand Square Feet
1974	1.3
1976	5.8
1978	10.9
1980	19.4
1982	18.6
1984	16.4
1986	4.9

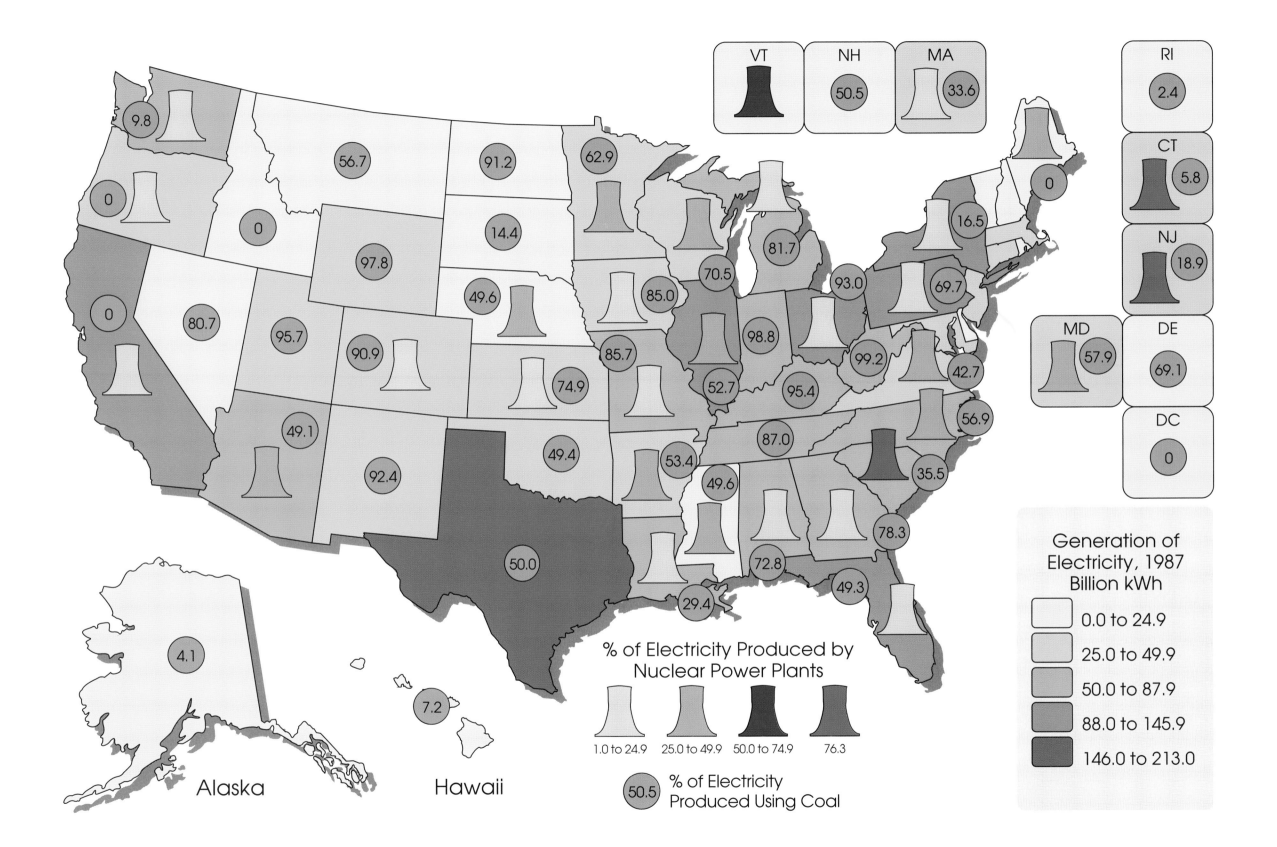

VT — [nuclear plant symbol]

NH — 50.5

MA — [nuclear plant symbol] 33.6

RI — 2.4

CT — [nuclear plant symbol] 5.8

NJ — [nuclear plant symbol] 18.9

MD — [nuclear plant symbol] 57.9

DE — 69.1

DC — 0

9.8

0

56.7

91.2

62.9

0

0

14.4

16.5

0

97.8

81.7

49.6

70.5

93.0

69.7

0

80.7

95.7

90.9

85.0

98.8

99.2

42.7

74.9

85.7

52.7

95.4

56.9

49.1

87.0

35.5

49.4

53.4

78.3

92.4

49.6

72.8

49.3

29.4

Alaska — 4.1

Hawaii — 7.2

% of Electricity Produced by Nuclear Power Plants

[plant symbol] 1.0 to 24.9   [plant symbol] 25.0 to 49.9   [plant symbol] 50.0 to 74.9   [plant symbol] 76.3

50.5 — % of Electricity Produced Using Coal

Generation of Electricity, 1987 Billion kWh

	0.0 to 24.9
	25.0 to 49.9
	50.0 to 87.9
	88.0 to 145.9
	146.0 to 213.0

The chances of being injured on the job vary greatly with occupation. Injury rates are lowest in office and professional jobs. The rate of injury has stayed approximately the same for most job categories, but improved safety standards and specialized training for employees have lowered accident rates in factories and, in particular, in mining.

The number of strikes has decreased greatly since 1970, reflecting improved working conditions and the loss of manufacturing jobs to foreign competition.

Union membership has decreased along with the number of factory jobs. In general, industrial employment has declined while non-factory jobs have increased. Traditionally, mines and factories have been the chief source of union members. Movement of factories to new locations in states without a strong union tradition has undoubtedly contributed to the decline in union membership among factory workers. Recent union increases reflect unionization of government employees, teachers, office workers, and retail salespeople.

The strength of unions among workers in the aircraft, auto, and machine industries, as well as among dock and construction workers, stands out on the map on page 93. The states with the highest rates of unionization are specialized in those types of work. The states of the traditional Manufacturing Belt, the coal mining states of the Appalachian region, and the industrial or mining states of the West stand out in bold patterns. The growth of manufacturing in the South has not been accompanied by the growth of unions in many cases. Service workers in the Northeast and Midwest have high rates of union membership, but New England's technical employees do not.

Previously, the presence or absence of unions had a great effect on pay scales and earnings. Today, this is less often the case. Pay is most directly related to the local cost of living. With the exception of Michigan, the highest pay rates are found in states with high taxes and housing costs. Alaska, because of its relative isolation, has the highest cost of living in the nation. The lowest pay rates are found in the rural farm states of the Great Plains and parts of the South.

Pay rates also reflect the types of jobs available in an area. The concentrations of media, banking, investment, and company headquarters functions (with a dominance of high paying jobs) in New York, San Francisco, and Los Angeles are also notable. New York's functions and employees spill over into Connecticut and New Jersey. States shown in the intermediate pattern all contain major cities with similar functions. The exception is Georgia, where Atlanta's role as a major regional center seems to be counterbalanced by the large number of lower paying jobs in the rest of state.

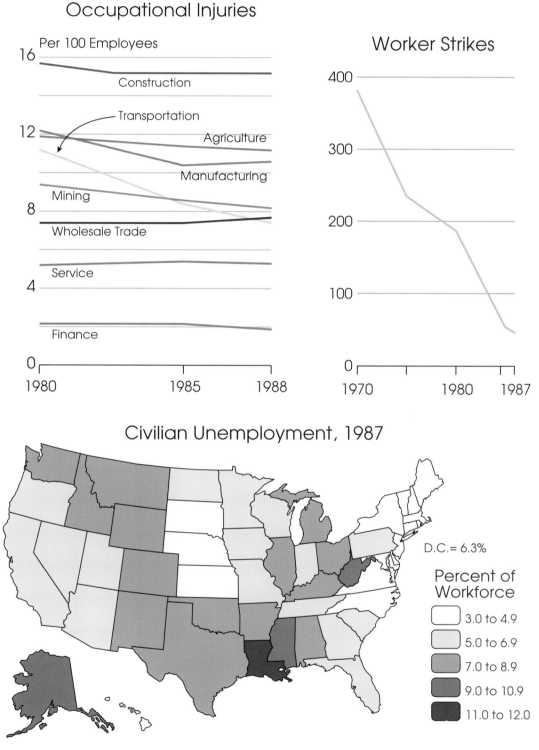

Occupational Injuries

Per 100 Employees

Construction
Transportation
Agriculture
Manufacturing
Mining
Wholesale Trade
Service
Finance

16 · 12 · 8 · 4 · 0

1980 · 1985 · 1988

Worker Strikes

400 · 300 · 200 · 100 · 0

1970 · 1980 · 1987

Civilian Unemployment, 1987

D.C.= 6.3%

Percent of Workforce

- 3.0 to 4.9
- 5.0 to 6.9
- 7.0 to 8.9
- 9.0 to 10.9
- 11.0 to 12.0

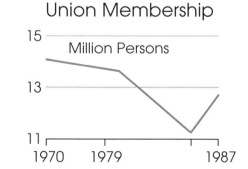

Union Membership

Million Persons

15 · 13 · 11

1970 · 1979 · 1987

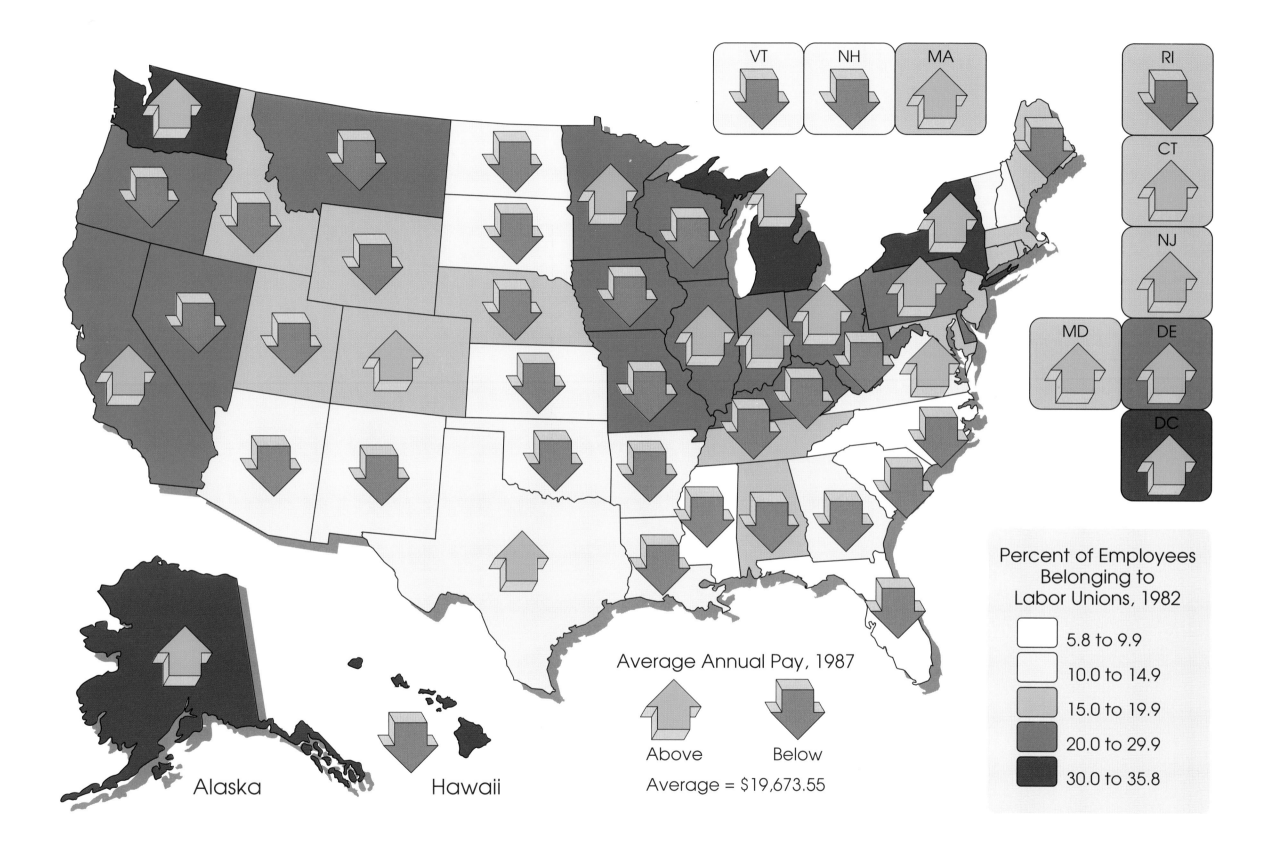

Average Annual Pay, 1987

Above   Below

Average = $19,673.55

Alaska

Hawaii

Percent of Employees
Belonging to
Labor Unions, 1982

5.8 to 9.9
10.0 to 14.9
15.0 to 19.9
20.0 to 29.9
30.0 to 35.8

VT   NH   MA   RI   CT   NJ   MD   DE   DC

TRANSPORTATION & COMMUNICATION

There are almost 110 million drivers in the United States and over 180 million automobiles, buses, and trucks on the highways. Americans drive a total of nearly two billion miles a year. The majority of American drivers are between 25 and 54 years old. Most adults drive on highways, where accident rates are highest among drivers under 21 years of age.

Personal and family business accounts for over half of all auto trips. Miles traveled to work and shopping are fewer in number. The fact that a quarter of all trips are work-related indicates that the automobile is vital to the American economy.

Roads and highways vary with population. The densely settled east has the greatest road density per square mile. Automobile registrations show a different pattern. States like Wyoming, Utah, and Alaska are sparsely populated but have a very young population containing large numbers of citizens of driving age. See page 43 for information on age of America's driving population.

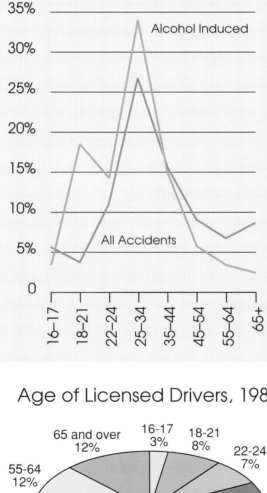

Percent of Motor Vehicle Fatalities Occurring in Different Age Groups, 1987

Household Vehicles, 1985

	Number of		Miles Driven		Gallons Consumed		Expenditures	
	Vehicles	Vehicles/ household	Total (billions)	Percent	Total (billions)	Percent	Total (billions)	Percent
Metropolitan	103	1.7	1029	76.1	62.6	74.6	73.8	74.5
Central City	62	1.8	646	47.8	38.7	46.1	45.6	46
Outside Central City	41	1.6	383	28.3	23.9	28.5	28.3	28.5
Nonmetropolitan	34.3	1.8	324	23.9	21.3	25.4	25.2	25.5

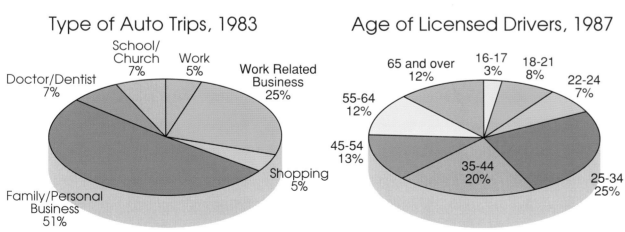

Type of Auto Trips, 1983

Age of Licensed Drivers, 1987

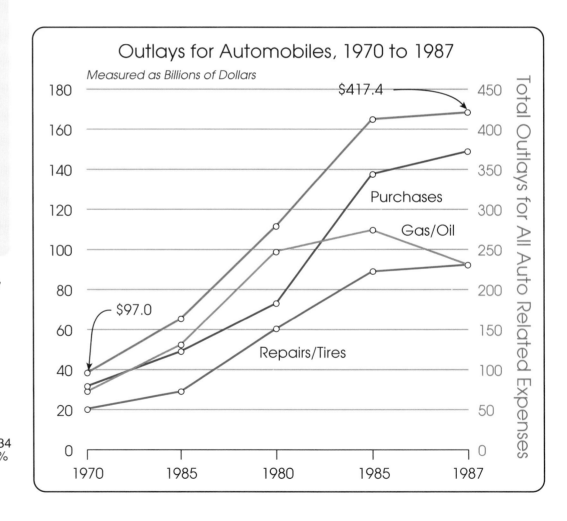

Outlays for Automobiles, 1970 to 1987

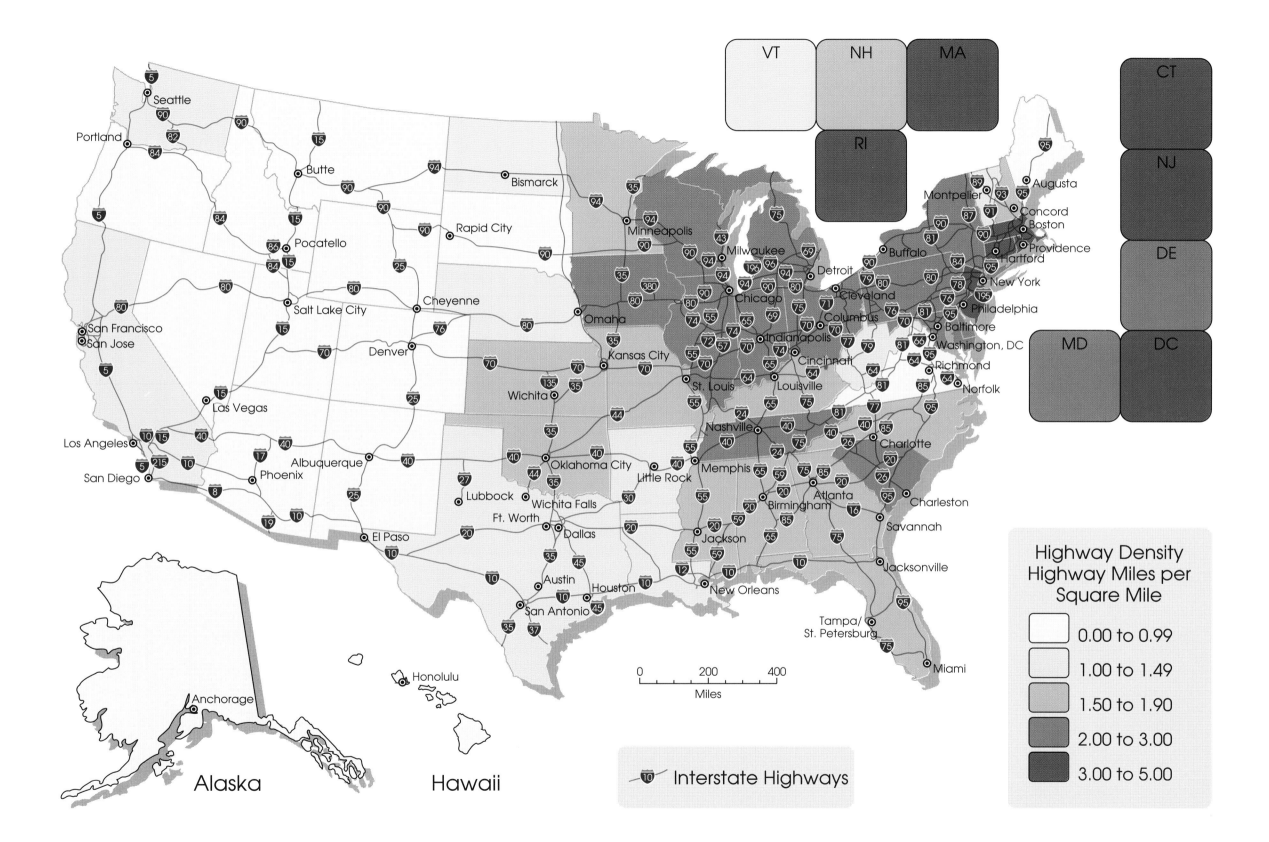

Highway Density
Highway Miles per Square Mile

0.00 to 0.99	
1.00 to 1.49	
1.50 to 1.90	
2.00 to 3.00	
3.00 to 5.00	

Interstate Highways

0   200   400
Miles

Alaska

Hawaii

VT   NH   MA
RI

CT
NJ
DE
MD   DC

America's growth has been linked closely to the growth and development of transportation. Throughout history, the U.S. government has played a key role in developing transportation and transportation technology. Each innovation, in turn, has led to a national unity aided by the connectivity of one place to another through modern transportation systems.

Transportation started with water transport. Railroads reached their peak in 1920. In 1916, the government began to develop a national system of paved highways throughout the country. By 1930, it was possible to drive from coast to coast. The rapid increase in the number of trucks used to haul freight resulted in the creation of the Interstate Highway System in the 1960s and 1970s.

Air traffic developed last. Mail was the chief freight carried. Passenger travel was insignificant until the 1930s when government took an active role in the development of airports and the centralizing authority for air travel.

Railroads, Class 1 Line-Haul, Thousands of Carloads, 1987

Coal	5,430
Farm Products	1,907
Chemicals, Allied Products	1,410
Food, Kindred Products	1,326
Nonmetallic Minerals	1,188
Transportation Equipment	1,085
Lumber, Wood Products	986
Pulp, Paper, Allied Products	561
Stone, Clay, Glass Products	559
Petroleum, Coal Products	520
Metallic Ores	494
Waste, Scrap Materials	440
Primary Metal Products	428
Machinery, Exc. Electrical	33
Fabricated Metal Products	24

Amtrak Passengers

Million Passengers

(line graph with y-axis: 22, 20, 18; x-axis: 1982, 1982, 1984, 1985, 1986, 1987)

Miles Between Air Traffic Hubs

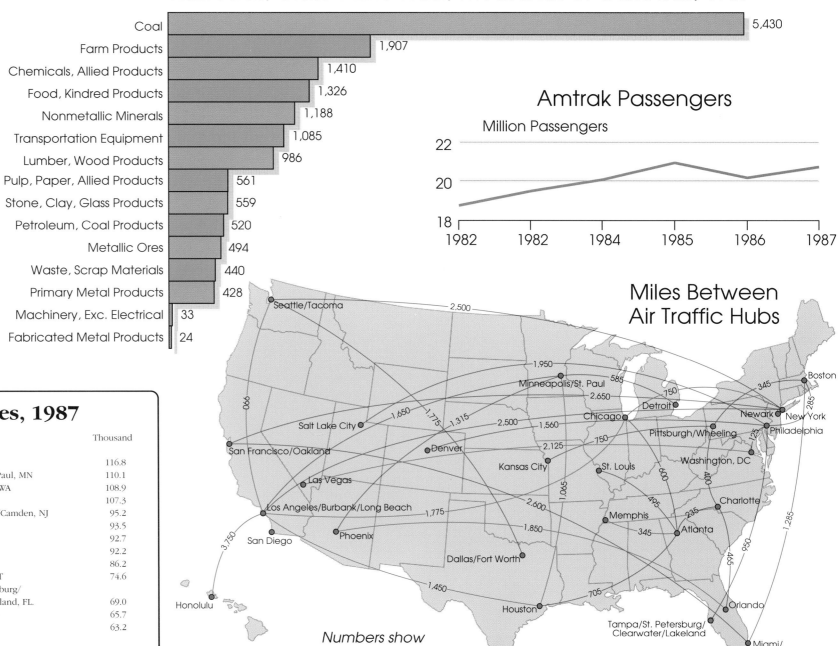

Numbers show approximate air miles

Total Aircraft Departures, 1987

	Thousand Departures		Thousand
Chicago, IL	375.8	Boston, MA	116.8
Atlanta, GA	281.9	Minneapolis/St. Paul, MN	110.1
Los Angeles/Long Beach, CA	269.2	Seattle/Tacoma, WA	108.9
Dallas-Ft. Worth, TX	266.6	Memphis, TN	107.3
New York, NY	201.7	Philadelphia, PA/Camden, NJ	95.2
Denver, CO	201.2	Charlotte, NC	93.5
San Francisco/Oakland, CA	192.3	Las Vegas, NV	92.7
Washington, DC	186.5	Honolulu, HI	92.2
Houston, TX	160.2	Orlando, FL	86.2
Miami/Ft. Lauderdale, FL	149.4	Salt Lake City, UT	74.6
St. Louis, MO	138.3	Tampa/St. Petersburg/	
Detroit/Ann Arbor, MI	137.0	Clearwater/Lakeland, FL.	69.0
Newark, NJ	136.5	Kansas City, MO	65.7
Phoenix, AZ	128.5	San Deigo, CA	63.2
Pittsburgh, PA/Wheeling, WV	119.9		

In the same way that transportation grew to move goods and people over vast distances, communications grew to move information.

Newspapers and mail service are the oldest media, existing since colonial times. Mail service, in fact, was considered so important in the early years of the United States that the Postmaster General was a full member of the first presidential cabinet. These two forms of communication dominated until the middle of the 19th century when the telegraph added new dimensions to communications. By the turn of the 20th century, science had provided telephones and the radios.

Newspapers, then and today, are a major form of advertising. Big cities contain the largest newspapers with the largest circulations. Newspaper circulation is greatest in the Northeast and Midwest, and least in the South.

Television, which debuted in the 1940s, is present in almost every household today, but was available only in major markets until the early 1950s. Today hundreds of cable systems throughout the country have made it possible to bring television to virtually all areas. In addition, most households have several radios.

Advertising on Network Television, 1987

Million Dollars

Category	Million Dollars
Detergents/Polishes/Cleansers	322
Household Furnishings/Items	330
Confectionery/Soft Drinks	384
Consumer Service	392
Restaurants/Drive-ins	498
Beer/Wine	514
Proprietary Medicines	773
Toiletries/Toilet Goods	868
Automotive	1,029
Food/Food Products	1,615

Advertising Expenditures, 1987

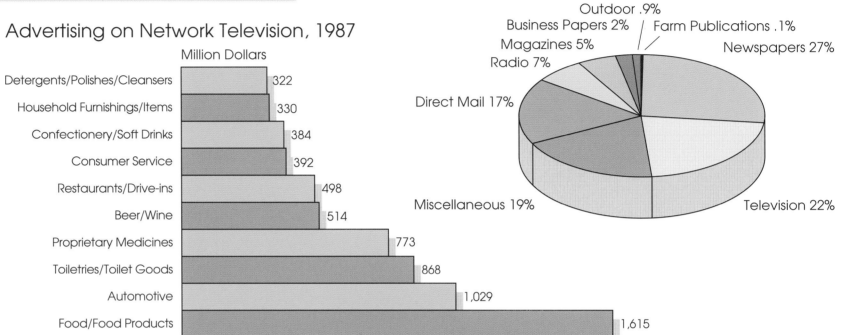

- Outdoor .9%
- Business Papers 2%
- Farm Publications .1%
- Magazines 5%
- Radio 7%
- Newspapers 27%
- Direct Mail 17%
- Miscellaneous 19%
- Television 22%

Percent of Households With . . .

	Telephone	Radio	Television	Cable TV	VCR
1950	•	92.6	9	•	•
1955	78.5	96.3	67	•	•
1960	81.0	98.6	87	•	•
1965	87.0	98.6	93	•	•
1970	•	99.0	95	1.5	•
1975	93.0	99.0	97	19.8	•
1985	91.8	99.0	98	44.6	20.8
1988	92.9	99.0	98	51.1	58.1

• not available

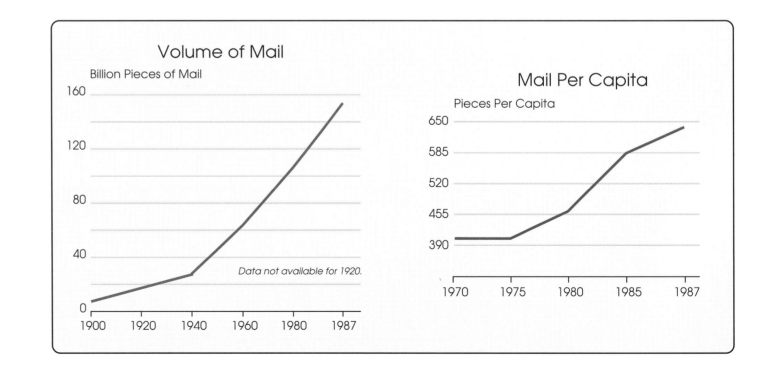

Volume of Mail

Billion Pieces of Mail

Data not available for 1920.

Mail Per Capita

Pieces Per Capita

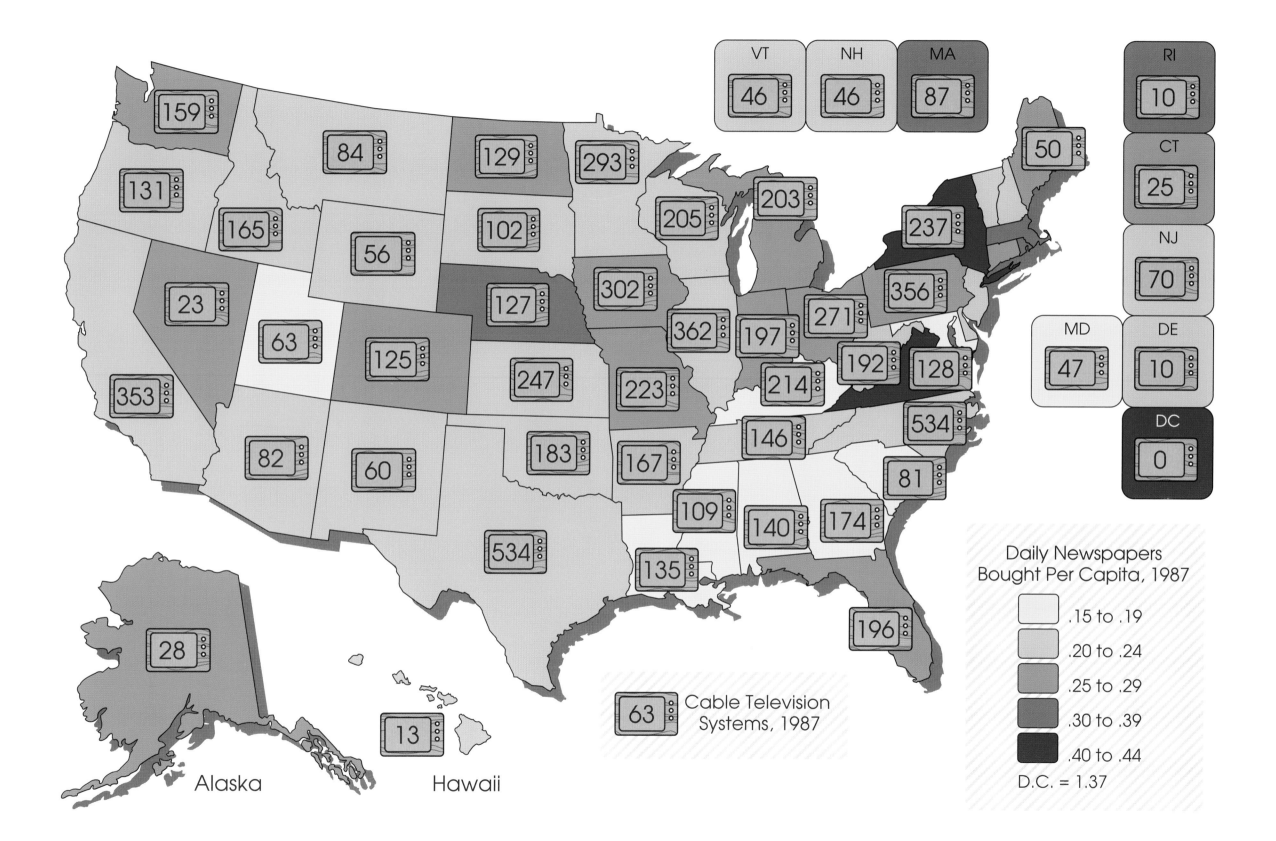

Daily Newspapers
Bought Per Capita, 1987

.15 to .19
.20 to .24
.25 to .29
.30 to .39
.40 to .44

D.C. = 1.37

Cable Television
Systems, 1987

Alaska

Hawaii

The division of government responsibility between the state and national levels is reflected in the areas in which each spends its tax money.

Education is by far the greatest single cost in most states. States, together with local property taxes, pay a large share of public school costs. States also provide a major portion of higher education costs by supporting state colleges and universities. Highways and welfare are the other leading expenditures for states. The federal government spends the greatest proportion of its budget maintaining the social security and medicare systems and, of course, on the national defense. Almost $173 billion is spent on interest payments for the national debt alone. Two-thirds of the total national debt has been built up in the years since 1980.

States earn their revenues from income and sales taxes. Corporations, as well as individuals, are subject to income taxes. Cigarette, alcohol, and gasoline taxes are other sources. There is a geography of state taxes. States tend to group in tax categories with similar tax rates among neighboring states. Two sets of states have the highest income taxes: a belt of northwestern states that includes Oregon, Idaho, North Dakota, Iowa, and Minnesota; and another in the southwest that includes California, Arizona, and New Mexico. Maine, Hawaii, and the District of Columbia also have high income taxes

Gasoline taxes are lowest in Alaska, California, Florida, New Jersey, New York,

and Wyoming. Surprisingly, gasoline taxes are very high in many of the oil-producing states. They are also high in most of the states in the South Atlantic region. Wisconsin has the highest gasoline taxes, and Minnesota has the highest taxes on cigarettes. Connecticut has the highest sales taxes, though food and drugs are exempt. However, without any exemption for food, the sales taxes in Washington and Mississippi may cost taxpayers more.

Sales tax rates range from 3 percent in Colorado and Wyoming to 7.5 percent in Connecticut. Five states have no sales tax. They are New Hampshire, Delaware, Montana, Oregon, and Alaska.

Federal taxes, of course, are uniform throughout the country. Federal aid to states, however, is not. Northeastern states frequently complain that they pay the highest federal taxes and receive the least in return. Similar complaints are heard in California, Nevada, Florida, and Illinois.

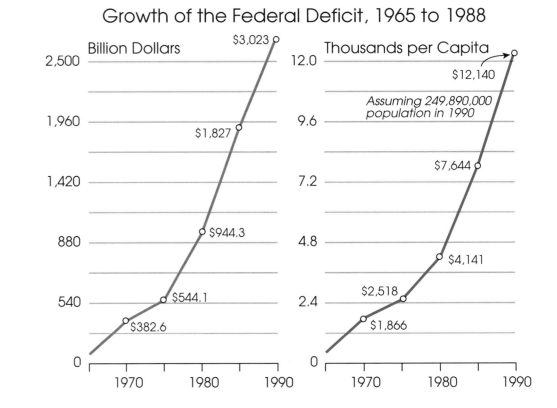

Growth of the Federal Deficit, 1965 to 1988

State Spending, 1986

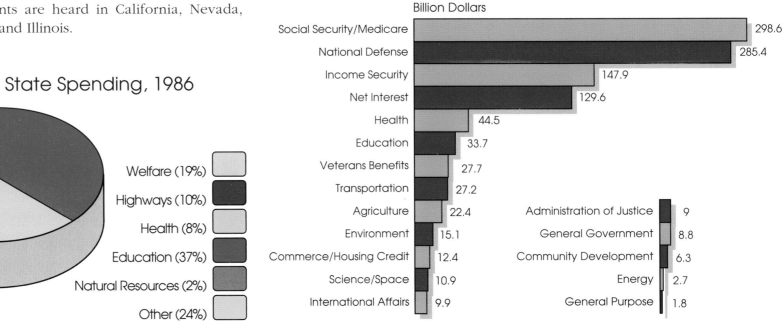

Welfare (19%)

Highways (10%)

Health (8%)

Education (37%)

Natural Resources (2%)

Other (24%)

Federal Government Spending, 1988

Billion Dollars

Social Security/Medicare	298.6
National Defense	285.4
Income Security	147.9
Net Interest	129.6
Health	44.5
Education	33.7
Veterans Benefits	27.7
Transportation	27.2
Agriculture	22.4
Environment	15.1
Commerce/Housing Credit	12.4
Science/Space	10.9
International Affairs	9.9

Administration of Justice	9
General Government	8.8
Community Development	6.3
Energy	2.7
General Purpose	1.8

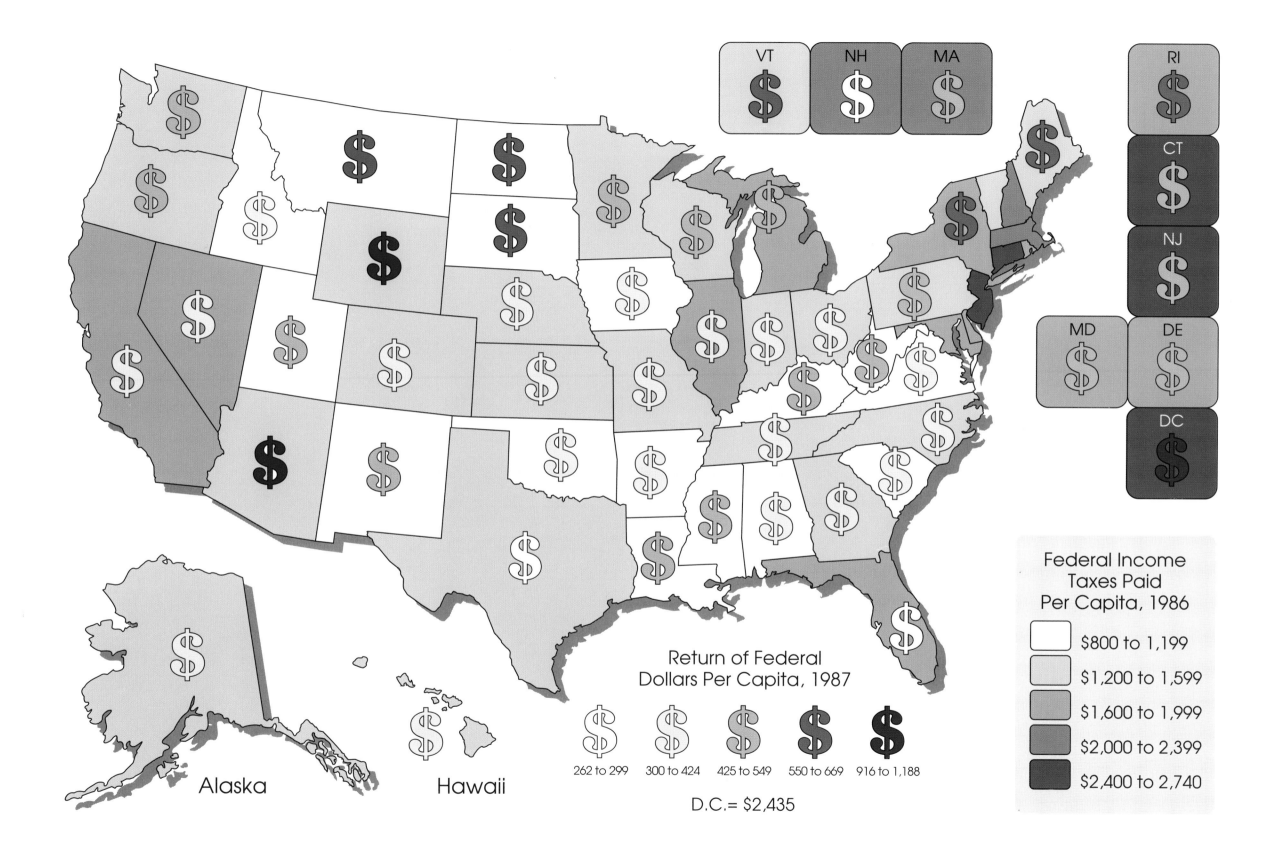

Federal Income Taxes Paid Per Capita, 1986

- $800 to 1,199
- $1,200 to 1,599
- $1,600 to 1,999
- $2,000 to 2,399
- $2,400 to 2,740

Return of Federal Dollars Per Capita, 1987

262 to 299 | 300 to 424 | 425 to 549 | 550 to 669 | 916 to 1,188

D.C.= $2,435

Alaska

Hawaii

The American system of government is based on checks and balances. The president and members of both houses of Congress are elected separately and do, in theory, balance power. Each state selects its own congressmen and senators; only the president is elected by voters from the entire country.

Democrats dominated the presidency from 1933 to 1952. Since that time, the presidency has alternated between parties, but more Republicans have been elected. This has not been the case, however, in Congress. Democrats have controlled the House of Representatives for 48 of the last 50 years. Republicans fared only a little better in the Senate, controlling that house for only 12 of the last 50 years.

In recent years, only a few states have voted consistently for the Democratic presidential candidate: Rhode Island, West Virginia, Minnesota, and Hawaii. In all cases, the prominence and popularity of the Democratic Party (or local conditions) in those states probably influenced the popular vote more than the presidential candidate did.

One of the great concerns of today's voters is the role of Political Action Committees in influencing the election and voting behavior of members of Congress. These PAC's are lobbying groups that represent special interests or groups, and not necessarily individuals. Campaigns are very expensive to run, and members of Congress are grateful for contributions. Increasingly, PAC's are a major source of campaign funding. The largest of these is the AARP, an organization representing the interests of senior citizens. Others represent specific industries like oil or steel. Still others represent services like insurance.

Not all Americans take advantage of the right to vote. The percentage of voters registered varies greatly. Generally, rural areas are most completely registered, while urban areas and the South are under-registered.

Under the American political system, voters are represented in the lower house of Congress in proportion to population. Each state must have at least one representative, regardless of population. Larger states have one representative for every 550,000 people. Regardless of size, each state elects two senators. Electoral votes are apportioned by combining the number of representatives and senators elected by each state and are used in a winner-take-all fashion when electing a president every four years.

Voting behavior, like registration, varies regionally. Generally, a smaller percentage of residents cast votes in the sunbelt states.

Senate, House and Presidential Power

	President	Congress	House Majority	House Minority	House Other	Senate Majority	Senate Minority
1939	D Roosevelt	76	D 261	R 169	4	D 69	R 23
1941	D Roosevelt	77	D 268	R 162	5	D 66	R 28
1943	D Roosevelt	78	D 218	R 208	4	D 58	R 37
1945	D Roosevelt	79	D 242	R 190	2	D 56	R 38
1947	D Truman	80	D 245	D 188	1	R 51	D 45
1949	D Truman	81	D 263	R 171	1	D 54	R 42
1951	D Truman	82	D 234	R 199	1	D 49	R 47
1953	R Eisenhower	83	R 221	D 211	1	R 48	D 47
1955	R Eisenhower	84	D 232	R 203	0	D 48	R 47
1957	R Eisenhower	85	D 233	R 200	0	D 49	R 47
1959	R Eisenhower	86	D 284	R 153	0	D 65	R 35
1961	D Kennedy	87	D 263	R 174	0	D 65	R 35
1963	D Kennedy	88	D 258	R 177	0	D 67	R 33
1965	D Johnson	89	D 295	R 140	0	D 68	R 32
1967	D Johnson	90	D 247	R 187	0	D 64	R 36
1969	R Nixon	91	D 243	R 192	0	D 57	R 43
1971	R Nixon	92	D 254	R 180	0	D 54	R 44
1973	R Nixon	93	D 239	R 192	1	D 56	R 42
1975	R Ford	94	D 291	R 144	0	D 60	R 37
1977	D Carter	95	D 292	R 143	0	D 61	R 38
1979	D Carter	96	D 276	R 157	0	R 58	R 41
1981	R Reagan	97	D 243	R 192	0	R 53	D 46
1983	R Reagan	98	D 269	R 165	0	R 54	D 46
1985	R Reagan	99	D 252	R 182	0	R 53	D 47
1987	R Reagan	100	D 258	R 177	0	D 55	R 45
1988	R Bush	101	D 262	R 173	0	D 56	R 44

D   Democrat   R   Republican

Voting Trend For US Senate Since 1984

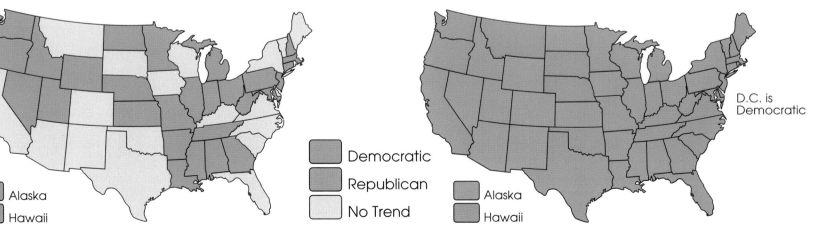

Alaska

Hawaii

Democratic

Republican

No Trend

Voting Trend For US House Since 1982

D.C. is Democratic

Alaska

Hawaii

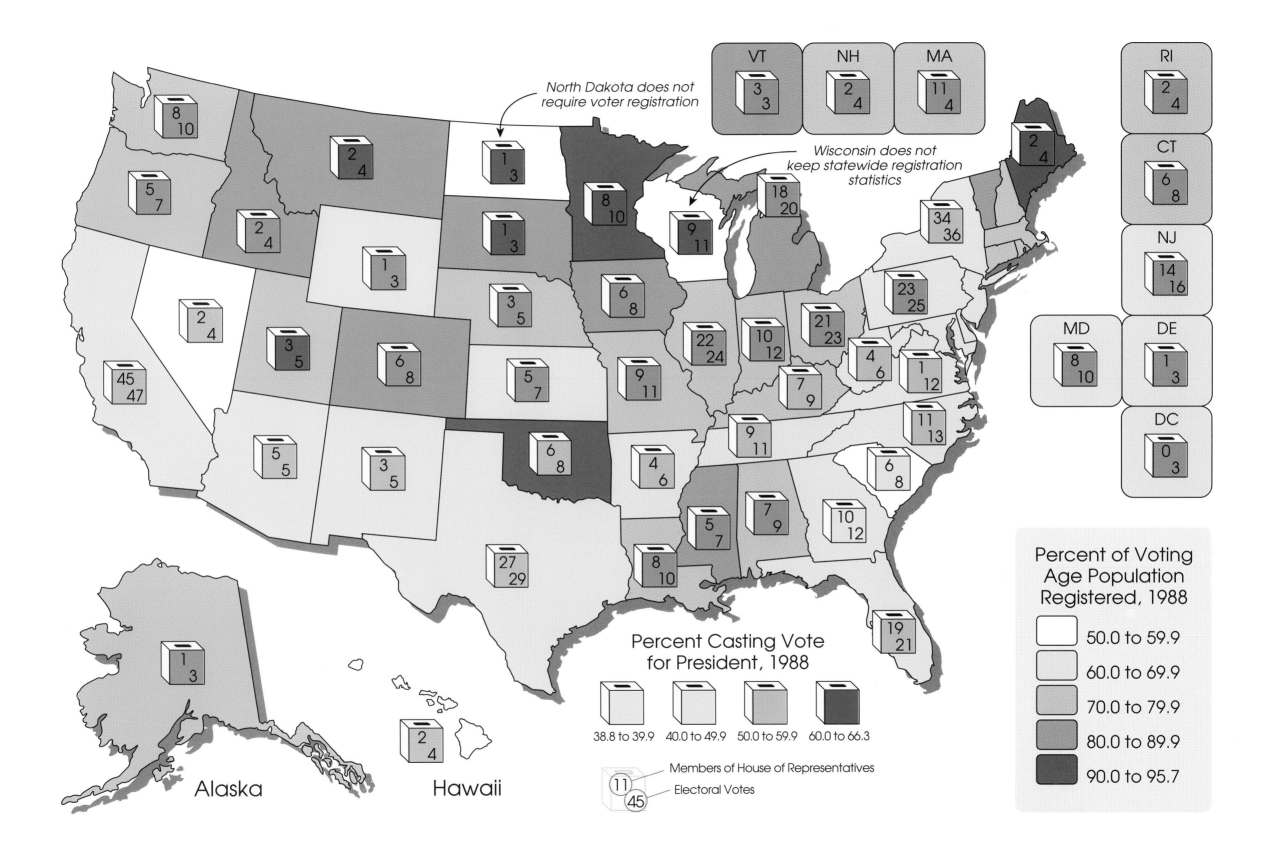

North Dakota does not require voter registration

Wisconsin does not keep statewide registration statistics

Percent Casting Vote for President, 1988

38.8 to 39.9 · 40.0 to 49.9 · 50.0 to 59.9 · 60.0 to 66.3

Members of House of Representatives
Electoral Votes

Alaska

Hawaii

Percent of Voting Age Population Registered, 1988

50.0 to 59.9
60.0 to 69.9
70.0 to 79.9
80.0 to 89.9
90.0 to 95.7

THE ENVIRONMENT   109

So important are America's wetlands that much environmental attention is focused on their conservation and use. Environmentalists, in both private and governmental organizations, point out that wetlands are not only scenic, but also are the principle habitat and breeding grounds for many of America's indigenous species.

Where man has come into conflict with areas permanently or periodically inundated with water, the American society, as a whole, has paid a high price. Dredging, filling, or other modifications for economic activities have interfered with or destroyed the natural value of wetlands. Environmental scientists have come to understand that beyond being habitats for wildlife, wetlands, particularly those poorly drained swampy areas that were once considered worthless, work as natural filtration systems that guard lakes, streams, and aquifers from pollution and undesirable and excessive nutrients.

Another of America's most pressing environmental issues is the control of acid rain. Acid rain results when natural precipitation becomes acidic after reacting to chemical pollutants released into the air.

The acidity of rain increases west to east as sulfur-containing pollutants move eastwardly and upward toward Canada with the natural movement of the U.S. stormtracks (see page 21). Acidification and the damage caused by acid rain is greatest in the northeast and Canada. Billions of dollars in damage to building structures has resulted. In addition, acid rain has killed entire fish populations in thousands of lakes throughout North America.

States That Do Not Have Programs to Acquire Wetlands

Alaska	Nevada
Alabama	North Dakota
Hawaii	Oklahoma
Kansas	Utah
Montana	Wyoming

Wetland Conversion

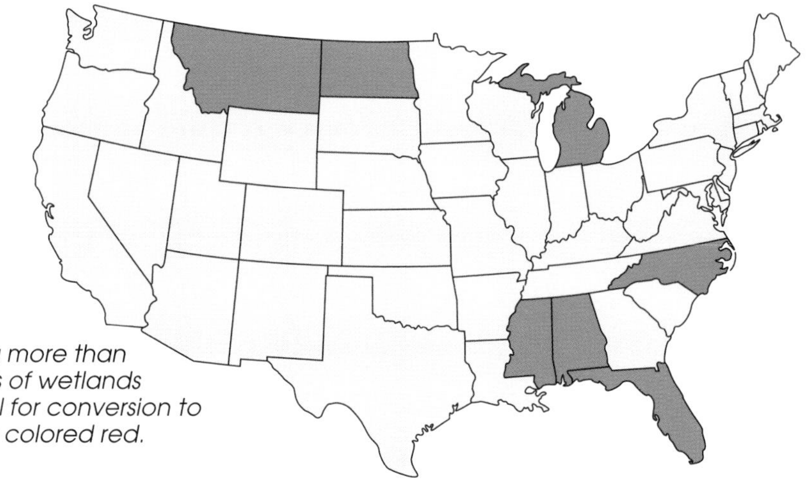

States having more than 200,000 acres of wetlands with potential for conversion to cropland are colored red.

Wetlands and Wetland Protection

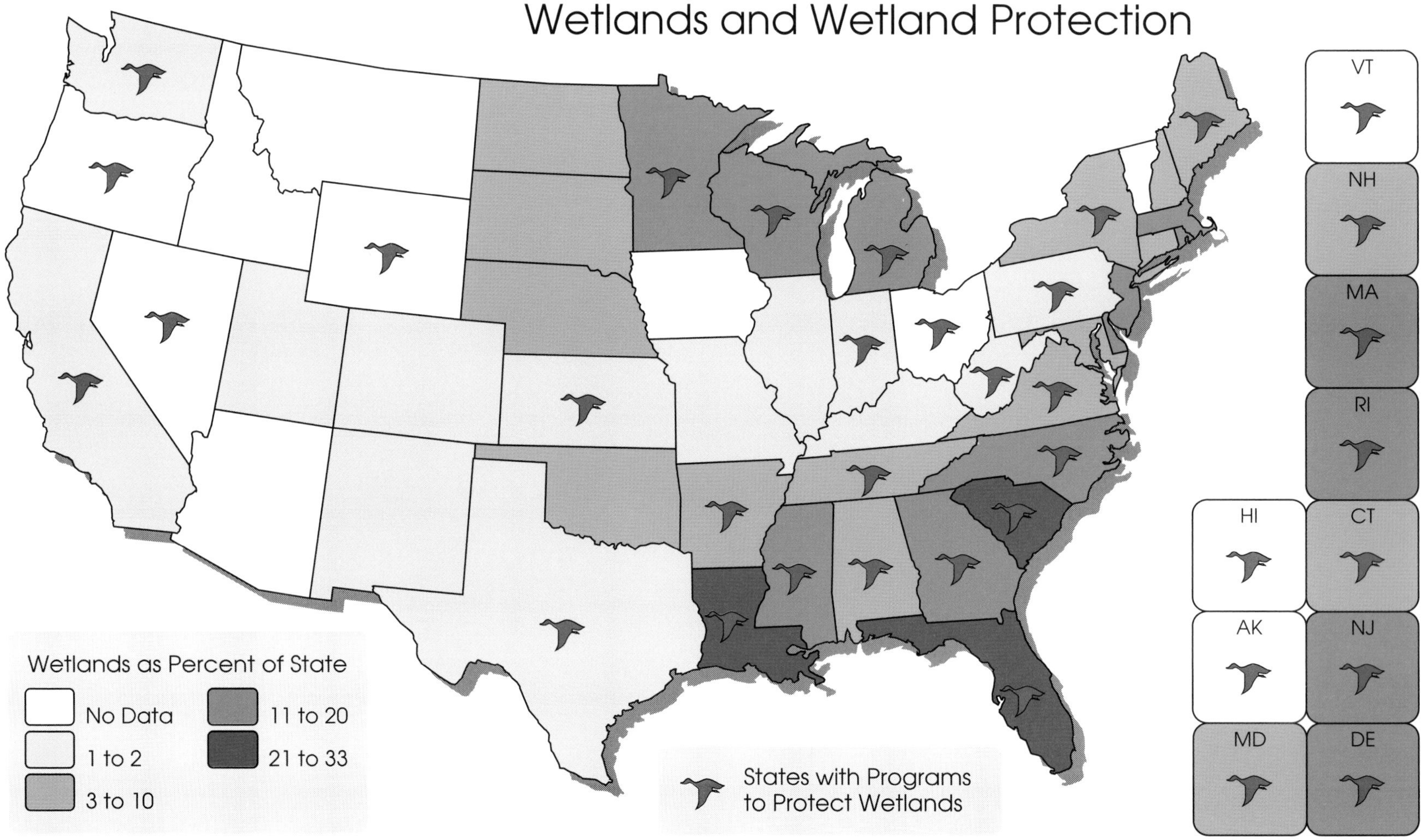

Wetlands as Percent of State

- No Data
- 1 to 2
- 3 to 10
- 11 to 20
- 21 to 33

States with Programs to Protect Wetlands

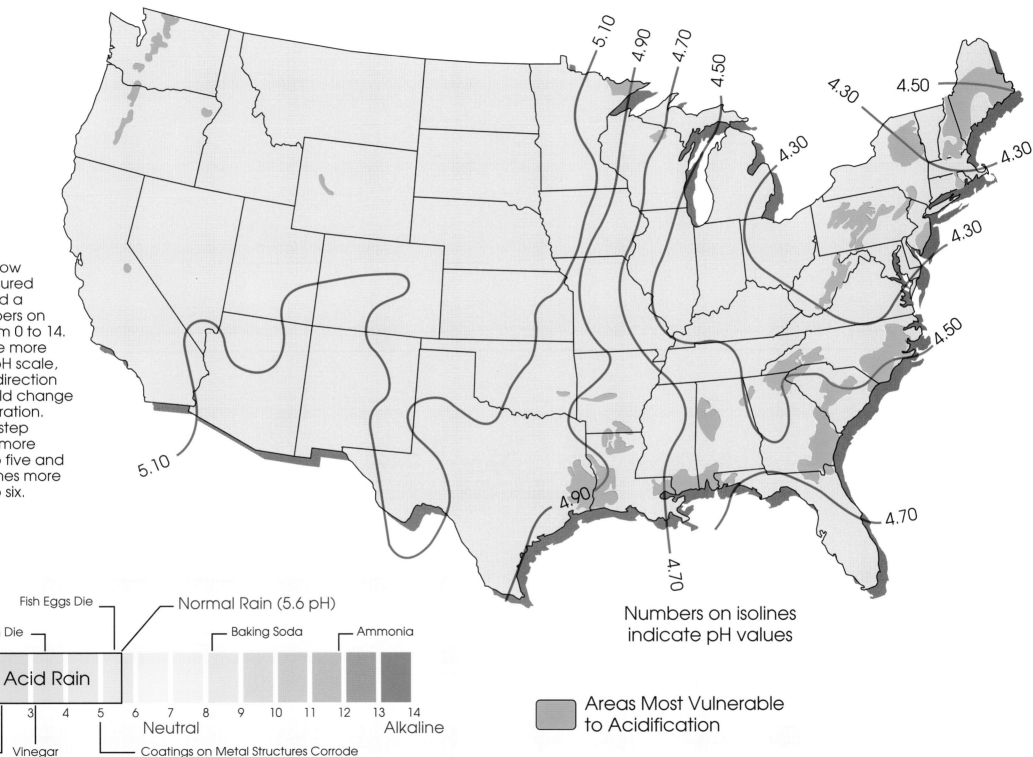

The acidity of snow and rain is measured on a scale called a pH scale. Numbers on the scale go from 0 to 14. Lower values are more acidic. On the pH scale, a step in either direction results in a tenfold change in acid concentration. This means that step four is ten times more acidic than step five and one hundred times more acidic than step six.

Numbers on isolines indicate pH values

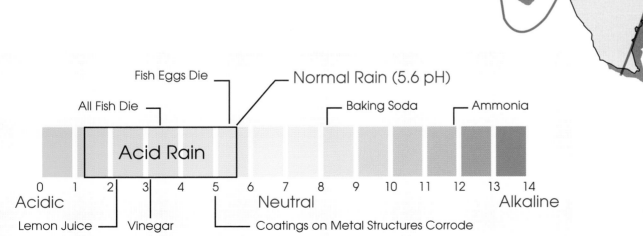

Normal Rain (5.6 pH)

Fish Eggs Die

All Fish Die

Baking Soda

Ammonia

Acid Rain

| 0 | 1 | 2 | 3 | 4 | 5 | 6 | 7 | 8 | 9 | 10 | 11 | 12 | 13 | 14 |

Acidic

Neutral

Alkaline

Lemon Juice

Vinegar

Coatings on Metal Structures Corrode

Areas Most Vulnerable to Acidification

Americans create 280 billion pounds of waste yearly or 1,167 pounds for every man, woman, and child. Not only are many streets and highways littered with bottles and trash, vast areas called "landfills," which are designated for solid waste disposal, are overfilled and/or closed to further dumping. No less than 27 states are running out of room to dump and have resorted to shipping trash to other states and countries for disposal.

Alternatives to dumping are recycling and refuse burning. Eighteen states, primarily those on either coast and along the Great Lakes, have current laws requiring recycling.

Radon emissions have also surfaced as a major environmental and health concern. Being a naturally occurring, inert but radioactive gas, radon—formed through the decay of uranium to lead—has been found in many American homes and is thought to produce lung cancer. Radon gas is emitted from certain kinds of soils and rock materials the locations of which have been shown in the following map as "Radon Hot Spots." Also shown are the percent of homes that have radon problems.

Landfill Capacity Problems
(N = None, M = Moderate, S = Severe)

AL	S	IN	?	MT	M	PA	S
AK	N	IA	N	NE	M	RI	M
AZ	M	LA	M	NV	N	SC	M
AR	N	KS	N	NH	M	SD	M
CA	M	KY	?	NJ	S	TN	M
CO	S	ME	M	NM	M	TX	?
CT	S	MD	M	NY	?	UT	N
DE	N	MA	M	NC	?	VT	?
FL	M	MI	?	ND	N	VA	M
GA	M	MN	N	OH	M	WA	N
HI	M	MS	N	OK	M	WV	S
ID	M	MO	?	OR	N	WI	N
						WY	M

Volume and Composition of Solid Waste

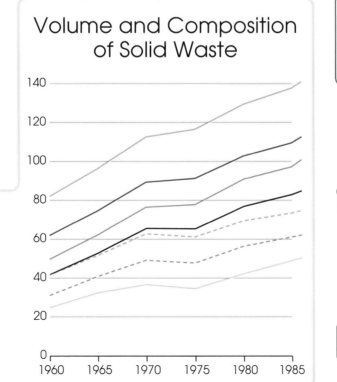

- Yard Wastes
- Food Wastes
- Rubber, Leather, Textiles, Wood, Misc. Inorganics
- Plastics
- Metals
- Glass
- Paper

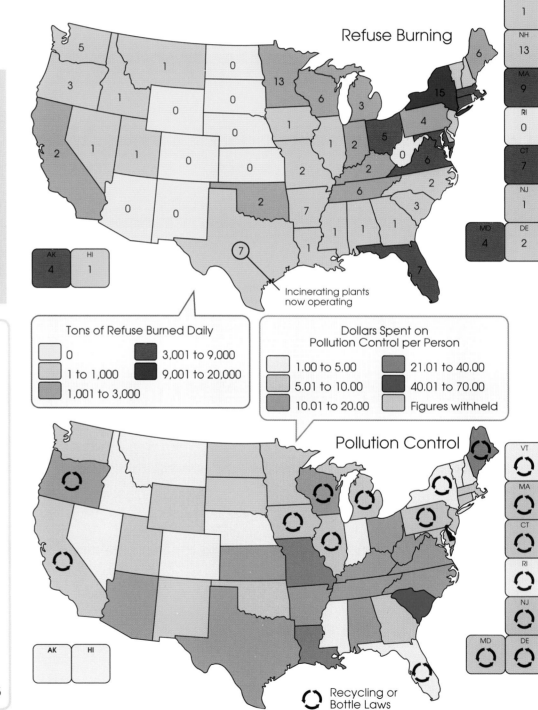

Refuse Burning

Incinerating plants now operating

Tons of Refuse Burned Daily
- 0
- 1 to 1,000
- 1,001 to 3,000
- 3,001 to 9,000
- 9,001 to 20,000

Dollars Spent on Pollution Control per Person
- 1.00 to 5.00
- 5.01 to 10.00
- 10.01 to 20.00
- 21.01 to 40.00
- 40.01 to 70.00
- Figures withheld

Pollution Control

Recycling or Bottle Laws

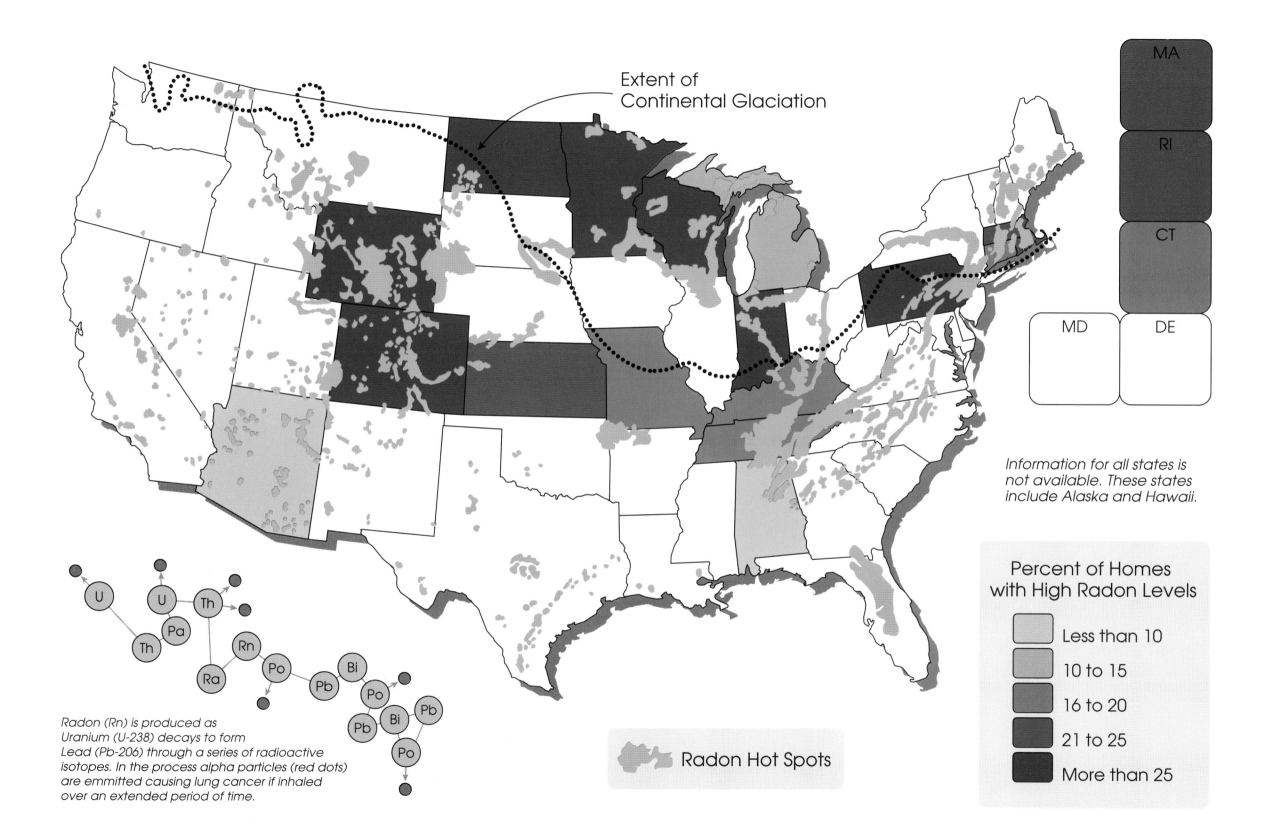

Extent of
Continental Glaciation

MA

RI

CT

MD   DE

Information for all states is
not available. These states
include Alaska and Hawaii.

Radon (Rn) is produced as
Uranium (U-238) decays to form
Lead (Pb-206) through a series of radioactive
isotopes. In the process alpha particles (red dots)
are emmitted causing lung cancer if inhaled
over an extended period of time.

Radon Hot Spots

Percent of Homes
with High Radon Levels

Less than 10

10 to 15

16 to 20

21 to 25

More than 25

Since 1983, Democratic members of Congress have voted for and have supported acts for clean air and clean water twice as often as their Republican counterparts. This information and information like it has been gathered by groups such as the League of Conservation Voters and has been used not only to grade elected officials but also to rank individual states in terms of their overall response to environmental issues. Among the states that rank high on issues of conservation and the environment are California, Florida, North Carolina, Michigan, and Massachusetts. The entire Northwest Region, the Lake States, the Mid-Atlantic Region, and New England are regarded as excellent examples of environmental managers.

One of the most disturbing environmental problems is the discharge of toxic waste. Between 100 and 7,000 pounds of toxic waste per person per year are deposited into the environment in various states. Although many states have commercial facilities engaged in the disposal of such toxins, millions of pounds of chemicals are discharged directly into the ground, the air, or into waterways. Americans, disgusted with medical wastes on beaches and/or drums of discarded chemicals near public places, have called upon legislators to identify and clean-up some 1,400 "Superfund Sites." These sites, resulting from indiscriminate and often illegal dumping, are known to affect the health of adults, retard neuro-development in children, kill wildlife, and in some cases render entire communities unlivable. The sites are concentrated in the East and scattered throughout the Lake States.

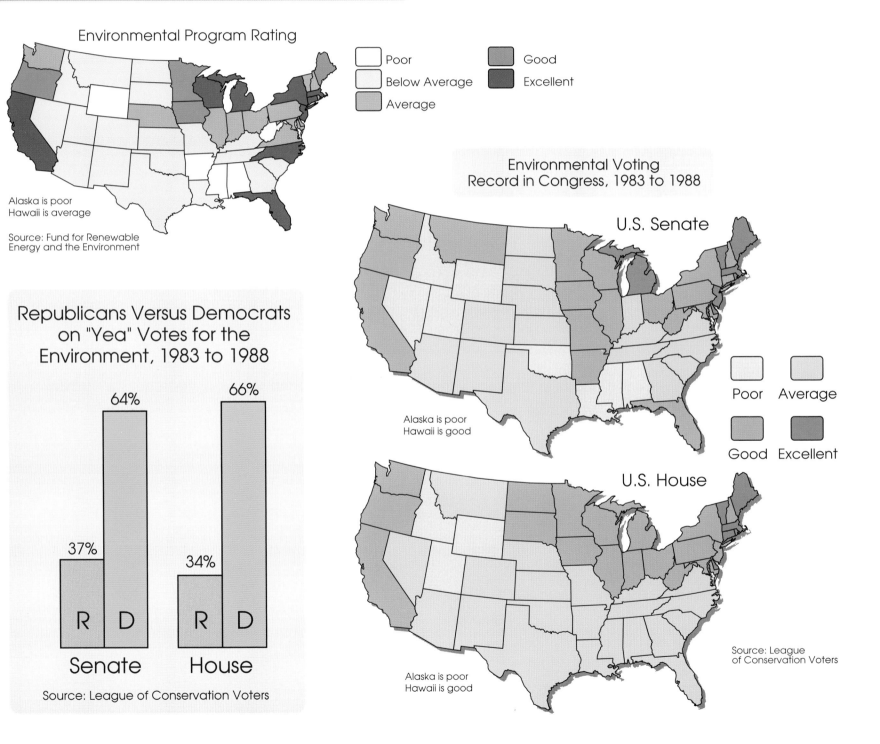

Environmental Program Rating

Poor
Below Average
Average
Good
Excellent

Alaska is poor
Hawaii is average

Source: Fund for Renewable Energy and the Environment

Republicans Versus Democrats on "Yea" Votes for the Environment, 1983 to 1988

64%
66%
37%
34%

R D   R D
Senate   House

Source: League of Conservation Voters

Environmental Voting Record in Congress, 1983 to 1988

U.S. Senate

Poor   Average
Good   Excellent

Alaska is poor
Hawaii is good

U.S. House

Alaska is poor
Hawaii is good

Source: League of Conservation Voters

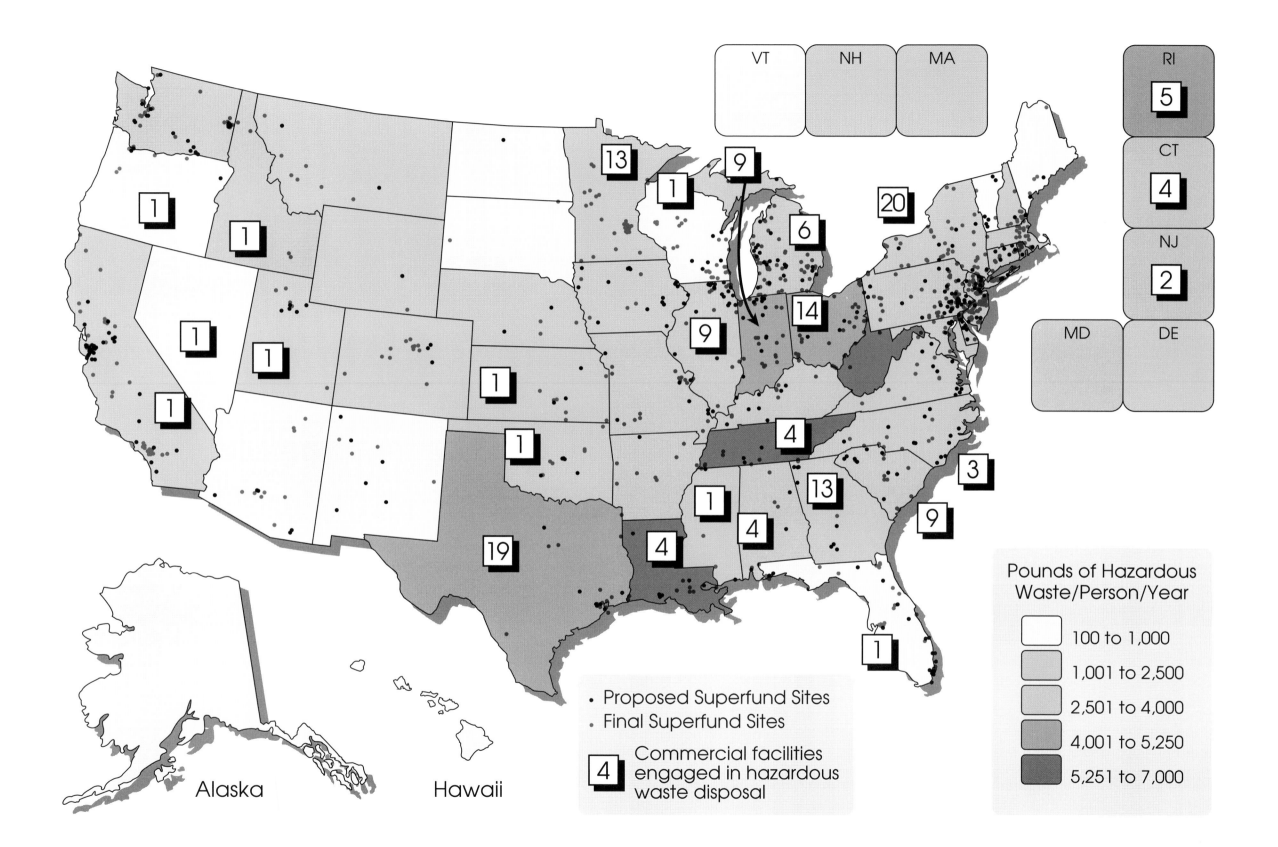

Pounds of Hazardous Waste/Person/Year

- 100 to 1,000
- 1,001 to 2,500
- 2,501 to 4,000
- 4,001 to 5,250
- 5,251 to 7,000

• Proposed Superfund Sites
• Final Superfund Sites

4 Commercial facilities engaged in hazardous waste disposal

VT   NH   MA

RI 5
CT 4
NJ 2
MD   DE

Alaska   Hawaii

AGRICULTURE

Vogeler, Ingolf. The Myth of the Family Farm: Agribusiness' Dominance of United States Agriculture. Boulder, CO: Westview Press, 1981. 352 p. *An attack on agribusiness using many facts to support the good sense in family farming. Useful information about generalized rural economy.*

CITIES

Brunn, Stanley D., et al. The American Metropolitan System: Present and Future. New York: Halsted Press, John Wiley and Sons, 1980. 216 p. *A substantial overview of economic, social, and political problems of U.S. cities covering inner-city revitalization, mortgage-lending, corporate control, communication technology, and the demands and consumption of energy.*

Christian, Charles M., et al. Modern Metropolitan Systems. Columbus, OH: C.E. Merrill, 1982. 495 p. *Urban processes and interactions in the United States related in a broad ranged compendium.*

Yeates, Maurice H., et al. The North American City. 3rd ed. San Francisco, CA; New York; London: Harper and Row, 1980. 536 p. *An excellent and complete treatment dealing with the city as system with inherent structure and problems. Good reading for students.*

Mumford, Lewis. The City in History: Its Origins, Its Transformations, and Its Prospects. New York: Harcourt, Brace and World, 1961. 657 p. *Mumford addresses basic questions about cities for students of all ages. A must for those seeking a groundfloor framework. Considered a classic. Enjoyable, invigorating prose captures students with timeless insight.*

CLIMATOLOGY

U.S. National Oceanic and Atmospheric Administration. Climates of the States: A Practical Reference Containing Basic Climatology Data of the U.S. Port Washington, NY: Water Information Center, 1974. 2 v. 1004 p. *A reference dealing with general climactic conditions in individual states. Temperature and precipitation data presented in tabular form.*

Barry, Roger G., et al. Atmosphere, Weather, and Climate. 4th ed. London; New York: Methuen, 1982. 407 p. *A readable well thought out text presenting principals of both meteorology and climatology.*

Critchfield, Howard J. General Climatology. 4th ed. Englewood Cliffs, NJ: Prentice-Hall, 1983. 453 p. *A non-technical primer dealing with applied climatology.*

Oliver, John E. Climate and Man's Environment: An Introduction to Applied Climatology. New York: John Wiley, 1973. 517 p. *A broad treatment elaborating on the relationship between human activities and climate.*

Trewartha, Glenn T., et al. An Introduction to Climate. 5th ed. New York: McGraw Hill, 1980. 416 p. *A good overview made clear through the use of a non-technical approach. An excellent first book.*

COASTAL AREAS

Bascom, Willard. Waves and Beaches: The Dynamics of the Ocean Surface. Garden City, New Jersey: Anchor Press/Doubleday, 1980. 366 p. *This volume describes waves, currents,*

and sediment transport in a non-technical fashion. Easy to read information in a colloquial style.

COMMUNICATIONS

Pool, Ithiel di Sola, ed. The Social Impact of the Telephone. Cambridge, MA: MIT Press, 1977. 502 p. *An informative collection of original papers showing how the telephone has shaped American society.*

Toffler, Alvin. The Third Wave. New York: William Morrow, 1980. 544 p. *Examines how media, new communication technology, and the micro-computer are being used to shape production, consumption patterns, and politics.*

CONSERVATION AND ENVIRONMENT

Brown, Lester R., et al. State of the World. New York: W.W. Norton and Company, 1989. 256 p. illus. *"State of the World" is an examination of the world's environmental health. This issue focuses upon environmental concerns (greenhouse effect, deforestation, and acid rain) and their causes and promotes public awareness of the issues at hand.*

Cloud, Preston. Cosmos, Earth, and Man: A Short History of the Universe. New Haven, CT: Yale University Press, 1978. 372 p. *Highly recommended all encompassing treatment that encourages students to see the inter-relationships evident between man, universe, and environment.*

Conservation Foundation Letter. 1– (1966–). Bimonthly. Conservation Foundation, Inc., 1717 Massachusetts Ave., N.W., Washington, DC 20036. *Bimonthly issues combine insights and commentary on singular environmental themes.*

Environment. 1– (1958–). Ten Issues. Scientists' Institute for Public Information, Heldref Publications, 4000 Albemarle St., N.W., Washington, DC 20016 (Formerly Scientists and Citizen). *Reviews aimed at providing factual information on leading environmental problems.*

Miller, G. Tyler, Jr. (George). Living in the Environment: An Introduction to Environmental Science. 4th ed. Belmont, CA: Wadsworth, 1984. 460 p. *Rudimentary ecology supported by thousands of references, editorials, and suggested readings.*

Science. 1– (1880–). Weekly. American Association of the Advancement of Science, 1515 Massachusetts Ave., N.W., Washington, DC 20005. *An excellent, readily available weekly providing coverage about a wide range of sciences. Commentary on environmental affairs is outstanding. Well illustrated.*

Toxic Release Inventory: A National Perspective. 1– (1989). Yearly. United States Environmental Protection Agency, Washington, D.C. 20540. *Data about air, water, and ground pollution. From information released by industrial polluters. Discloses toxin type, amount, and location of release. Sobering facts about the true state of U.S. environment.*

CRIME

Herbert, David T. The Geography of Urban Crime. London; New York: Longman, 1982. 120 p. *Introductory text dealing with the growing field of social geography.*

Bureau of Labor Statistics, U.S. Department of Justice. Report to the Nation on Crime. 2nd ed. Washington, DC: Gov-

ernment Printing Office, 1988. 135 p. *This yearly report is highly recommended for both student and professional. Supported with many maps, graphs, and tables, the Department of Justice explains crime patterns while telling readers about criminals and their motivations. An excellent diagrammatic treatment.*

ECONOMICS

Conkling, Edgar C., et al. Man's Economic Environment. New York: McGraw-Hill, 1976. 308 p. *Economic geography as it relates to space, location analysis, transportation, trade, and development. Surprisingly refreshing despite usually dull material. Recommended for student who want new perspectives on day-by-day interactions.*

Wheeler, James O., et al. Economic Geography. New York: John Wiley and Sons, 1981. 395 p. *Standard college level text covering agriculture, manufacturing, service economies, energy, and urbanization. Particularly strong explanations of how transportation is related to economy and space.*

ELDERLY

Golant, Stephen M., ed. Location and Environment of Elderly Population. New York; Toronto; London: John Wiley, 1979. 214 p. *Contributions by 18 authors edited by Golant. Descriptive of migration and movement of the elderly in the United States. Sections on methodology, planning, and planning of movement of retirees.*

ENERGY

Cuff, David J., and William J. Young. The United States Energy Atlas. 2nd ed. New York: Free Press, 1984. 416 p. *The best source for U.S. resources, transportation, production, consumption. Well conceived and illustrated. Many maps, graphs, and diagrams.*

Glasstone, Samuel, et al. Nuclear Power and Its Environmental Effects. La Grange Park, IL: American Nuclear Society, 1980. 395 p. *Very good overview of environmental impact. Of particular interest are chapters on transportation and disposal of nuclear waste.*

McMullan, John T., et al. Energy Resources. 2nd ed. London; New York: Edward Arnold, 1983. 177 p. *A non-technical introduction to basic energy facts and principals. Highly readable. A recommended first book.*

FISHING

Shapiro, Sidney, ed. Our Changing Fisheries. Washington, DC: Government Printing Office, 1971. 534 p. *A handsome, non-technical account of fisheries in the United States. Although some data statistics are dated, the issues remain largely current.*

GENERAL FACTS

Cole, J.P. Geography of World Affairs. 6th ed. London: Butterworths, 1983. 267 p. *An "objective factual survey of geographical factors relating to world affairs." Cole discusses ways of reviewing world affairs, distribution of population, resources, production and consumption. Lastly, he reviews twelve regions of the world and laments over present problems and future prospects of these regions. This edition is hoped to serve as a reference and source of ideas for the discussion of world affairs.*

U.S. Bureau of the Census. County and City Data Book, 1983. 10th ed. Washington, DC: Government Printing Office, 1983. 996 p. *A veritable cornucopia of geographical information. The three enormous tables for states, counties, and cities present statistics on 216, 216, and 170 items, respectively.*

U.S. Bureau of the Census. State and Metropolitan Area Data Book, 1982: A Statistical Abstract Supplement. Washington, DC: Government Printing Office, 1982. 611 p. *Valuable companion to "County and City Data Book, 1983" providing detailed data on 320 items for 318 standard metropolitan areas and for each county within these areas, 73 items for 429 central cities, and 2,018 items for the United States as a whole, for four major regions, nine smaller regions, 50 states, and the District of Columbia.*

U.S. Bureau of the Census. Statistical Abstract of the United States. Washington DC: Government Printing Office, 1879– . Annual. *The one publication that is absolutely indispensable for anyone concerned with the United States. In addition to the 1,500 tables furnishing data on virtually every conceivable subject, this volume is a guide to sources.*

HOUSING

Adams, John S. Housing America in the 1980's. New York: Russell Sage Foundation, 1987. 328 p. illus., maps. *The information in this book uses census data and housing surveys in order to describe changes and trends in the history of housing in America. Adams discusses patterns of housing use, supply and demand, and issues concerning housing policies reveling housing to be "a document of settlement pattern on the land."*

INDUSTRY

Bluestone, Barry, et al. The Deindustrialization of America: Plant Closings, Community Abandonment, and the Dismantling of Basic Industry. New York: Basic Books, 1982. 323 p. *A readable, disturbing text analyzing management motives for plant closings and consequent impacts on workers, families, and communities.*

LANDSCAPE

Pirkle, E.C. (Earl), et al. Natural Landscape of the United States. 3rd ed. Dubuque, IA: Kendall-Hunt, 1982. 399 p. *An introductory description of geomorphology and landform regions in the United States.*

Thornbury, William D. Regional Geomorphology of the United States. New York: Wiley, 1965. 609 p. *Text relating to landforms and physical regions in the U.S..*

LAND USE

Jackson, Richard H. Land Use in America. New York: Halsted Press, 1982. 226 p. *A good look at the successes and failures of land-use planning as it relates to environmental protection, the suburbs, and agricultural lands.*

MINERALS

Dixon, Colin J. Atlas of Economic Mineral Deposits. Ithaca, NY: Cornell University Press, 1979. 143 p. *Shows mineral deposits, what they consist of, and their size.*

Fishman, Leonard L. World Mineral Trends and U.S. Supply Problems. (Resources for the Future, research paper no. R-20).

Baltimore, MD: Johns Hopkins, 1981. 535 p. *Considers long-term supply and price problems aluminum, chromium, cobalt, copper, lead, manganese, and zinc.*

U.S. Bureau of Mines. Minerals Yearbook. Washington, DC: Government Printing Office, 1932/33–. Annual. 3 v. *Detailed annual review of the U.S. and world mineral industry. Volume one is devoted to individual metallic and non-metallic mineral commodities. Volume two reports on the United States. Volume three examines individual countries throughout the world.*

Weston, Rae. Strategic Materials: A World Survey. Totowa, NJ: Rowman and Allanfeld, 1984. 189 p. *A survey of strategic mineral resources, their vulnerability, and the development of potential new sources.*

NATIONAL PARKS

Foresta, Ronald A. America's National Parks and Their Keepers. Baltimore, MD: Johns Hopkins University Press for Resources for the Future, 1984. 382 p. *An excellent analysis of U.S. national parks and the National Park Service. Emphasized is the changing role of parks in society. Includes first rate bibliography. Must reading for those who seek to understand recreation and social change.*

NATIVE AMERICANS

Bureau of Indian Affairs. Indian Service Population and Labor Force Estimates. Washington, DC: U.S. Department of Interior, 1989. 24 p. *Information on the status of the Indian labor force. This study is limited to Indian populations over the age of sixteen living on federal reservations or in the surrounding Indian communities .*

OCEANS AND LAKES

Marx, Wesley. The Oceans: Our Last Resource. San Francisco, CA: Sierra Club, 1981. 332 p. *Topics such as ocean dumping of sludge and nuclear waste combined with issues of sea farming and mining make this Sierra Club offering a must for environmentally concerned students.*

PEOPLE AND CULTURE

Allen, James P., et al. We the People. New York: Macmillan, 1988. 315 p. 115 maps, color. *Data from the 1980 U.S. Census. Presented to show how 67 ethnic groups are distributed throughout the country. Intelligent and aware of issues of statistical sampling. A must for school libraries.*

de Blij, Harm J. Human Geography: Culture, Society, and Space. 2nd ed. New York: Wiley, 1982. 656 p. *A splendid introduction to demography, economics, and politics as they relate to human geography. As always with de Blij, smooth, highly readable prose.*

Fischer, Eric. Minorities and Minority Problems. New York: Vantage Books, 1980. 475 p. *An encyclopedic account of minorities throughout the world giving readers a feeling for the position and historical importance of minorities among world cultures.*

Gastill, Raymond D. Cultural Regions of the United States. Seattle, WA: University of Washington Press, 1976. 382 p. *Covering religion with the use of text, maps, and illustrations, principal American denominations are discussed in*

the context of their relationship and importance in various regions of the conterminous United States.

PHYSICAL GEOGRAPHY

Gabler, Robert E., et al. Essentials of Physical Geography. 2nd ed. Philadelphia, PA: Saunders College, 1982. 568 p. *A comprehensive introductory text combining environmental science and physical geography.*

Strahler, Arthur N., et al. Elements of Physical Geography. 3rd ed. New York: John Wiley and Sons, 1984. 538 p. *The most widely used introductory text. Current, concisely written, well illustrated, book that has grown with the publication of newer editions.*

POLITICS

Glassner, Martin Ira, et al. Systematic Political Geography. 3rd ed. New York: John Wiley and Sons, 1980. 537 p. *The most widely used text of its kind. Readable and enlightening for students in high school and college. Good treatment of basic political systems as they relate to society.*

POPULATION

Demography. 1– (1965–). Twice Yearly, 1965–68. Quarterly since 1969. Population Association of America, P.O. Box 14182, Benjamin Franklin Station, Washington, DC, 20044. *The principal journal covering population in the United States.*

Population Bulletin. 1– (1945–). Quarterly. Population Reference Bureau, Inc., 2213 M Street, NW, Washington, DC, 20037. *Issues are devoted to particular demographic topics. Intended for the general audience, issues are valuable sources of demographic information.*

Newman, James L., et al. Population: Patterns, Dynamics, and Prospects. Englewood Cliffs, NJ: Prentice-Hall, 1984. 306 p. *Basic population geography coupled with elements of demography explains relationships among population, resources, and politics.*

Shnell, George A., et al. The study of population: Elements, Patterns, Processes. Columbus, OH: Merrill, 1983. 371 p. *Major elements of population geography are covered in an historical context. World scale maps demonstrate population patterns in a cartogrammatic form where countries are shown in a size relative to the size of their population.*

RECREATION

Chubb, Michael, et al. One Third of our Time? An Introduction to Recreation Behavior and Resources. New York; Chichester, U.K.: John Wiley and Sons, 1981. *An emphasis on recreational facts and figures provides an excellent introduction to a most important and often overlooked aspect of human study.*

Clawson, Marion, et al. Economics of Outdoor Recreation. Baltimore, MD: Johns Hopkins University Press for Resources for the Future, 1966. 328 p. *Dated but sound treatment demonstrating relationships between recreational resources and demand and how these factors relate to policy formulation.*

Gunn, Clare A. Vacationscape: Designing Tourist Regions. Austin, TX: University of Texas, Bureau of Business Research, 1972. 238 p. *Sheds light on the processes involved in recreation*

planning. Subjects covered include design of regional tourist zones, planning of recreational regions, and human ecological approaches to balancing social and environmental concerns in recreational planning. Well illustrated concepts with poor bibliography.

Mathieson, Alister, et al. Tourism: Economic, Physical, and Social Impacts. London; New York: Longman, 1982. 208 p. *Covers tourism and its effects on spatial economics and physical environments. Also understood are social consequences of tourism, both positive and negative. Good book that underscores existing theory while introducing new concepts and structures relating to tourism and trade.*

SOILS

Basile, Robert M. A Geography of Soils. Dubuque, IA: Wm C. Brown, 1971. 152 p. *A basic introductory level book dealing with soil classification, the utilization and distributions of soils. Good glossary, maps, diagrams, and annotations.*

Brady, Nyle C. The Nature and Properties of Soils. 9th ed. New York: Macmillan, 1984. 750 p. *Soil science discussed with emphasis on processes as they relate to agriculture and the environment.*

Foth, Henry D. Fundamentals of Soil Science. 7th ed. New York: John Wiley and Sons, 1984. 436 p. *New illustrations and diagrams make the 7th ed. of Foth's introductory college level text worth buying. Processes of soil formation and the relationships between soils, plants, and animals are illuminated.*

Steila, Donald. The Geography of Soils: Formation, Distribution, and Management. Englewood Cliffs, NJ: Prentice-Hall, 1976. 222 p. *An introductory text in soil science for non-specialists addressing issues of soil use and abuse. Illustrations and maps in highly readable format for general student population.*

SPORTS

Rooney, John F. Jr. A Geography of American Sport: From Cabin Creek to Anaheim. Reading, MA: Addison-Wesley, 1974. 306 p. *The first text on American sports that deals with its geographical dimensions. Emphasis on major American sports on both the university and professional levels. Sports included are baseball, football, and basketball. Lovers of statistics will love this academic yet fascinating spatial approach to understanding sports information.*

SUBURBAN AMERICA

Hawley, Amos H., et al, eds. Nonmetropolitan America in Transition. Chapel Hill, NC: University of North Carolina Press, 1981. 833 p. *A collection of 21 essays by 29 authors. Comprehensive and useful. An economic and sociological approach to understanding America at the non-metropolitan level. Broad coverage includes topics such as population de-concentration, the dynamics of economic opportunity, access to opportunity, non-metropolitan amenities, environmental impacts of non-urban growth, and planning as related to growth.*

Muller, Peter O. Contemporary Suburban America. Englewood Cliffs, NJ: Prentice-Hall, 1981. 218 p. *The first comprehensive treatment of the suburban zone surrounding American cities is still one of the best in terms of conceptualization and design.*

Platt, Rutherford H., et al. Beyond the Urban Fringe: Land-use Issues of Nonmetropolitan America. Minneapolis, MN:

University of Minnesota Press, 1983. 416 p. *A collection of 27 essays. Thought by many to be the best book in its subject area due to its even-handed coverage of political, social, environmental, and technological matters pertaining to land-use in non-metropolitan areas. Information is presented in an indisciplinary approach.*

TRANSPORTATION

Lowe, John C., et al. The Geography of Movement. Prospects Heights, IL: Waveland, 1984. 333 p. *A modern look at transportation as related to human and economic activities.*

Stilgoe, John R. Metropolitan Corridor: Railroads and the American Scene. New Haven, CT: Yale University Press, 1983. 416 p. *A look at the impact of railroads on landscape, society, and culture between 1880 and 1930. Important reading for those who wish to see how and why rail systems have changed during the past century.*

VEGETATION

Collinson, A.S. Introduction to World Vegetation. London; Boston, MA: George Allen and Unwin, 1977. 201 p. *Numerous figures highlight a text that deals with the patterns of vegetation throughout the United States and the world.*

WATER RESOURCES

Geraghty, James J., et al. Water Atlas of the United States. 3rd ed. Syosset, NY: Water Information Center, 1973. 190 p. *Updated from 1962, this water atlas, contains 122 plates covering atmospheric, hydrolic, and water-use data for all fifty states.*

Leopold, Luna B. Water: a Primer. San Francisco, CA: W.H. Freeman, 1974. 172 p. *A "must" for those seeking a clear introduction to one of America's most valuable resources. Leopold's explanations of the drainage network, floodplains, and the water budget are especially helpful to students. Text is accompanied by excellent illustrations. Although dated in some respects, concepts remain relevant in what will be considered the new environmental decade.*

Powledge, Fred. Water: the Nature, Uses, and Future of Our Most Abused Resource. New York: Farrar, Straus Giroux, 1982. 423 p. *A work intended to motivate the general reader through education on topics such as water quantity and the absence of a national water policy. Powledge teaches as well as provokes new thoughts.*

U.S. Water Resources Council. The Nation's Water Resources, 1975–2000: Second National Water Assessment. Washington, DC: Government Printing Office, 1978. 4 v. *A four volume appraisal. Volume 1 is an overview. Volume 2, covers water resources, demands, and quality. Volume 3, is a compilation of supportive information and statistics. Volume 4 is a compendium of regional water resource reports.*

WOMEN

Mazey, Mary Ellen, et al. Her Space, Her Place: A Geography of Women. Washington DC: Association of American Geographers, 1983. 83 p. *Pertinent without being "preachy" the authors demonstrate a good grasp of geographic concepts in a study of women in the United States. Good reading. Essential for youthful readers who are otherwise not encouraged to see women in American society. Recommended reading for both males and females.*